La Strada

Rutgers Films in Print
Mirella Jona Affron, Robert Lyons,
and E. Rubinstein, editors

My Darling Clementine, John Ford, director
edited by Robert Lyons

The Last Metro, François Truffaut, director
edited by Mirella Jona Affron and E. Rubinstein

Touch of Evil, Orson Welles, director
edited by Terry Comito

The Marriage of Maria Braun, Rainer Werner Fassbinder, director
edited by Joyce Rheuban

Letter from an Unknown Woman, Max Ophuls, director
edited by Virginia Wright Wexman, with Karen Hollinger

Rashomon, Akira Kurosawa, director
edited by Donald Richie

8½, Federico Fellini, director
edited by Charles Affron

La Strada, Federico Fellini, director
edited by Peter Bondanella and Manuela Gieri

La Strada

Federico Fellini,
director

Peter Bondanella and

Manuela Gieri, editors

Rutgers University Press

New Brunswick and London

La Strada is volume 8 in the *Rutgers Films in Print* Series

Library of Congress Cataloging-in-Publication Data

La Strada.

  (Rutgers films in print ; v. 8)
  Filmography: p.
  Bibliography: p.
  1. Strada (Motion picture) I. Fellini, Federico. II. Bondanella, Peter, 1943–
III. Gieri, Manuela. IV. Strada (Motion picture) V. Series.
PN1997.S774 1987   791.43′72   86-27960
ISBN 0-8135-1236-0
ISBN 0-98135-1237-9 (pbk.)

Contents

Introduction

Fellini's *La Strada* and the Cinema of Poetry / 3
Peter Bondanella and Manuela Gieri

Federico Fellini: A Biographical Sketch / 23

La Strada

Credits and Cast / 32

The Continuity Script / 35

Notes on the Continuity Script / 165

Contexts

The Making of *La Strada*
    The Genesis of *La Strada* / 181
    Federico Fellini
    The History of a Collaboration:
A Complementary Diversity / 185
    Tullio Pinelli
I Spoke Badly of *La Strada* / 187
    Ennio Flaiano
Fellini and the Phantom Horse / 188
    Moraldo Rossi
The Most Strenuous Film in a Career of Forty-Three Years / 190
    Luigi Giacosi
An "Active" Character: Gelsomina Senses the Life of the Trees / 192
    Giulietta Masina
The Crisis of Neo-Realism
    La Strada / 199
    André Bazin
    Italian Cinema / 204
    Guido Aristarco

An Interview with Federico
Fellini / 206
George Bluestone
Guido Aristarco Answers
Fellini / 208
Guido Aristarco
Letter to a Marxist Critic / 211
Federico Fellini
The Road Beyond Neo-
Realism / 215
Federico Fellini

Reviews and Commentaries

Reviews
Films in Review / 225
Francis Koval
Sight and Sound / 226
Gavin Lambert
The Times (London) / 228
Newsweek / 229

Saturday Review / 230
Arthur Knight
The New Yorker / 232
John McCarten
Harper's Magazine / 233
"Mr. Harper"
Hudson Review / 235
Vernon Young

Commentaries
The Secret Life of Federico
Fellini / 239
Peter Harcourt
La Strada / 253
Frank Burke

Filmography and Bibliography

Fellini Filmography, 1950–
1985 / 265

Selected Bibliography / 267

Introduction

Fellini's *La Strada* and the Cinema of Poetry

Peter Bondanella
and Manuela Gieri

t is difficult to understand either the artistic and historical significance of *La Strada* or the immediate critical response to this film without reference to the cinema movement known as neo-realism. Fellini's career as a film-maker had its start in the immediate postwar period in Italy at the same time that the world noticed a dynamic new film style emerging from the dissipating smoke of the only recently silenced guns and bombs. With directors such as Roberto Rossellini (*Open City*, 1945; *Paisan*, 1946), Vittorio De Sica (*Shoeshine*, 1946; *Bicycle Thief*, 1948; *Umberto D.*, 1951), Luchino Visconti (*La Terra Trema*, 1948), Giuseppe De Santis (*Bitter Rice*, 1948), Luigi Zampa (*To Live in Peace*, 1946), Alberto Lattuada (*Without Pity*, 1948), and Pietro Germi (*The Path of Hope*, 1950), it seemed to critics both inside and outside Italy that the cinema had suddenly abandoned the Hollywood "dream factory" for the actual streets and squares of war-torn Europe.

Film critics and film historians of this period believed that the neo-realist prototypes constituted a victory of social realism over fantasy and fiction. The necessary characteristics of neo-realism that emerged from their writings stressed a definite social context; a sense of historical actuality and immediacy; political commitment to progressive or even violent social change; "authentic" on-location shooting as opposed to the "artificiality" of the studio; a rejection of classical Hollywood acting styles, generic codes, and cinematic conventions; extensive use of nonprofessional actors whenever possible; and a documentary style of cinematography, aiming at a faithful reproduction of Italian life and popular culture. The best critic of the era, André Bazin, proclaimed neo-realism as a cinema of "fact" and "reconstituted reportage" which rejected both dramatic and cinematic conventions and which "respected" the ontological wholeness of the reality it captured, just as the narrated screen time in neo-realist films often "respected" the actual duration of the story. Bazin sharply distinguished the style of Rossellini and his Italian contemporaries from the montage style of Sergei Eisenstein with its ideologically motivated juxtaposition of images, seeing the new Italian school as closer in spirit to the deep-focus, extended shot techniques of Orson Welles and Jean Renoir.[1]

Less well known outside Italy was the existence of an important Italian literary current, best represented by the early novels of such writers as Elio Vittorini (*In Sicily*, 1941), Cesare Pavese (*The Harvesters*, 1941; *The Moon and the Bonfires*, 1951), Carlo Levi (*Christ Stopped at Eboli*, 1945), and Italo Calvino (*The Path to the Nest of Spiders*, 1947). Italian neo-realist cinema was part of a larger revitalization of Italian culture after the defeat of the Fascist regime, which had attempted to monopolize Italian culture from its seizure of power in 1922 until its downfall in 1943. If film critics and film historians in the immediate postwar period had approached neo-realist cinema from a broader cultural perpective, their emphasis upon the "realism" of such films might well have been tempered. They would have been forced to recognize that the major works of neo-realist fiction which appeared almost contemporaneously with the best films embodied an esthetic that could not be encompassed simply by traditional notions of "realism." The novels of Levi, Vittorini, Calvino, and Pavese all deal with social reality in a symbolic or mythical fashion, and all employ a subjective and often unreliable narrative voice, thereby embracing a clearly antinaturalistic narrative stance quite contrary to the canons of literary realism established by the novel in the nineteenth century.

An additional problem arose within Italian criticism of neo-realism between 1945 and 1955. Whereas almost all critics, no matter what their ideological persuasions, stressed the "realism" of Italian neo-realist cinema in the immediate postwar period, an especially influential and highly vocal group of Marxist critics turned this *description* of neo-realism into a programmatic *prescription* for all Italian films. Led by Guido Aristarco, the foremost Marxist film historian in Italy and the editor of the influential journal *Cinema Nuovo*, this group of intel-

---

1. For Bazin's seminal essays on Italian neo-realism, see *What Is Cinema?: Vol. II*, trans. Hugh Gray (Berkeley and Los Angeles University of California Press, 1971).

lectuals advocated a "realist" cinema as a dynamic social force working for radical social and political change in Italy. Their writings attempted to replace the generally Catholic tone of prewar Italian culture with that of Marxist ideology, and they would be especially insensitive or opposed to any film that ignored concrete social and economic concerns or embodied a nonmaterialist view of Italy.

In their haste to canonize certain stylistic traits admittedly present in the greatest of neo-realist films, as well as their progressive, reformist, or even revolutionary content, Aristarco and other like-minded leftist critics usually overlooked or minimized the creative imagination and artistic motivation that had produced the best of these "realistic" films. Moreover, in their desire to see a particular ideology prevail within Italian cinema, such leftist critics tended to believe that neo-realism was a movement based upon universally agreed-upon stylistic principles and thematic concerns. Thus, when a director such as Federico Fellini expanded the boundaries of the critics' definition of what constituted neo-realism and began producing films that seemed to reflect an individualist, nonmaterialist perspective, it was construed by them as a "betrayal" and bitterly opposed in polemical reviews and essays. Of course, a few Italian directors (especially Luchino Visconti and Giuseppe De Santis) were Marxists and saw film-making as a means of changing Italian society. But it was primarily the Marxist film critics, far more than any directors or scriptwriters, who not only insisted upon the "realism" of Italian neo-realism but also advanced the sometimes dogmatic claims for cinema as a political force that should agitate for radical transformations in Italy's social and economic order.

Some four decades after the appearance of Rosselini's *Open City,* which was universally hailed as the first masterpiece of a new cinematic "movement" by critics in Europe and America, our understanding of Italian neo-realism has changed considerably. In retrospect, it now seems clear that the early critics' rather simplistic view of neo-realism as a cinema of pure, unmediated realism was never a satisfactory description of its great variety or its originality. Nor do the very different works of such directors as Rossellini, De Sica, and Visconti, to mention only the most important directors, reflect a single unified style or thematic content. There never existed a self-conscious neo-realist "movement" as such, except in the writings of the Marxist ideologues who used that notion to attack directors and films that did not fit their prescriptive norms.

In fact, Italian film-makers were trying to accomplish in the cinema not unlike what their contemporaries in Italian literature hoped to achieve: the creation of a new artistic language that would enable them to deal poetically with important social and political issues. Italo Calvino perhaps expressed this desire best when he wrote that neo-realists in both film and literature "knew all too well that what counted was the music and not the libretto . . . there were never more dogged formalists than we; and never were lyric poets as effusive as those objective reporters we were supposed to be."[2] Calvino goes on to suggest that since the neo-realists were so far removed from the canons of traditional literary realism, "perhaps the right name for that Italian season, instead of 'neo-realism,' should be 'neo-expressionism.'"[3] Cesare Pavese seems also to be describing the Italian film-makers or novelists of the postwar generation when he says that American novelists sought to "readjust language to the new reality of the world, in order to create, in effect, a *new* language, down-to-earth and symbolic, that would justify itself solely in terms of itself and not in terms of any traditional complacency."[4] Men such as Rossellini and De Sica were, above all else, attempting to see their world afresh from novel perspectives, thereby creating a "new" reality in their art.

Certainly, the best neo-realist films and novels dealt with universal human problems, contemporary stories, and believable characters from everyday life. But in spite of these general and rather vague similarities that united directors of very different artistic or political temperaments, Italian neo-realist films never completely rejected the conventions of Hollywood codes, nor did they completely obscure the role of fantasy and imagination (as opposed to documentary "facts") in their works. Many of the best neo-realist films (in particular the films listed above by Germi, De Santis, Lattuada, and De Sica) reworked Hollywood genres (the western, the gangster film, the musical), and most used professional actors, even stars, in their films.[5] The basis for the fundamental change in cin-

---

2. Italo Calvino, preface to *The Path to the Nest of Spiders*, trans. Archibald Colquhoun (New York: Ecco Press, 1976), p. vii.

3. Ibid., p. xi.

4. Cesare Pavese, *American Literature: Essays and Opinions*, trans. Edwin Fussell (Berkeley and Los Angeles: University of California Press, 1970), p. 197.

5. The classic study of Italian neo-realism in English, primarily a reflection of the "realist" approach to the subject, is Roy Armes, *Patterns of Realism: A Study of Italian Neo-Realism* (Cranbury, N.J.: A. S. Barnes, 1971). Other influential books on Italian cinema which view neo-realism from a realist perspective include: Carlo Lizzani, *Il cinema italiano 1895–1979*, 2 vols. (Rome: Editori Riuniti, 1979); Pierre Leprohon, *The Italian Cinema* (rev. ed. of 1966 French ed.; London: Secker & Warburg, 1972); and especially the essays of the major neo-realist scriptwriter, Cesare Zavattini, in *Neorealismo ecc.*, ed. Mino Argentieri (Milan: Bompiani, 1979). An

ematic history marked by Italian neo-realism was less an agreement on a single, unified cinematic style than a common aspiration to reject Fascist cultural prescription and view Italy afresh, employing a more honest, ethical, but no less poetic cinematic language in the process.

Federico Fellini has consistently maintained that he was influenced by Roberto Rossellini more than any other single film-maker. He has always insisted, however, that the legacy of Rossellini was not merely stylistic. Instead, in Fellini's words, what Rossellini taught him about film-making was a moral attitude, an "example of humility, or better, a way of facing reality in a totally simplified way; an effort of not interfering with one's own ideas, culture, feelings."[6] For Fellini, Italian neo-realism meant primarily a way of seeing the world and its problems honestly and without prejudice, but it also required remaining open to the poetic potential of even the most banal daily events. And Fellini was not the first or only Italian director who began his career in the neo-realist era but eventually felt constrained by the ideological demands of leftist critics for films which would follow a particular political slant or embody a specific "realist" style. Many other directors also began to view such demands as an imposition upon their artistic freedom.

Perhaps the most important theoretical issue which emerged in reaction to the ideological strictures of the leftist critics concerned the concept of film character. Most neo-realist films, regardless of their stylistic or thematic content, usually viewed their characters from a strictly social perspective. Environment shapes and ultimately determines a character's fate. The unemployed worker in De Sica's *Bicycle Thief,* a classic example of a neo-realist protagonist, derived almost all of

---

anthology of writings following this traditional approach may be found in David Overby, ed., *Springtime in Italy: A Reader in Neorealism* (Hamden, Ct.: Archon Books, 1979).

A number of important recent publications alter radically the traditional "realist" interpretation of Italian neo-realism in favor of a more balanced approach stressing the element of fantasy and the use of traditional cinematic codes and conventions in Italian neo-realism. In particular, see: Lino Miccichè, ed., *Il neorealismo cinematografico italiano* (Venice: Marsilio Editori, 1975); Ben Lawton, "Italian Neorealism: A Mirror Construction of Reality," *Film Criticism* 3 (1979): 8–23; Peter Bondanella, *Italian Cinema: From Neorealism to the Present* (New York: Frederick Ungar, 1983); *idem,* "America and the Italian Cinema," *Rivista di Studi Italiani* 2 (1984): 106–25; Robert P. Kolker, *The Altering Eye: Contemporary International Cinema* (New York: Oxford University Press, 1983), and Millicent Marcus, *Italian Film in the Light of Neorealism* (Princeton: Princeton University Press, 1986).

6. Federico Fellini, "My Experiences as a Director," in *Federido Fellini: Essays in Criticism,* ed. Peter Bondanella (New York: Oxford University Press, 1978), p. 3.

his pathetic dramatic force from the fact that without a bicycle, he would lose his hard-won job hanging posters on city walls, and without his job, his family would be doomed to a life of deprivation. His material circumstances determined much of his essential nature. Moreover, since he was typical of the workers in Italy immediately after the end of the war and before the economic boom that thrust Italy into the vanguard of newly emerging industrial nations, he could also be seen as a social *type,* a figure typical of an entire class or generation of Italians.

Roberto Rossellini, universally (Marxists included) acknowledged as the father of Italian neo-realism, became concerned about the unidimensionality of such characters. In 1954, the same year *La Strada* was released in Italy (where it was greeted by a chorus of hostile attacks from the Left), Rossellini declared that neo-realism had to be transcended if Italian cinema was to progress and to reflect the much altered "reality" of the postwar world: "One can't help being interested in other subjects and problems and trying new directions; one can't forever shoot films in bombed cities. . . . Life has changed, the war is over, the cities have been reconstructed. What we needed was a cinema of the Reconstruction."[7] As early as 1949 in *Stromboli* and later in such films as *Voyage in Italy* (1953), two works starring Ingrid Bergman, Rossellini moved toward a cinema that explored dimensions of the human condition unrelated to strictly social or political problems—in particular, human loneliness, alienation, and the search for meaningful emotional relationships between men and women.

Michelangelo Antonioni was equally impatient with the leftist critics' demands for more and more "neo-realistic" treatments of Italian life and responded directly to their insistence upon the portrayal of social *types* in the cinema. And it is significant that in his discussion of this issue, he focuses specifically upon De Sica's unemployed worker who is forced to steal a bicycle after having lost his own:

> The neo-realism of the postwar period, when reality itself was so searing and immediate, attracted attention to the relationship existing between the character and surrounding reality. . . . Now, however, when for better or worse reality has been normalized once again, it seems to me more interesting to examine what remains in the characters from their past experiences. This is why it no longer seems to me important to make a film about a man who has his bicycle stolen. That is to say, about a man whose importance resides (primarily and exclusively) in the fact that he has his bicycle stolen. . . .

7. Cited in Bondanella, *Italian Cinema: From Neorealism to the Present,* p. 105.

Now that we have eliminated the problem of the bicycle (I am speaking metaphorically), it is important to see what there is in the mind and the heart of this man who has had his bicycle stolen, how he has adapted himself, what remains in him of his past experiences.[8]

Like Rossellini's films of the late 1940s and early 1950s, Antonioni's films in this same period (*Story of a Love Affair,* 1950; *The Vanquished,* 1952; *The Girl Friends,* 1955) moved away from strictly social or economic problems and toward an analysis of individual solitude and alienation. Moreover, Antonioni's characteristic camera style avoided the documentary effects usually associated with neo-realism in favor of a modernist and abstract photographic style.

When Federico Fellini turned from writing screenplays for neo-realist directors to making his own films in the early 1950s, his works began to distance themselves immediately from a conception of cinema that would be acceptable to Marxist critics. In the three films Fellini produced before *La Strada—Variety Lights, The White Sheik,* and *I Vitelloni*—the film character conceived of as a social *type,* the typical neo-realist hero, is modified and ultimately superseded. Rather than concentrating upon how a protagonist's environment shapes his character and his destiny, Fellini turned instead in this "trilogy of character" to reflect upon the significance of the clash between a character's social "role" or "mask"—how a character tends to act in society—and the character's authentic "face"—represented by his subconscious aspirations, ideals, and instincts.[9] With Fellini's subsequent "trilogy of salvation or grace"—*La Strada, Nights of Cabiria,* and *Il Bidone,* but most clearly in *La Strada*—we witness an even clearer transition from a neo-realist cinematic world, based upon character types who reflect social or economic conditions, to a more fanciful world of the director's own invention. Fellini shifts attention from a character's environment to a character's emotions, dreams, and psychology. Far from representing social types by their environment, the protagonists of these early Fellini films are totally atypical creatures, owing more to the world of adolescent dreams or to the personal myths of their creator than to any attempt on the director's part to represent a simple reflection of his society. *La Strada,* Fellini has declared, is "really the

---

8. Cited in ibid., p. 108.
9. For a more detailed discussion of Fellini's "trilogy of character" and his subsequent "trilogy of grace or salvation," of which *La Strada* is the classic expression, see Peter Bondanella, "Early Fellini: *Variety Lights, The White Sheik, The Vitelloni,* in *Federico Fellini: Essays in Criticism,* ed. Bondanella, pp. 220–238; or the same author's more detailed treatment in *Italian Cinema: From Neorealism to the Present,* pp. 113–141.

complete catalogue of my entire mythical world."[10] In this film, Fellini completes his evolution toward a cinema of self-consciously poetic images and personal symbols or myths. While the surroundings of the film's characters are directly from a textbook definition of Italian neo-realism—stark landscapes, poverty-stricken peasant families, real locations in the small towns of provincial Italy, nonprofessional actors playing minor roles—no film could be farther from realist aims than *La Strada*.

Fellini agreed with both Rossellini and Antonioni that Italian cinema needed to pass beyond a dogmatic approach to social reality, dealing poetically with other equally compelling personal or emotional problems. Communication of information, especially information of an ideological kind, was not Fellini's goal in creating a film. As he has so aptly put it, "I don't want to demonstrate anything; I want to show it."[11] In contrast to what leftist critics maintained, Fellini suggests that there should be no privileged subject matter for the Italian cinema. If a director feels that he cannot express himself except in a realistic style, that is perfectly acceptable to Fellini, although he himself felt no strong commitment to create realistic films designed to convince audiences of the need for political change in Italy. Rather than viewing human relationships with a Marxist emphasis upon class struggle or social conflict, Fellini retains, in spite of his distaste for the institutions of the Church, a profoundly Christian emphasis upon the individual and the essential loneliness of the human condition. As Fellini has explained, "Zampanò and Gelsomina are not exceptions, as people reproach me for creating. There are more Zampanòs in the world than bicycle thieves, and the story of a man who discovers his neighbor is just as important and as real as the story of a strike. What separates us [Fellini versus his critics on the Left] is no doubt a materialist or spiritualist vision of the world."[12]

Fellini's interest in a poetic cinema rather than a "realistic" cinema is immediately evident in his choice of protagonists for *La Strada*. Far from wishing to portray characters who were products of their environment, Fellini's characters reflect a multilayered array of symbolic possibilities not exhausted by their socioeconomic conditions. Gelsomina, the young woman who is bought from her impoverished mother by Zampanò, a performer and strongman in a traveling circus, is described by her mother as "a bit strange" (shot 9) and "not like the other girls" (shot 13). A more uncharitable view of Gelsomina might even call

10. Cited by Tullio Kezich in "The Long Interview" in *Juliet of the Spirits,* ed. Tullio Kezich (New York: Grossman, 1965), p. 30.
11. Cited in *Fellini on Fellini,* trans. Isabel Quigly (New York: Dell, 1976), p. 52.
12. Cited in Bondanella, *Italian Cinema: From Neorealism to the Present,* p. 134.

her retarded or dim-witted. Yet, this sympathetic waif who knows almost nothing about the real world possésses a special capacity for communicating with children, animals, or even inanimate objects. She knows, for example, when it is about to rain (shot 60). She has a strange affinity with nature and seems most at home by the seashore. Once, in a moving shot (133), Gelsomina walks by a solitary tree and imitates with her arms the angle of its only branch. Immediately afterwards, she listens enraptured to the almost musical sound of the telegraph wires that only she is capable of hearing. When she confronts Osvaldo, a truly freakish child in the farmhouse attic (shots 163–175), only Gelsomina understands the nature of his suffering, his loneliness, and his inner pain.

Gelsomina thus possesses a Franciscan simplicity and a purity of spirit which more than compensates for her diminished intellectual capacity, and this emotional potential makes her the perfect vehicle for Fellini's poetic mythology. Later, she is photographed (shot 236) against a wall upon which is affixed a poster reading "Immaculate Madonna," for Gelsomina will become the means through which her companion Zampanò learns to feel—learns, in effect, what it means to become a human being. This vocation of Gelsomina's becomes clear to her in a conversation with the Fool, who relates to Gelsomina the celebrated "parable of the pebble" (shots 462–469): "I don't know what purpose this pebble serves, but it must serve some purpose. Because if it is useless, then everything is useless" (shot 466). Here, the Fool convinces Gelsomina that she must be meant to stay with Zampanò. In spite of his brutish insensitivity, Zampanò nevertheless cares for her a little. This realization confirms Gelsomina in her vocation until her death from grief over Zampanò's accidental killing of the Fool.

Fellini's complex characterization of Gelsomina is paralleled by an equally ambiguous portrayal of the two male figures in her life, the Fool and Zampanò. When we first see the Fool in the film, he is skillfully performing his tightwire act high above the crowd, wearing a pair of angel's wings (shot 244). Thus, the religious associations that began by picturing Gelsomina as a Madonna or Virgin figure continue with the Fool's initial characterization as an angel, the heavenly figure traditionally linked to the delivery of special messages from the other world, as in the case of Gabriel and the Virgin Mary. At first, the Fool seems to serve precisely such a function in Fellini's poetic mythology. But the Fool also possesses a darker side to his character, a touch of Lucifer as well as Gabriel. Although he is the vehicle for confirming Gelsomina in her spiritual vocation, delivering the message that all human beings need others and serve some positive function, he himself rejects this very same belief in his own life: "I don't need anybody!" (shot 473). In his claim that he can survive perfectly well without others, the Fool resembles Zampanò in spite of his seemingly wise, even religious nature.

Much of the same kind of ambiguity can be found in the character of Zampanò. He is constantly compared to animals in his speech, his behavior, his coarse treatment of Gelsomina, and his promiscuous sexuality. Even his strongman routine seems devoid of any intelligence or style and focuses, instead, upon brute force and muscle. Unlike Gelsomina, who has a special affinity for children and nature, or the Fool, who is most at home in the air high above the admiring crowds as he performs his amazing feats on the high wire, Zampanò's element is the solid earth. It is there on his knees that he shatters the chains around his chest, and it is there he lies in a drunken stupor on not a few occasions. Although Zampanò embodies brute strength and may be contrasted to the agility and quickwittedness of the Fool, both men nevertheless share a similar selfishness. Each of them feels that he can live without the love of his neighbor. When Zampanò staggers drunkenly out of a bar after learning of Gelsomina's death, his pathetic cry echoes that of the Fool earlier: "Cowards . . . ! I don't need . . . I don't need anybody! . . . I . . . I want to be alone . . . alone" (shot 740). But unlike the Fool, we soon realize that Zampanò does not mean what he says. As Zampanò staggers toward the beach, that special place frought with symbolic associations with Gelsomina, he slowly looks up toward the stars, overcome by emotion. And it is in that moment that we discover how Gelsomina has profoundly changed Zampanò's character. It is a mark of Fellini's genius that he never specifies exactly what kind of an experience Zampanò undergoes at the close of the film. It may well be a private revelation of an important truth. It may be the feeling of an emotion never before experienced. While such an event can perhaps most easily be paralleled to the religious experience of conversion, Fellini quite clearly stops short of providing his audience with a simple, unequivocal significance for his closing shot. There is no "message" to conclude the film. Rather, the film concludes on an eloquent and moving image—Zampanò, prostrate upon the beach as he grasps the sand in desperation and finally sheds a tear.

Fellini pursues his search for a poetic cinema on a number of levels—in his ambiguous characterization of the protagonists, in his imaginative choice of visuals, and in his heuristic collaboration with Nino Rota, the composer whose original music embellishes the majority of the films Fellini has made during his career. A number of the most familiar and most suggestive visual images in *La Strada* have already been discussed in connection with the three central protagonists. But it may be even more instructive in describing Fellini's cinema of poetry to analyze briefly two series of shots which stand out in the film precisely because they are devoid of dramatic action or of crucial dialogue. The first series consists of three shots in ELS, each dissolving into the next: first a herd of horses grazing (shot 579); then a small lake seen from a mountain road (shot 580); and finally a peaceful countryside (shot 581). The second series consists of five shots—three in ELS and two in LS—which also move forward by dissolves: a valley shot from a mountain road (shot 634); a wood seen from road-level (shot 635); leafless trees (shot 636); a town built into a hillside (shot 637); and a snowy field (shot 638).

The above shots are traveling shots, taken as if from Zampanò's moving caravan. Traditional cinematic narrative frequently employs such traveling shots and dissolves to reflect rapid passages through time or space. But Fellini also employs them poetically to say something of importance about Gelsomina. The first series immediately follows the convent sequence, where Gelsomina learned from the young nun who befriended her that she, too, had a vocation: just as the nun was the bride of Christ, Gelsomina was destined to live with Zampanò. This important sequence thus confirmed the message contained in the Fool's earlier "parable of the pebble." As a result, the views of nature contained in the first series of traveling shots are ordered, calm, comforting, and even domestic. The second series of five shots immediately follows the killing of the Fool by Zampanò. Now, the earlier view of nature is replaced by a more foreboding, wintry, threatening, and desolate landscape: even the town is an uninviting fortress-like structure which repels rather than welcomes us.

Even in what might be a series of insignificant shots, employed by a lesser director only to move his narrative forward in time or space, Fellini's lyrical touch is evident. In retrospect, we realize that each of the shots discussed above was a subjective shot from Gelsomina's point of view. Ultimately, Fellini skillfully used these two series of shots devoid of dramatic action both as reflections of a crucial development that took place earlier in the narrative and as concrete poetic metaphors for Gelsomina's states of mind. Earlier, Gelsomina was content over the reconfirmation of her vocation in life. Later, her composure and self-assurance have been tragically destroyed by the death of the Fool, the character who first suggested to her that her life might have some purpose.

In *La Strada,* Fellini and Rota also demonstrate the poetic power of film music. It might not be surprising in a film such as *La Strada* for the musical score to pass relatively unnoticed, given the dominant place imagery or camera movement plays in Fellini's works. Originally, the central musical motif in the film was intended to be a seventeenth-century melody by an Italian composer. Moreover, in the initial shooting script (see n. 9, "Notes on the Continuity Script" in this volume), the music that eventually became identified as Gelsomina's theme song was introduced by means of a radio off-screen, which Gelsomina overheard as she was standing under the eaves of a house in the rain waiting, along with Zampanò, for a mechanic to repair his motorcycle.

In the final version of the film, Fellini and Rota wisely rejected this version of the music's origin. Instead, they substituted for the music of the past an entirely original composition by Rota. Moreover, this tune is introduced (shot 375) not by an anonymous radio but by the Fool, who is rendering it on his violin. It is infinitely more appropriate for this transference of the melody to take place through the intervention of the Fool, since it is precisely the Fool who at this point in the film is encouraging Gelsomina to work in the circus independently of Zampanò and implicitly urging her to explore the untapped potential of her personality. Later on, in the often discussed "parable of the pebble" (shots 462–469), the Fool provides for Gelsomina a philosophical rationalization for what is here merely implied.

What has traditionally been recognized as Gelsomina's theme begins first, to be more precise, as the Fool's theme. Because of the Fool's influence, Gelsomina recognizes her function in the world, and her means of expressing this realization becomes her habitual playing of the melody, now *her* theme. This process of transference of the central musical motif in *La Strada* still remains incomplete, however, until it is finally associated with her even by the brutish Zampanò years after Gelsomina's death. Now sung unaccompanied by an anonymous woman (shots 721–735), who informs Zampanò that Gelsomina has died, its poetic evocation manages to awaken Zampanò's deadened conscience and has quite frequently moved audiences to tears. As a perceptive discussion of Fellini and Rota has pointed out, the poetic power of the musical motif in *La Strada* depends not only upon the fact that it represents a "static or redundant identifying tag" but also on its function as a "true signifier that accumulates and communicates meaning not explicit in the images or dialogue."[13]

As *La Strada* fades out to its concluding end title, we are left with a number of possible interpretations for the events we have just witnessed. And that is precisely what Fellini intended in producing such a lyrical cinematic work, an openended narrative colored by his own personal mythology and populated by

13. Claudia Gorbman, "Music as Salvation: Notes on Fellini and Rota," in *Federico Fellini: Essays in Criticism,* ed. Bondanella, p. 82.

ambiguous figures who derive their meaning not from their socioeconomic environment but, instead, from their emotional impact upon us and their potential symbolic importance. As the title of the film itself suggests ("the road"), the work is a picaresque, nonlinear narrative that traces the journey of Gelsomina and Zampanò from one ocean beach (where Gelsomina is purchased by Zampanò to assist him in his routines) to another, where Zampanò finally senses a feeling of remorse and loneliness over his loss. The literal journey from one shore to another is far less important, of course, than the figurative distance the characters travel. The quest motif, from Homer's *Odyssey* on, usually embodies a journey of self-discovery, and Fellini's *La Strada* follows this venerable literary tradition. Fellini's treatment of this inner journey in the film and his creation of unusual but highly evocative characters explain the many different interpretations that have been advanced to analyze the film's meaning. For some, the relationship between Gelsomina and Zampanò is a complex metaphor for the failure of communication in the modern world. For others, it is the visual and lyrical embodiment of a timeless fairy tale, Beauty and the Beast, wherein the Beast (Zampanò) is transformed by the suffering of Beauty (Gelsomina). Zampanò's slow transformation from a brutish and insensitive lout to a human being at least capable of shedding tears may also be viewed as a sentimental romance structure—the love of a good woman changes a bad man. And, of course, an even more complicated interpretation of the film can also be advanced, one that would emphasize its Christian overtones—the "parable of the pebble," Gelsomina's visual associations with the Madonna, and the Fool's "angelic" message announcing Gelsomina's spiritual vocation.

It is rare to discover a viewer of *La Strada* who has not been profoundly touched by the film. Yet, any critical attempt to reduce to discursive terms the emotional and poetic appeal of the film seems doomed to failure. Moreover, close scrutiny of the content of the film (what, for Fellini, always represents the least important aspect of his cinema) may even make the film appear simpleminded. Perhaps Peter Harcourt summed up this irreducibly lyric or poetic quality of *La Strada* better than anyone else when he wrote that the most moving sequences of the film are "essentially dumb" and "defy confident interpretation"; unless the viewer remains open to what he calls "a subliminal level, a level largely of images plus the complex association of scarcely perceived sound," a viewing of *La Strada* will remain unsatisfying.[14]

---

14. Peter Harcourt, "The Secret Life of Federico Fellini," cited in *Federico Fellini: Essays in Criticism*, ed. Bondanella, pp. 241, 247.

Perhaps nothing reveals so clearly Fellini's essentially poetic approach to his film-making than a consideration of how *La Strada* was made. When Fellini began making the film, as he notes in "The Genesis of *La Strada*" (reprinted in this volume), there "merely existed a confused feeling of the film," "a sense of guilt as pervasive as a shadow, vague and consuming, composed of memories and forebodings." In this initial stage of creativity (which unites the unconscious with past memories), all seems vague and amorphous. This is evident again from "The Genesis of *La Strada*," when Fellini speaks of his first ideas about the work—he imagines silence as snow falls on the ocean, various compositions of clouds, or a nightingale's song. None of these images eventually finds a specific place in the completed film, although they are a necessary stage in Fellini's creative process, and they will eventually be replaced by equally subjective and personal poetic images as the film takes clearer shape.

The "reality" that interests Fellini and that eventually becomes the center of any film produced by him is thus not a reflection of the objective world around him. He feels little or no need to photograph the world as it is, since he is far more interested in shaping the world into a product of his own imagination. Fellini's cinema presents a distorted mirror of reality, or better still, a recreated reality embodying his private fantasies and symbols. Even the apparently autobiographical elements in Fellini's cinema are creations of the director's fantasy: "I have invented myself entirely: a childhood, a personality, longings, dreams and memories, all in order to enable myself to tell them." [15]

Fellini furthermore believes that the idea for a film and the film itself have an independent existence quite apart from the director's relationship to it. Rather than creating the film, the film confronts the director and demands to be created. "Everything goes ahead as if, at the beginning, there were an agreement between the film that is to be born and me. As if the finished film already existed quite outside me, just as—on a very different scale—the law of gravity existed before Newton discovered it." [16] And the film presents itself to the director's consciousness in the form of images rather than rational ideas. Such images are influenced by Fellini's own memories and dreams, and may actually have a history in the director's past. Yet, before they can take on artistic form, they must be reinvented in order to be transformed into images of collective memories and dreams that his audience can share and appreciate. Thus transformed, they become meta-

15. *Fellini on Fellini,* p. 51.
16. Ibid., p. 104.

phorical images, now removed from the private fantasy world of the director and connected with the collective fantasy of his public.

Because the first stage of this process involves the recollection of ideas that present themselves through images, drawing and sketching become important to Fellini at this point:

> In general, the drawings I make have only a functional purpose, and are closely linked with my work as a director. Just as the screenplay represents the literary, the verbal phase in the realization of a film, it often happens that in the work of preparation I make sketches, designs, figures, in an attempt to fix and visually clarify a setting, a situation, a character, the costume of a certain personage, a feeling. . . . For me, drawing, designing, although coming from a very natural instinct, never has an esthetic finality. It is only an instrument, a means, a link in the chain by which fancy and imagination are anchored in a cinematic result.[17]

This habitual tendency to render in visual terms everything connected with the genesis of a film was particularly important in the case of *La Strada,* by Fellini's own testimony:

> When I am preparing for a film, I write very little. I prefer to draw the characters and the sets. This is something I learnt to do when I was working in provincial music halls. From then onwards I have liked drawing the ideas that come to me, and translating every idea into an image. There are even ideas that are born all at once in the form of an image. "Reading" it all comes later. This was particularly so with the character of Gelsomina.[18]

From the formative idea and the drawings or sketches that evolve from it, Fellini moves to the shooting script, which he usually writes in collaboration with one or more of his close associates. The shooting script is, for Fellini, more of a necessity of production than an artistic requirement. Without a shooting script, or at least a general scenario outline, it would be impossible for him to obtain the backing of a producer. Since he himself conceives the film in completely visual terms, and this essentially personal collection of images and symbols represents the essence of what the film will eventually become, it would be unthinkable for Fellini to film a screenplay written by someone else. This very procedure, of

17. Ibid., p. 101.
18. Ibid., p. 100.

ZAMPANÒ

course, occurs constantly in Hollywood productions of films or television series. For Fellini, the shooting script serves the purpose of organizing the preexisting visual images and thus constitutes the "literary" phase in the process of film-making. In the case of *La Strada* as well as every other film Fellini has made, the film he ultimately creates is quite different from the published Italian shooting script. His scripts represent an intermediate stage in the process. They are really only a general outline of the narrative material the director and his associates have agreed upon *before* they actually begin filming.

It is significant that the original Italian shooting script of *La Strada,* published in 1955 after the release of the film, contained absolutely no directions for camera movements or angles, and almost nothing to indicate how the film would be edited. The only indication of what might occur in the final editing process were general transitions between the major sequences (usually "fade out," "dissolve" and the like). This shooting script became a film of 745 discrete shots, and almost none of these shots were specifically demanded by the shooting script. Dialogue is naturally present in the shooting script, and there are relatively few changes in this dialogue between the shooting script and the final film. Yet, dialogue plays a secondary role in all of Fellini's films. He distrusts dialogue and uses it merely for informational purposes, since dialogue and sound effects are intended only to support the image. The present edition of the continuity script for *La Strada* contains extensive descriptions of the camera movements precisely because, for Fellini, the poetry of cinema resides primarily in movement, and in everything that supports movement—camera angles, lighting, and editing.

Pier Paolo Pasolini, an Italian director who wrote important theoretical essays on the semiotics of the cinema and its essentially oneiric and poetic nature, has been one of the few directors to have analyzed the shooting script in theoretical terms. In an essay entitled "The Scenario as a Structure Designed to Become Another Structure" (originally written in 1966), Pasolini defined the shooting script as an amorphous and indeterminate text "whose principal structure is the intrinsic reference to a cinematographic work in the making."[19] This definition fits the description of a Fellini shooting script only in part, however. With *La Strada,* the shooting script was never precisely a structure designed to become

---

19. Pier Paolo Pasolini, "The Scenario as a Structure Designed to Become Another Structure," *Wide Angle* 2 (1977):41. For Pasolini's famous formulation of the thesis that cinema is essentially poetic in nature, see "The Cinema of Poetry," reprinted in *Movies and Methods: An Anthology,* ed. Bill Nichols (Berkeley and Los Angeles: University of California Press, 1976), pp. 542–558.

another *visual* structure, since Fellini's scripts scrupulously avoid a language specific to the cinema. There is almost no reference in the shooting script to the manner in which a scene will be shot. On the other hand, the foundation of Fellini's cinematic language is based upon a complex of images that are the product both of the environment (the objects represented) and of the director's private fantasy world. Thus, Fellini's cinema is oneiric and poetic by its very nature, as Pasolini argued, and its imagery is of an irrational type similar to the language of poetry. In Fellini's case, the shooting script and the final version of the completed film are united by at least one similar feature: they both embody a language that is poetic in nature.

After the shooting script is completed, the delicate work of transforming Fellini's images into a film takes place on the set, on location, and later during the final editing process. In no sense, however, do these steps in Fellini's creative process entail a mere adaptation of the existing script. In the first place, Fellini believes in improvisation, in remaining open to all potentially heuristic discoveries on the set or on location. His is a controlled improvisation, of course, since the director is totally responsible for the completed work. Some idea of the atmosphere that reigns during the production of a Fellini film may be gained from reading the several articles reprinted in this volume about the making of *La Strada*. It is clear from Moraldo Rossi's description of Fellini's nocturnal encounter with a phantom horse (which later became incorporated into one of the most celebrated and mysterious sections of the film), or Giulietta Masina's account of her acting, or Luigi Giacosi's problems encountered in the production, or even the nature of the collaboration which Fellini's co-scriptwriters contributed to the final work, that the atmosphere on a Fellini set is one closer to that of a carnival or an ocean voyage than an efficient Hollywood operation. Its very lack of what a Hollywood producer would call a rational structure or a detailed schedule of shooting, organized shot by shot from a preestablished and very detailed screenplay, is for Fellini the guarantee that the process of making a film will be always open to free flights of the imagination. In no sense, therefore, does Fellini's original shooting script control what he actually films or, more importantly, *how* he actually films it. Fellini's very conception of film-making involves few direct links between shooting script and film, except insofar as the general storyline or dialogue is concerned, and presupposes—indeed, demands—constant alteration and experiment as the film is being created. The present edition of the continuity script of *La Strada* was prepared with the hope that this more complete description of the film's dialogue, camera movements, and editing will introduce the viewer to the visual poetry embodied in Fellini's virtuoso style. But the reader is urged never to forget that for Fellini, any linguistic description, any verbalized account, any rational narrative of what is essentially for him a *lyrical* and *visual* experience must of necessity pale before the work of art itself.

Federico Fellini: A Biographical Sketch

Federico Fellini was born in 1920 of middle-class parents at Rimini in the province of Emilia Romagna. Very little is known about his early childhood, except for the information and misinformation he himself has provided in a number of interviews. While the story about the young Fellini running away from home to join a traveling circus may well be the director's invention, every form of entertainment—the circus, the cinema, comic strips, the music hall, the theater—fascinated him as a youngster—a fascination later reflected in almost all of his films. He soon drifted away from his hometown to Rome, where he made an abortive attempt to complete law school. He supported himself by sketching caricature portraits in Roman restaurants and writing for *Marc'-Aurelio,* an Italian humor magazine. When Mussolini banned American comic strips in Italy, Fellini invented an Italian version of *Flash Gordon.* His talent as a sketch artist and cartoonist would in the future always play a role in the preparations for his films.

During the Second World War, Fellini met and married Giulietta Masina, falling in love with her voice, which he heard for the first time on the Italian state radio network. According to the director's testimony, during the occupation of Rome, he twice narrowly escaped arrest and possible deportation by the Germans in several of the dragnet operations the Nazis carried out to surprise suspected Resistance leaders. In the first instance, he was saved by the fortuitous destruction of his papers in an Allied bombing raid. In a second case, he avoided arrest by pretending to be the friend of a German officer who happened to be passing his home when soldiers arrived to take him into custody. With the liberation of Rome, Fellini eked out a living of sorts by making caricature sketches of American soldiers in the Eternal City.

Fellini lacked any formal training in cinematography and developed his personal style only after a long apprenticeship as a scriptwriter. His introduction to the world of the cinema came about as a result of a fortunate friendship with the actor Aldo Fabrizi, who introduced Fellini to the soon-to-be famous neo-realist director, Roberto Rossellini. Fabrizi would play the partisan priest in Rossellini's *Open City* (1945), and Fellini collaborated on the script of this film, a work of genius which alerted the entire world to the fact that a new artistic movement had arisen in Italy from the rubble of the war.

Besides his work with Rossellini on *Open City,* Fellini embarked on a series of associations that led from minor gag writer to major scriptwriter and, ultimately, to direction in 1950. He coilaborated on the story and screenplay for Rossellini's *Paisan,* being especially responsible for the enigmatic monastery sequence. He was co-author of the screenplay for Alberto Lattuada's *The Crime of Giovanni Episcopo* (1946) and Lattuada's *Without Pity* (1947), the latter of which was a denunciation of racism and other negative aspects of American culture in post-war Italy. It featured a daring interracial love affair between a black G.I. and an Italian girl from Livorno. Fellini not only wrote the script for Rossellini's *The Miracle* in 1948 but also acted a leading role in the controversial film in which a simple-minded village woman (Anna Magnani) is seduced by a stranger (Fellini); the woman is convinced that he is St. Joseph and she is to become a second Virgin. With the hostile critical reaction in some Church circles that greeted *The Miracle,* Fellini encountered for the first of many times the force of censorship. The other important neo-realist films to which Fellini made major script contributions include Pietro Germi's *In the Name of the Law* (1948); Lattuada's *The Mill on the Po* (1949); Rossellini's *The Flowers of St. Francis* (1949); Germi's *The Path of Hope* (1950); and Rossellini's *Europe '51* (1951).

Fellini's debut as a director on *Variety Lights* (1950) was made in collaboration with Alberto Lattuada, a veteran director whose career had begun long before Fellini became interested in the cinema and whose best works were made during the neo-realist period. This early work and Fellini's second film, *The White Sheik* (1952), avoided the political and socioeconomic concerns typical of neo-realist cinema and concentrated, instead, upon the world of the personal daydreams and aspirations of his often pathetic but likable characters, most of whom are associated in some way with the entertainment world. *I Vitelloni* (1953) was Fellini's first critical and popular success within Italy, and a number of leftist critics usually unfavorable to Fellini's work viewed his bittersweet portrait of life in the Italian provinces as a work of trenchant social criticism. Fellini also contributed a brief episode to a film entitled *Love in the City* (1953), which was organized by Cesare Zavattini, the most famous of all neo-realist scriptwriters.

The international success of *La Strada* (1954), Fellini's fourth feature film, assured Fellini of a lifelong career in the cinema while opening a sometimes acrimonious polemical debate with a number of Marxist critics, who attacked Fellini's poetic and highly personal cinema for helping to turn Italian neo-realism away from the goals of social reform or revolution. Quite without intending to do so, Fellini found himself involved in an ideological "crisis of neo-realism." Yet, Fellini continued to make the kinds of films he wanted to make, garnering not only Academy Awards for *La Strada* but also for *Nights of Cabiria* (1957) and *8½* (1963), as well as achieving an unprecedented international commercial success with *La Dolce Vita* (1959), which even added new words to the English vocabulary—the adjective "Fellinian," referring to fanciful, baroque imagery; the noun *paparazzi* for the bothersome photographers who flocked around celebrities on Rome's Via Veneto; and the term "la dolce vita," describing the decadence of the jet-set life illuminated by the bright lights of the news media.

With *La Dolce Vita, 8½,* and *Juliet of the Spirits* (1965), Fellini reached the pinnacle of artistic, critical, and commercial success. In 1967, however, he was hospitalized and almost died from a mysterious disease. He had been working on a new film, *The Voyage of G. Mastorna,* which was never realized, and his illness may have been caused by a creative crisis. Nevertheless, with *Fellini Satyricon* (1969), Fellini's genius seemed to have been reinvigorated, and the focus of his films became increasingly poetic and personal. *Fellini: A Director's Notebook* (1969), *The Clowns* (1970), and *Fellini's Roma* (1972) dealt with meta-cinematic questions on the nature of the cinematic medium itself. *Amarcord* (1973), the most commercially successful of all his works since the 1960s, treated the period of his childhood in Fascist Italy with a rare blend of nostalgia and critical distance. *Fellini's Casanova* (1976) and the more recent *City of Women* (1980) examined Fellinian myths of sexuality. *Orchestra Rehearsal* (1979), a rare political film made for Italian television, offered a bleak image of strife-torn Italy as an orchestra out of control and in revolt against its conductor. *And the Ship Sails On* (1983) presented a dark allegory of the end of the world, a contemporary "ship of fools" in which we see not only the beginnings of the military conflicts that have destroyed modern Europe but also the birth of

Dino De Laurentiis receives the Oscar statuettes for *La Strada* in 1956.

the cinema. And in his latest work, *Ginger and Fred* (1985), Fellini examines the power of television to produce contemporary mythologies.

There is probably no living director who has received so many awards and maintained so high a critical reputation over such a length of time as Fellini. Besides Oscars (Best Foreign Film) for *La Strada, Nights of Cabiria,* and *8½,* Fellini's works have received numerous major prizes at many film festivals around the world. Broadway musicals (*Sweet Charity* and *Nine*) have been based on two of his films (*Nights of Cabiria* and *8½*). At least two popular American directors—Woody Allen and Bob Fosse—have declared their indebtedness to Fellini's cinema, and there is little doubt that his particular brand of cinema has served as a positive example for countless others. Fellini's entire work has been recently honored in 1985 with prestigious retrospectives at both the Venice Film Festival and at New York's Lincoln Center Film Festival.

Giulietta Masina and Federico Fellini at Lincoln Center in 1985.

La Strada

La Strada

This transcription of the verbal and visual continuity script of Federico Fellini's *La Strada* is based upon both the Italian release print from the Centro Sperimentale di Cinematografia in Rome and the American release print from Films, Incorporated (the Janus Classic Films Collection). As much as possible we have tried to retain the flavor of Fellini's own language whenever the shooting script conforms closely to the final film. Included in our notes are some important segments of the shooting script, translated into English for the first time, that originally appeared in *La strada: Sceneggiatura originale di Federico Fellini e Tullio Pinelli* (1955) and were later reprinted in Renzo Renzi's edition of *Il primo Fellini* (1969).

The abbreviations used to describe camera distance follow the usual English-language conventions (ELS = extreme long shot; LS = long shot; MS = medium shot; MCU = medium close-up; CU = close-up; POV = point of view). We urge the reader to remember that these terms are, at best, approximate. We have been especially careful to provide the reader with an extremely precise record of camera movements, since they are so essential to Fellini's cinematic style.

Credits and Cast

Director
Federico Fellini

Producers
Carlo Ponti, Dino De Laurentiis

Production Company
Trans-Lux

U.S. Distributor
Paramount

Screenplay
Federico Fellini, Tullio Pinelli, with
the collaboration of Ennio Flaiano,
based on a story by Fellini and Pinelli

Dialogue
Ennio Flaiano

Director of Photography
Otello Martelli

Cameraman
Roberto Girardi

Sets
Mario Ravasco

Costumes
Margherita Marinari

Makeup
Eligio Trani

Music
Nino Rota

Music Director
Franco Ferrara

Sound
A. Calpini, R. Boggio

Editor
Leo Catozzo

Assistant Editor
Lina Caterini

Artistic Collaborators
Brunello Rondi, Paolo Nuzzi

Assistant Director
Moraldo Rossi

Production Director
Luigi Giacosi

Locations
Viterbo, Ovindoli, Bagnoregio, and
various small towns in Central and
Southern Italy

Process
Black and White

Release Data
18 September 1954 (Italy)
16 July 1956 (United States)

Length
107 minutes

Gelsomina Di Constanzo
Giulietta Masina

Zampanò
Anthony Quinn

The Fool
Richard Basehart

Giraffa
Aldo Silvani

Two main characters

Widow
Marcella Rovere

The Nun
Livia Venturini

Other roles are played by uncredited actors.

The Continuity Script

1. *Fade in.* ELS: *a deserted shore bordered by white surf. A small female figure enters the frame from the bottom left, carrying something toward the sea in the background.*

   CHILDREN'S VOICES (*off*): Gelsomina! . . . Gelsomina!

   Four little girls between six and eight years of age, barefoot, dressed in rags, enter the frame from the left background and head toward the girl. She advances toward the children while they continue to call out.

   CHILDREN: Gelsomina! . . . Gelsomina!

   Gelsomina is like the others, barefoot and dressed in rags. She is carrying on her back some firewood she has gathered. At first, the voices do not cause her to hasten her steps. The children reach her on the run. They are puffing and very excited.

   CHILDREN: Your mother says to come quickly. . . . A man with an enormous motorcycle has arrived. . . . He says that Rosa is dead.

   They all begin running toward the sea and the background of the frame. Dissolve.

2. LS *of a house. The children and Gelsomina enter the foreground of the frame and head toward it. In front of the shack by a little patio stand Gelsomina's Mother, holding a baby in her arms, and a tall, heavyset man wearing a leather jacket. When she sees Gelsomina, she calls out to her.*

3. MS: *Gelsomina glancing toward the ground. One of her sisters stands beside her to the left of frame.*

   MOTHER (*off*): Gelsomina . . . do you remember Zampanò who took Rosa away? (*She suddenly breaks into tears.*)

4. MS: *Zampanò leaning against the patio.*

   MOTHER (*off*): My poor daughter!

5. MCU: *Mother with baby in her arms.*

   MOTHER: I'll never even see where they buried her! She's dead. Poor
   little thing. She's dead. She was so pretty, so good, she was so clever in
   everything . . . !

6. MS: *Gelsomina, as she lets the firewood fall from her back.*

   MOTHER (*off*): Zampanò, do you see how this other daughter of mine
   resembles Rosa? . . . This is Gelsomina.

7. MCU: *Zampanò, blowing on the half-lighted end of his cigarette.*

   MOTHER (*off*): Ah! How miserable we are!

8. MCU: *Gelsomina as she looks up.*

   MOTHER (*off*): Now, Zampanò, I did tell you that this girl is not like
   Rosa. This one, poor thing, is very good.

9. MCU: *Zampanò with the cigarette in his mouth.*

   MOTHER (*off*): She does everything you tell her. . . . Gelsomina, she's
   just a bit strange . . . but if she eats every day, perhaps she'll change.

10. MS: *Gelsomina, her mother embracing her while her sister stands in the
    left background of frame.*

    MOTHER: Do you want to go with Zampanò to take Rosa's place? He'll
    teach you a trade, too . . . you'll earn a bit of money and here at home
    there'll be one less mouth to feed . . . (*She begins to kiss and hug
    Gelsomina.*) Hey, Gelsomina? Zampanò is a good man, you know?
    He'll treat you well. He'll take you all over the world. You'll sing and
    dance . . .

11. MCU: *Zampanò puffing his cigarette.*

MOTHER (*off*): . . . and do you know what he gave me, Gelsomina? He gave me ten thousand lire![1]

12. MS *of Zampanò.*

MOTHER (*off*): See, I have it right here . . . ten thousand lire! Now I can fix the roof, and these little creatures can eat a little bit.

13. MS: *Gelsomina, her mother, and sister, all crying.*

MOTHER: Oh, why did your father leave us? My Gelsomina! You've grown up, you've never had a job, it's not my fault, poor thing, if you're not like the other girls. . . .

14. MCU *of Zampanò.*

MOTHER (*off*): Don't you want to help your mother a little?

15. *As in 13.*

MOTHER: And you'll teach her a trade, won't you, Zampanò?

Listening all the while, her eyes puffy from tears, Gelsomina stands up, overwhelmed and disturbed, staring out of frame at Zampanò. She wears a bewildered smile.

16. MS *of Zampanò.*

ZAMPANÒ (*crudely*): Sure! I can even train dogs! Hey, kids, go buy a kilo of salami . . .

17. MS: *Zampanò's back, as he hands some money to one of the little girls; the others are standing in the background.*

ZAMPANÒ: . . . half a kilo of cheese . . .

18. MS *of Zampanò.*
    ZAMPANÒ: . . . and two flasks of wine.

19. *As in 17.*

ZAMPANÒ: That's the kind of guy I am. Take it, come on—now run along.
MOTHER: Go on, go on, children. Thank him!

*Two children run to the left out of frame. Looking disturbed, her eyes
downcast, Gelsomina turns toward the beach, and without saying a word
walks toward the ocean. Alarmed, her mother calls to her.*

MOTHER: Where are you going? Come back here, Gelsomina!

20. MS: *Zampanò, looking out of frame at the scene.*

21. *As in 19.*

MOTHER: Why are you acting like that? Oh, Zampanò! Gelsomina!

In the distant background, Gelsomina makes no reply. She kneels down.

22. MCU: *Gelsomina in profile, against the beach in the background. Her expression passes quickly from a tearful anxiety to a momentary childish smile. Dissolve.*

23. MS: *Gelsomina and her mother entering frame left. Camera tracks right following them, then stops as Gelsomina and her mother head toward a woman in the background.*

MOTHER: Hurry! Hurry!
WOMAN: Where are you going?
GELSOMINA: I'm going to work. I'll learn a trade, then I'll send money home. . . . He's a performer. I'll be a performer too, I'll dance and sing . . . just like Rosa did . . .

WOMAN: And when are you coming back?

GELSOMINA (*bewildered*): When will I come back?

Gelsomina and her mother hurry to the right, followed by the children. Camera tracks right and frames them all in a MLS, *with Zampanò and his motorcycle and van in the far background. Her mother cries out sorrowfully to Gelsomina, suddenly grief-stricken.*

MOTHER: Don't go away! Don't go away, daughter! (*Crying pitifully, the mother embraces and hugs Gelsomina in an exaggerated, awkward manner. Then Gelsomina leans over to embrace her little sisters.*) My little baby! . . . My little daughter! . . . I don't want you to leave!

24. LS: *Zampanò standing in front of his van, which is parked on top of a ridge. The canvas-covered van, which is attached to a motorcycle, bears the name "Zampanò" and the picture of a mermaid.*

ZAMPANÒ: I said we'd come back soon!

25. ELS: *Gelsomina and her family running toward Zampanò.*

26. MCU: *Gelsomina, with Zampanò preparing to leave in the background, as she turns toward the others out of frame and waves good-bye.*

GELSOMINA: All aboard! (*Gelsomina gives a military salute with a clownish expression, her jacket then covering her face.*)

MOTHER (*off*): Your things, Gelsomina!

27. MS: *Mother waving a shawl.*

MOTHER: Your shawl! . . . your shawl!

28. MCU: *Gelsomina, suddenly saddened by her departure. Seated on his motorcycle in the background, Zampanò impatiently cries out.*

ZAMPANÒ: Jump in!

Gelsomina climbs up the ridge to the rear of the van. She turns toward her mother out of frame.

29. MCU: *Mother in tears.*

    MOTHER: My daughter!

30. LS *of the van.*

    MOTHER (*off*): My poor little girl!

    Camera pans left to follow Zampanò's departing van.

31. LS: *The family from Gelsomina's* POV *in the van; as the vehicle pulls away, the children run after it along the road.*

32. MS: *Gelsomina, inside the van, waving good-bye.*

33. ELS *of the road with the family far in the background.*

34. MS: *Gelsomina in the van. Her face becomes sadder and sadder as she draws the van's canvas flaps closed. Dissolve.*

35. ELS: *Zampanò's motorcycle-van drives down the road diagonally toward the camera. Camera pans to right, following the van's progress. Dissolve.*[2]

36. CU *of Zampanò's right arm, as he enters the screen from the left. Camera follows behind Zampanò as he enters the middle of a circle of spectators. Camera then tracks on Zampanò as he walks around behind the van, revealing Gelsomina (MS), who sits in the rear of the van without missing a gesture or a word. Zampanò is performing, repeating his usual spiel.*

    ZAMPANÒ: This chain here is a piece of metal a half centimeter thick . . . it's made of pig iron, which is stronger than steel. With only the expansion of my pectoral muscles—that is, my chest . . .

37. MCU: *Gelsomina in the van.*

ZAMPANÒ (*off*): . . . I'll shatter the hook.

38. LS *of Zampanò from a high angle in the midst of his audience as they toss him some change.*

ZAMPANÒ: Thank you, thank you, thank you, ladies and gentlemen. In order to do this . . .

39. MS: *Zampanò rises to his feet and wraps the chain around his chest.*

ZAMPANÒ: . . . I'll have to inflate my lungs like an inner tube. (*Camera pans on Zampanò a full 360 degrees as he walks around the audience in a circle, continuing his spiel.*) A vein might burst, and I might spit up some blood. One time in Milan, a man who weighed some two hundred and sixty pounds lost his eyesight doing this feat. This happened because it's the optic nerve that does all the work, and when you've lost your sight, you've had it. If there are some squeamish people in the audience, they'd better not look, since there might be some blood. (*The pan ends on a* MS *of Zampanò, kneeling on the ground and preparing to shatter the chain. He begins to inflate his chest.*)

40. MCU: *Gelsomina in the rear of the van, her eyes wide open in amazement.*

41. MS: *Zampanò shatters the chain.*

42. MCU: *Gelsomina, who applauds with a puzzled look.*

ZAMPANÒ (*off*): Thank you, thank you.

Dissolve.

43. LS: *Zampanò is seated upon a tin drum, slowing eating his soup by the fire while Gelsomina stands in the background, gingerly tasting her soup. Zampanò's motorcycle is parked in the left foreground of frame. The scene is an empty field by the road.*

44. MS: *Zampanò eating in silence. Church bells are tolling in the distance.*

45. MS: *Gelsomina, with a bemused expression, tosses a spoonful of soup behind her.*

46. MS: *Zampanò, who meticulously eats his soup in silence.*

47. MS: *Gelsomina, after a momentary hesitation, tosses away all of her soup from her messtin, staring out of frame at Zampanò.*

48. *As in 43. Finishing his soup in obvious exasperation, Zampanò looks first at Gelsomina, then away from her; he stands up. Camera tracks backward as he walks to the rear of the van.*

ZAMPANÒ: Didn't you ever make soup at your house? . . . Hey?
GELSOMINA (*off*): No . . .

Camera stops on a MS *of Zampanò's back while he searches around in the rear of the van.*

ZAMPANÒ (*calmly, without anger*): It's fit for pigs! (*Gelsomina is framed through the open flaps of the van in the distant background.*) Now, there's enough stuff here to dress ten people—shoes, dresses, everything.

As Gelsomina puts down her messtin, the camera pans right, following her approach to where Zampanò is standing at the rear of the van.

ZAMPANÒ: Come here: maybe there's something that fits you.

Gelsomina is now standing alone in MS, *the empty field in the background.*

ZAMPANÒ (*off*): You have to look elegant. I don't want rags worn around Zampanò. My women have always cut a fine figure. Here. (*Zampanò enters the frame from left foreground; he approaches Gelsomina, hands her a pile of clothes and hats with his right hand while carrying a drum and a trumpet with his left hand. He tries a staved-in top hat on her.*) Try saying, "Zampanò is here."

GELSOMINA (*in a faint voice*): Zampanò is here.

*Zampanò scratches his ear, walks around Gelsomina to consider the effect,
and exchanges the top hat for a bowler. As she stands with an apprehensive
look, Zampanò adjusts the bowler to a more jaunty angle.*

ZAMPANÒ: Zampanò is here!
GELSOMINA: Zampanò is here!

Zampanò walks away from her to the background as Gelsomina, in MS,
*overwhelmed with exuberance by her new costume, suddenly makes a
series of funny faces and clownish hops of unrestrained and childish
pleasure. In the background, Zampanò turns around to look back at
Gelsomina; he is surprised and instinctively hostile.*

ZAMPANÒ: Hey! . . .

49. MS: *Zampanò, back to camera, as he calls out.*

ZAMPANÒ: Come over here!

50. MS: *Zampanò, back to camera. He then turns around, walks toward the camera, and sits down. Gelsomina hastens to obey, crouching near him. With the smugness of a teacher, Zampanò takes up each musical instrument, naming them in turn.*

ZAMPANÒ: This one here is a trumpet.

He brings the trumpet to his lips and with fanfare, plays a few notes intended to impress as a virtuoso sound. As soon as he puts the trumpet down, Gelsomina seizes it. As Zampanò is about to show her how the drum is played, she blows the trumpet. An out-of-tune squeal issues forth. With an icy calm, Zampanò strikes the trumpet with the drumsticks and takes it away from her, saying in a cold, menacing tone of voice:

ZAMPANÒ: Always do only what I tell you. (*He takes up the drum and puts it around Gelsomina's neck.*) This one here is a drum.

Gelsomina impetuously strikes the drum at random with her fists. As Zampanò glances coldly toward her, Gelsomina's enthusiastic smile turns into a worried frown. Zampanò grasps the drumsticks and strikes the instrument properly so that it gives off a dry and precise roll.

ZAMPANÒ: Zampanò is here.

He gives the drumsticks to Gelsomina, who tries but fails to imitate Zampanò's precise drumbeat.

GELSOMINA: Zampanò is here.

51. MS: *Zampanò takes back the drumsticks to demonstrate once more the proper procedure. He repeats with obvious irritation:*

ZAMPANÒ: Zampanò is here! (*He hands the drumsticks back to Gelsomina, out of frame.*)

52. MS: *Gelsomina, full of childish enthusiasm, as she exclaims, after having beaten the drum:*

GELSOMINA: Zampanò has arrived! (*She rolls the drum once again improperly.*)

53. *As in 51. Wearing a sullen expression, Zampanò begins to stand up.*

54. LS: *Zampanò and Gelsomina. Camera pans left to follow Zampanò as he walks slowly toward the bushes. He rips off a branch and tears off its leaves; then the camera follows him as he goes back to where Gelsomina is standing, wearing a naive smile.*

ZAMPANÒ: Go on, try again.
GELSOMINA (*shouting*): Zampanò has arrived!

Without warning, in a sudden, calculated motion Zampanò gives her a stroke on the legs with the switch. Gelsomina, stupefied, emits a suffocated cry, as she hops backward on one foot, rubbing her injured leg with her left hand.

GELSOMINA: Ouch!
ZAMPANÒ (*with an icy calm*): Come here.

Gelsomina distrustfully returns to her original place, as Zampanò points the switch to the spot.

ZAMPANÒ: Right there . . . try it.

Apprehensive, Gelsomina tries again.

GELSOMINA: Zampanò has arrived.

Zampanò strikes her a second time.

GELSOMINA: Ouch! (*Gelsomina backs away quickly, rubbing her bruised leg once more as the camera tracks right to follow her, leaving Zampanò out of frame.*)

ZAMPANÒ (*off*): You have to say it like this . . .

55. MS *of Zampanò.*

> ZAMPANÒ: . . . Zampanò is here! . . . Try it!
> GELSOMINA(*off*): Zampanò . . .

56. LS: *Gelsomina, terrified, bewildered, with tears in her eyes, begins to roll the drum again. The camera slowly tracks toward her. Several children observe the scene in the background.*

> GELSOMINA (*frantically*): . . . is here. Zampanò is here. Zampanò is here.
> YOUNG CHILD: Zampanò is here.

A woman enters the frame from the left background holding a child in her arms, and she calls out to the child who imitated Gelsomina's line.

> WOMAN: Come here immediately.

The tracking shot ends in a MCU *of Gelsomina in tears. Dissolve.*

57. MS: *Zampanò chewing a straw and sitting on the motorcycle. Through the rear of the van, in the distant background, we see a car traveling down a lonely road.*

> GELSOMINA (*off*): Slowly sparkle, shining fire . . .

58. LS: *Gelsomina, her back to the camera. Standing before the fire, Gelsomina recites some strange verses and moves her cape up and down, giving her the appearance of a bird flapping its wings.*

> GELSOMINA: . . . arise spark, the night whispers . . . boo, boo, boo . . .
> ZAMPANÒ (*off*): Hey . . .

Gelsomina turns and walks toward Zampanò out of frame.

59. *As in 57.*

ZAMPANÒ (*in a brusque tone*): . . . what are you doing there?

60. LS: *Gelsomina, walking to the left of frame, staring at the sky.*

GELSOMINA: Tomorrow, it'll rain.

61. *As in 59.*

ZAMPANÒ: And how do you know that?

62. *As in 60.*

GELSOMINA (*nodding*): Oh, it'll rain.

63. *As in 61.*

ZAMPANÒ: Come here.

64. *As in 62. Camera tracks to follow Gelsomina as she comes up to Zampanò sitting on the motorcycle. Gelsomina is visibly nervous and apprehensive.*

ZAMPANÒ: Climb in.

Gelsomina heads toward the rear of the van and momentarily disappears; then as Zampanò turns around toward the rear of the van to look at her, she disappears behind him, tapping his arm to attract his attention. Then, moving slightly away from the van, she says:

GELSOMINA: I sleep here outside.
ZAMPANÒ: Oh, you do? (*He climbs down from the motorcycle and walks behind her, asking matter-of-factly*): Tell me, what's your name?
GELSOMINA: Di Constanzo, Gelsomina.[3]
ZAMPANÒ: Come on, Gelsomina, get moving!

Zampanò pushes her forward toward the camera, which tracks backward. Then the camera stops as they go out of frame on the lower left side. Then

camera tracks forward to a CU *of the inside of the van, where an impro-*
vised bed can be seen. In the background, Zampanò and Gelsomina stand
looking inside the van. Zampanò rudely shoves Gelsomina inside.

GELSOMINA (*whispering*): Tomorrow!
ZAMPANÒ: Come on, get in!

Zampanò draws the flaps of the van closed as he enters behind her.
Fade out.

65. *Fade in. The interior of the van at night. Zampanò is lying in the fore-*
*ground, deep asleep. Gelsomina awakens and sits up (*MS*); she dries her*
tears, turns to Zampanò, and looks at him with frightened curiosity at
first; then, little by little, an almost maternal expression appears on
her face. Outside, sound of dogs barking. Gelsomina wipes her eyes
again. Behind her, a trumpet can be seen hanging on the wall of the van.
Fade out.

66. *Fade in.* MS: *Zampanò on his knees, performing his chain-breaking act.*
He is puffing, sweating, and grunting. Sound of drum roll over.

67. MS *of Gelsomina. Her face is covered with white greasepaint, her eyes*
are circled in black, and she is wearing a bowler hat. She stands be-
side the van, playing the drum with a listless expression, and looking at
Zampanò's act out of frame.

68. MS: *Zampanò shatters the chain around his chest.*

69. *As in 67. Gelsomina stops playing the drum and looks at the crowd.*

70. *As in 68: Zampanò rubs his eyes from the strain of his feat of strength.*
Camera tilts up as he rises to his feet and addresses the spectators. As he
speaks, camera first pans slightly right, then tracks left to follow him.

ZAMPANÒ: Thanks. And now, ladies and gentlemen, for the first time in
this city we are going to open a completely new little farce that'll make
you all laugh. (*To someone in the audience.*) Hello . . . hello, sir. . . .

now, if there's anyone with a heart condition, he'd better not watch, since he might die from laughing . . .

Zampanò (LS) walks behind the van and the camera comes to rest on a MS of Gelsomina in the foreground of frame standing in front of the van. Zampanò can be seen through the open flaps of the van itself as he begins changing his costume. Then Gelsomina turns around to look at Zampanò and picks up her cape. With an excited smile, she walks to the right into the middle of the circle of spectators, places her drum on the ground, and throws her cape over her shoulder with her back to the camera.

ZAMPANÒ: . . . and since we work in order to build up our appetites . . . my wife will pass a hat around later. (*To Gelsomina.*) Hey, come on, hurry up!

71. MS: *Gelsomina, spectators in background.*

72. MS: *Gelsomina with her back to the camera. Zampanò leaps from behind the van, dressed as a clown and holding a rifle in his hand.*

ZAMPANÒ: Good day, "lung rady" Gelsomina![4]

Gelsomina gives Zampanò a military salute.

GELSOMINA: Zampanò!

Camera tracks on Zampanò walking right.

ZAMPANÒ: Excuse the question, but does my "lifle" frighten you? (*Camera comes to rest on a MS of Zampanò as he nears Gelsomina, in the left of frame and in the center of the circle of spectators, who is not responding to his cue.*) I said, excuse the question, but does my "lifle" frighten you? (*He angrily strikes her with his top hat to prompt her. They are both in MS in the center of the frame.*) Well, if you're not afraid of it, then let's go "hinting" with my "lifle."

As Zampanò aims his rifle, Gelsomina breaks into laughter and walks in a

complete circle around him. Camera pans slightly right and left to follow her movement.

GELSOMINA: Ha! Ha! Ha! You don't say "lifle," you say "rifle," you ignoramus!

73. MS: *Gelsomina smiles in self-satisfaction as the audience applauds her remark on Zampanò's mispronunciation.*

74. LS: *Gelsomina at left of frame.* MS *of Zampanò, face to camera, in the right foreground. Zampanò turns toward Gelsomina, who stands first on one foot and then on the other, gazing into the distance.*

GELSOMINA: But where are those ducks?[5]

*Zampanò (*MS*) doffs his hat, making a left turn. Gelsomina and Zampanò now trace a circle in the midst of the audience.*

ZAMPANÒ: O.K., since there aren't any ducks, you play the duck and I'll play the "hinter."

Zampanò and Gelsomina have returned to the same frame composition as in the beginning of shot, but now their respective positions have been reversed.

GELSOMINA (*braying like a donkey*): Hee-haw, hee-haw.
ZAMPANÒ: No, that's a jackass, not a duck.

Gelsomina starts flapping her cape like a duck.

GELSOMINA: Quack, quack . . .

75. MS *of Gelsomina.*

GELSOMINA: . . . quack, quack. (*Camera pans slightly left as Gelsomina turns around quacking.*)

76. LS: *Zampanò moving slightly left, aiming his rifle out of frame at Gelsomina.*

77. *As in 75. Gelsomina continues to quack and turns around.*

78. MS: *Zampanò, stumbling clumsily and drawing a bead on Gelsomina out of frame. Then he fires his popgun, which explodes in a cloud of white powder.*

GELSOMINA (*off*): Quack, quack . . .

79. MCU: *Gelsomina falls to the ground, holding her ears.*

80. MS: *Zampanò falls to the ground from the recoil.*

81. MS: *Gelsomina rises to her feet.*

82. LS: *the entire audience, as the two performers rise to their feet in the center circle.*

    ZAMPANÒ: Thanks! . . . thanks again! . . .

83. MS: *Zampanò addresses the audience as he removes his cloak and rubber nose.*

    ZAMPANÒ: . . . And now my wife will pass the hat through the audience, and whoever wants to donate something, thanks . . .

84. MS: *Gelsomina, smiling as the crowd applauds enthusiastically behind her.*

    ZAMPANÒ (*off*): . . . to whoever doesn't want to give something, thanks just the same.

    Dissolve.

85. LS: *the inside of a* trattoria.[6] *A door leading onto the street opens and Zampanò enters after hesitating a moment on the threshold. The large room is filled with traveling pedlars, livestock merchants, and peasants. Zampanò looks around with ostentatious self-assurance and turns halfway toward the door and toward Gelsomina.*

    ZAMPANÒ: Good evening to everybody!
    CUSTOMER AT A TABLE: Now shut that door!

    Zampanò waves hello to a few acquaintances in a cordial manner, anxious to be recognized and greeted. Gelsomina follows Zampanò inside. Camera pans slightly right to follow their movement in the trattoria.

    ZAMPANÒ: Ciao! . . . Ciao, Schile.[7]
    SCHILE: Hey, ciao, Zampanò.

ZAMPANÒ: Hey, tightwad, how are you?
ANOTHER CLIENT: Hey, Zampanò, how's it going?
ZAMPANÒ: Meet my wife.
CLIENT: Your wife? This is another of your girlfriends. Pleased to meet
you. Sit down and join me.
ZAMPANÒ: No, no, no, I'll sit over here. . . . Waiter!

They sit down at a free table in the foreground.

GELSOMINA: Should I go over . . . ?
ZAMPANÒ: No, you stay there. (*Zampanò bangs impatiently on the table,
taking off his leather jacket.*) Waiter! . . .

86. MCU *of Gelsomina. She is visibly excited and happy at what seems to be
the novel experience of eating in a restaurant.*

WAITER (*off*): I'm coming, I'm coming. Here's the wine.

87. MCU *of Zampanò.*

ZAMPANÒ: Something to eat!

88. MS: *Zampanò and Gelsomina at the table as the waiter approaches from
the background, hands Zampanò a menu, and clears off the table.*

WAITER: There's roast lamb and veal stew ready.
ZAMPANÒ (*to Gelsomina*): What're you having?
GELSOMINA: That.
WAITER: Which? Roast lamb or veal stew?
GELSOMINA: Both.
WAITER: Both?
ZAMPANÒ: O.K., both for her. Pasta and roast lamb for me.
WAITER: All right. (*He walks away from the table and exits frame from
the right background.*)
ZAMPANÒ: And a liter of red wine.
WAITER: O.K.

89. MCU: *Zampanò picking his teeth with a toothpick, his elbows on the table.*

90. MCU: *Gelsomina, who glances at Zampanò, out of frame, in admiration and then, with a childish smile, she picks up a toothpick herself and imitates Zampanò. Dissolve.*

91. MCU: *Gelsomina, finishing her meal with gusto, carefully cleaning her plate with a piece of bread.*[8]

92. MCU: *Zampanò, drinking a glass of wine and obviously under the influence.*

93. *As in 91. Gelsomina in turn takes a glass of wine and drinks it all down at once, then sighs with satisfaction.*

94. *As in 92. Zampanò seems more solemn than before.*

95. *As in 93.*

GELSOMINA: But . . . where'd you come from?

96. *As in 94.*

ZAMPANÒ (*grinning slyly*): From my hometown . . . heh, heh, heh!

97. MCU: *two-shot of Zampanò and Gelsomina.*

GELSOMINA: You don't speak like the people from around where we live. Where were you born?
ZAMPANÒ: In my father's house.

Camera pans slightly left so as to follow Zampanò's movement as he turns to address the waiter at the counter in the background. Gelsomina is out of frame.

ZAMPANÒ: Waiter!
WAITER: I'm coming! (*The waiter approaches their table and takes the carafe Zampanò is handing him.*)
ZAMPANÒ: Bring the wine here. Come on!

The waiter then exits frame right.

PROSTITUTE (*to a pedlar, as they stand at the table near the counter in the background*): Well, marry me—that way, it'll stay in the family.

98. MCU: *Zampanò staring at the prostitute, out of frame.*

99. MS: *the prostitute and the pedlar, as she examines his wares.*

PROSTITUTE: My, my! What do you mean, wool? This is cotton padding. That's right—we wrap our toes up in it!

100. MCU *of Zampanò.*

   ZAMPANÒ: Hey, redhead! . . .

101. *As in 99.*

102. *As in 100.*

   ZAMPANÒ: Come over here! . . .

103. LS: *the prostitute and the pedlar, with Zampanò in the left foreground, back to camera. Camera pans slightly right as the prostitute approaches Zampanò and reveals Gelsomina, also in the foreground, with Zampanò at the table.*

   PROSTITUTE: You talking to me?
   ZAMPANÒ: Sure, come over here . . .

   The camera tracks backward, following the prostitute as she approaches their table, then stops in MS as she stands between the still-seated Zampanò and Gelsomina, both looking at her as she faces the camera.

   ZAMPANÒ (*back to camera, taking her hand*): What are you doing?

   Continuing to hold his hand, the prostitute walks around Zampanò.

   PROSTITUTE (*shrugging her shoulders*): Nothing.
   ZAMPANÒ: Well, sit down over here, then.

104. MCU: *two-shot of Zampanò and the prostitute. She sits down, still holding hands. Zampanò slaps her bottom playfully and she laughs.*

105. MCU: *Gelsomina laughs shyly along with the prostitute.*

106. *As in 104.*

ZAMPANÒ: Do you want something to drink?

PROSTITUTE: Thanks.

ZAMPANÒ (*to the waiter out of frame*): Where's that wine?

PROSTITUTE (*to Gelsomina out of frame*): I don't like this place one
bit . . . not at all.

107. *As in 105.*

108. *As in 106.*

ZAMPANÒ: Smoke a cigarette? (*He breaks a cigarette in half, hands one
part to the prostitute, who places it in a cigarette holder. Then Zampanò lights first her cigarette, then his, with a match.*)

PROSTITUTE: But I must have met you previously . . .

ZAMPANÒ: That's possible. I'm always traveling around . . .

PROSTITUTE: That's it.

WAITER (*off*): Here's the wine.

*Zampanò takes the carafe of wine that the waiter has just placed at the
edge of the table, and pours it into Gelsomina's glass, out of frame.*

PROSTITUTE (*to Gelsomina out of frame*): Have you already eaten?

109. MCU *of Gelsomina.*

ZAMPANÒ (*off, only his arm visible pouring the wine*): Yes.

*Gelsomina looks up and hands the glass to the prostitute out of frame with
a smile.*

110. MCU: *the prostitute, as Gelsomina's hand enters frame with the glass; the
prostitute takes the glass, raising it in a toast.*

PROSTITUTE: Cheers!

111. MCU: *Gelsomina, smiling with satisfaction.*

112. MCU: *the prostitute as she drinks the wine and then puts the glass on the table.*

113. *As in 108.*

> PROSTITUTE: Now, where have I seen you two before? What kind of work do you do?
> ZAMPANÒ: I'm a traveling performer. (*He gestures to Gelsomina.*)

114. *As in 111. Gelsomina smiling proudly.*

> ZAMPANÒ (*off*): She's my assistant. I've taught her everything. When I took her on . . .

115. MCU: *the prostitute, looking at Zampanò, out of frame, and puffing her cigarette.*

> ZAMPANÒ (*off*): . . . she didn't even know how to hee-haw!

The prostitute breaks into a vulgar burst of laughter.

116. *As in 114.*

117. MCU: *Zampanò and the prostitute, as he rolls up his left shirt-sleeve and flexes his arm.*

> ZAMPANÒ: Look here, look here. Feel . . . what muscles.

The prostitute feels his muscles and gives a shrill laugh of admiration.

> PROSTITUTE: Hey, what a man!

Zampanò then pulls a wad of crumpled-up bank notes from his pocket and puts them on the table.

> ZAMPANÒ: Look at this. In an hour. All earned with these.

The prostitute picks up one of the bank notes.

PROSTITUTE: Can I take one?

Zampanò slaps her hand playfully, as she giggles again.

118. MCU: *Gelsomina, clapping her hands and laughing.*

119. MCU: *Zampanò and the prostitute.*

ZAMPANÒ: Clever, aren't you?

120. LS: *the prostitute stands up with her back to the camera, doors and wall of trattoria in background. Zampanò and Gelsomina are still seated, facing camera.*

PROSTITUTE: Come on, you two! Come on, let's go outside . . . (*She walks behind Zampanò, hugging him from behind, as she continues*) . . . it stinks in here. Let's go see the fireworks.

Gelsomina stands up; Zampanò finishes his glass of wine and calls out to the waiter in the background.

ZAMPANÒ: All right. Let's go. Waiter! Give me two flasks of wine. How much do I owe?
WAITER: That makes 2,200 lire with the bottles.

As the prostitute heads for the door, Gelsomina puts on her coat and scarf, and Zampanò rises unsteadily to his feet, taking his money from the table and knocking over a chair as he picks up his jacket. Gelsomina replaces the chair while Zampanò takes the wine, and the three leave the trattoria.

121. LS: *the front door of the trattoria as they leave, passing by a pedlar's stand near the door.*

ZAMPANÒ: Hey, pedlar!
PEDLAR: Good evening.

After walking toward the foreground, they stop by the stand and camera frames them in LS.

ZAMPANÒ: How's business?
PEDLAR: Just so-so.

As the prostitute walks out of frame, the camera pans left slightly to frame just Zampanò and Gelsomina, as he hands her the flasks of wine.

ZAMPANÒ: Here, put these inside.

Camera tracks on them as they join the prostitute by the motorcycle.

ZAMPANÒ: Hey, redhead, where're you going? Get on!

Gelsomina heads toward the rear of the van and disappears behind it.

PROSTITUTE: Now, what's this contraption? Your car?

Zampanò seizes the prostitute's left arm and gives her a slap on the behind.

ZAMPANÒ: And maybe it doesn't suit you?

Giggling, the prostitute escapes his grasp and runs to the other side of the motorcycle. Camera pans slightly left so as to follow her movement.

PROSTITUTE: Hey, are you crazy?

Camera frames the van in MS *as they sit on the motorcycle and Gelsomina reappears from behind the van at right of frame.*

ZAMPANÒ: It's American . . . a Davis . . . in seven years it's never
  stopped running one time . . .
PROSTITUTE: Oh, my God!

Zampanò starts the motor as Gelsomina walks around the motorcycle toward the prostitute.

ZAMPANÒ: Just listen to that engine.

The prostitute laughs wildly.

GELSOMINA: I'll just get on in the back.
ZAMPANÒ: You wait here.

Camera remains motionless and frames Gelsomina in MS, *face to camera, as the motorcycle exits frame right.*

GELSOMINA: Where are you going?

Gelsomina, in MS, *stands in the center of the frame and in the middle of the road, now deserted. She looks around baffled, confused, and frightened. The distant roaring of the motorcycle engine is heard off. Gelsomina turns, back to camera, and starts walking slowly toward the background. Dissolve.*

122. ELS: *the same deserted, dimly lit road. Gelsomina (*LS*) is seated dejectedly on the curb in the right of frame. The clopping of hooves heralds the approach of a riderless horse. It enters frame right in the foreground and slowly passes by Gelsomina, casting a shadow over her as she looks up and watches it proceed down the lonely road. Dissolve.*

123. MS: *Gelsomina, still seated on the curb, after the break of day. A man pushing a bicycle walks behind her and down the sidewalk. Gelsomina glances up.*

124. MS: *high angle on two small children in the foreground and a small boy carrying an even smaller child in his arms in the background. They are all standing in the middle of the road.*

125. *As in 123. Gelsomina dejectedly props her head on her hand.*

126. *As in 124. The smaller of the two children heads toward Gelsomina. The camera pans right, following the child until it comes to rest in a* LS *with Gelsomina; the child hands Gelsomina a stick and sits at her right side on the curb. Gelsomina examines the stick curiously. There is a covered bowl of food to her left on the curb. Gelsomina turns to the child, then once again she dejectedly props her head up with her hand.*

127. MS: *a young woman pushing her bicycle.*

YOUNG WOMAN: Are you still here?

128. *As in 126. Gelsomina stomps her foot in anger.*

129. MS: *the young woman approaching Gelsomina. Camera pans on her as she moves right.*

YOUNG WOMAN: Now, why haven't you eaten your soup? (*The young woman stops on the sidewalk behind Gelsomina (who abruptly stands up, facing the camera), and she addresses another woman leaning out of a nearby window.*) Now, why hasn't she eaten her soup?
WOMAN AT THE WINDOW: She didn't want to eat. You can't figure anything out with this one.

Gelsomina stands in MS *in the middle of frame, still facing the camera, with the two women behind her.*

GELSOMINA (*angrily*): Fooey on this soup! (*She turns around and walks past both women.*) I'll just give a kick to this soup!
WOMAN: Do you see how she carries on?

Gelsomina stops and leans against the wall.

YOUNG WOMAN: Say, does your husband have a motorcycle with a van? . . . Were you in the square yesterday? . . . Well, will you believe it's the same man? . . . Near Zelve's garden, there's a man with a motorcycle and a van.

130. MCU: *Gelsomina's back as she turns left abruptly, looking at the woman out of frame, biting her nails and looking surprised.*

GELSOMINA: Where?
YOUNG WOMAN (*off*): Down there . . .

Gelsomina turns right to look down the street, then back to the woman, still out of frame.

YOUNG WOMAN (*off*): At the end of the street where the houses stop.

Gelsomina hastily runs down the street in the far background. Dissolve.

131. ELS: *a road by a deserted field. Gelsomina runs along the road from left background. She halts as she spots the van out of frame. Camera tracks on her as she runs to the left and reveals the abandoned van. The lower portion of Zampanò's prostrate body can be seen in the left foreground near two empty flasks of wine. Gelsomina walks toward Zampanò. Once she is next to him, camera moves slightly left and frames her in* MS.

GELSOMINA: Zampanò! (*Gelsomina moves slightly to left of frame, then kneels beside him.*) Zampanò! (*She wrings her hands in despair and listens to his heartbeat. When she lifts up one eyelid, he awakens momentarily from his drunken stupor. Then she smiles, reassured, as she realizes that Zampanò is not hurt. Becoming more apprehensive, she stands up.*)

132. MCU *of Gelsomina. Suppressing her tears, Gelsomina turns around and walks toward the motorcycle in the background, as a child appears from the rear of the van. Gelsomina (*LS*) looks at the child, then walks away from the van to the left of frame, while the child walks behind the van in the same direction.*

133. ELS: *some deserted fields. Gelsomina enters frame from the right. She walks along the near side of the road, then stops to pick up some flowers, while the child enters frame from the right, walking along the far side of the road. Gelsomina slowly walks into the field toward the left, followed*

by the young girl as the camera tracks with them both. Behind a solitary tree in the foreground, Gelsomina stoops to pick some more flowers, then stops and with her arms imitates the angle of the tree's only branch. The young girl laughs. Gelsomina continues left and encounters another young child, a boy, seated on the ground, playing in the sand.

YOUNG CHILD (*pointing to his left toward a yard enclosed by barbed wire fencing*): Did you know the dog died?

Gelsomina (MS) walks toward the gate and pauses; then, attracted by the subdued and almost musical buzzing of the telegraph wires that only she is capable of hearing, she places her head against the telegraph pole and listens in amazement. Dissolve.

134. MS: *a high angle of Zampanò still asleep. He awakens, sits up, and rubs his eyes with a grunt. Sound-over of a passing motorcycle. Zampanò stands up and stumbles to the right, carrying his jacket and his hat. Camera tracks with him, then past him to the right. He puts on his cap.*

GELSOMINA (*now visible in the distant background*): Are you awake? I planted some tomatoes . . .
ZAMPANÒ (*staggering to the right of frame and back to the motorcycle*): Tomatoes?

Gelsomina joins him by the motorcycle. Camera now frames them in LS.

GELSOMINA: I found some seeds there in the garden . . . real big seeds, so I planted them.

Zampanò grunts twice, feeling the effects of a hangover.

ZAMPANÒ: Go on, get moving . . . hah!
GELSOMINA: Why, are we leaving?
ZAMPANÒ: What do you want to wait for—for the tomatoes to grow? Come on, push!

In distress, she walks to the back of the van and starts pushing it. Dissolve.

135. MS: *Zampanò driving. Gelsomina is seated in the back of the van and facing the rear, watching the road disappear in the distant background. She then turns and taps Zampanò's shoulder to attract his attention.*

GELSOMINA: Did you used to act this way with Rosa, too?
ZAMPANÒ: What?
GELSOMINA (*shouting in his left ear*): With Rosa!
ZAMPANÒ: What the hell are you talking about?
GELSOMINA: Why did you go off with that woman? Did you used to act like that with Rosa, too?
ZAMPANÒ: Knock it off!

Gelsomina draws away from Zampanò, then taps his shoulder again.

ZAMPANÒ: What do you want?
GELSOMINA: So you're the kind of man who runs around with women?
ZAMPANÒ: What?
GELSOMINA (*shouting in his left ear*): . . . who runs around with women.
ZAMPANÒ: Listen, if you want to stay with me, learn one thing—keep your mouth shut! (*Then Zampanò changes his expression from a scowl to a bemused smile.*) Tomatoes! . . . What do you have in that head of yours? (*He hands her an apple to eat.*)

136. *A traveling* ELS *of the distant road ahead from Zampanò's* POV *at the wheel. Sound-over of the honking horn of the motorcycle. A flock of sheep and two shepherds block the path ahead in the center of the frame, but then begin to move aside. Fade out.*[9]

137. ELS: *a wedding party in a farmyard. Gelsomina and Zampanò are performing in the background, while some farm animals are eating in the left foreground.*

138. LS: *Gelsomina and Zampanò performing with tambourines and bells.*

139. *A tracking* MS *from left to right of a long table crowded with merry-making wedding guests. Camera speeds up to follow a young girl running*

*behind the table after a soldier who has stolen her dinner plate. Camera
stops in a* MS *of a man toasting the newlyweds.*

WEDDING GUEST: Here's to the bride . . .

140. MS: *the priest and the newlyweds seated at the table.*

WEDDING GUEST (*off*): . . . as fresh as a rose!

141. MS: *several male guests at one side of the table, as they raise their
glasses in a toast.*

142. MS: *Gelsomina and Zampanò, who look out of frame at the party. Then
they move backward into a* LS *and remove their caps-and-bells. Gelsomina
puts on her bowler and grabs a cane; Zampanò sits down with his drum,
as Gelsomina turns to the wedding party out of frame.*

GELSOMINA: It's Bajon's fault.[10]

143. LS: *Gelsomina and Zampanò performing. Gelsomina struts back and forth to the music.*

144. MS: *Gelsomina turns and continues her routine to the music, until a guest offers her a glass of wine. She sips a bit of it, then turns and hands the glass to Zampanò.*

145. *As in 140. The husband kisses the bride as everybody claps.*

146. MS: *Gelsomina clapping while Zampanò, still seated on the ground, finishes his wine. Some excited children in the background are staring at Gelsomina.*

147. MCU: *Mother-in-Law, mopping her brow and shouting to Gelsomina and Zampanò.*

MOTHER-IN-LAW: Hey!

148. *As in 146.*

GELSOMINA: Zampanò, they're calling us.

149. *As in 147.*

MOTHER-IN-LAW: Hey, come eat something!

150. LS: *Gelsomina and Zampanò, as he stands up and takes the bells off his feet.*

ZAMPANÒ: Thanks. We're coming right now.

151. MS: *looking along the table of guests. A woman in the left foreground calls out to Mother-in-Law.*

OLD WOMAN: Have a seat!

Then a priest seated beside the old woman says:

PRIEST (*to Mother-in-Law*): Come on, come on over here . . .

152. *As in 149. Mother-in-Law then exits frame from the left.*

MOTHER-IN-LAW: I don't have time now.

153. MS: *the soldier at the table, throwing food over the other guests.*

154. MS: *children and dog picking up food under the table.*

155. LS: *Zampanò walks toward foreground past the table and exits frame from the left. Gelsomina is about to follow him when a little girl grabs her coat.*

LITTLE GIRL: Come on! . . . Come on! . . . Come on . . . ! (*The little girl pulls Gelsomina toward the right foreground.*)
GELSOMINA: But I have to eat.
LITTLE GIRL: Eat later, eat later.

They exit frame from the right foreground.

156. LS: *the outside stairs of the farmhouse, as Gelsomina is pulled into the frame from the left foreground by the little girl. They walk toward the stairs and the background. Another little girl follows closely behind them.*

GELSOMINA: But where are you taking me? Where are we going?
LITTLE GIRL: We're going to see Osvaldo!

Gelsomina and the two girls climb the stairs, while another little girl enters frame from the background, singing through a megaphone in imitation of Gelsomina.

ANOTHER LITTLE GIRL: It's Bajon's fault.

An older girl, accompanied by a young boy in a black cape, enters frame from the left foreground. The older girl runs toward the child who is singing and takes the megaphone away from her, while the children who are climbing the stairs exit frame.

157. MS: *from the top of the stairs. Gelsomina and the little girl are climbing the stairs. The camera, behind the banister, tilts down, then up to follow their upward movement, ending in a* ELS *of the entire hallway with Gelsomina in* MCU *facing the camera and the little girl in the distant background.*

LITTLE GIRL (*to Gelsomina*): Over here, over here . . .

Gelsomina turns and runs after the girl.

158. *Reverse angle shot of the hallway. Camera pans right on the running girl who turns left in the hallway, then comes back out into the hallway to beckon to Gelsomina.*

CHILD (*off*): Osvaldo! Osvaldo!
LITTLE GIRL: Shh! Shh!

159. MS: *Gelsomina enters frame from the left, pushed by the other little girl. Camera pans right to follow them. She turns around and exclaims:*

GELSOMINA: Stop pushing or else I'll slap you!

Gelsomina makes a left turn, while the little girl turns to call the little boy in the black cape.

SECOND LITTLE GIRL: Natalino, Natalino, come on, you too!

160. LS: *a high angle of the little boy with the black cape as he enters frame from the left side and makes a left turn, following the others.*

161. MS: *the first little girl opens Osvaldo's door, first turning to Gelsomina out of frame and motioning to her to remain silent, then turning around and entering the room.*

LITTLE GIRL: Osvaldo! . . . Osvaldo! . . . Look who's here! (*She stops in* LS *in the center of the room, framed by the half-opened door. Then she turns and points to Gelsomina out of frame.*)

162. MS: *Gelsomina coming in the door. Camera pans with her as she enters.*

163. LS: *Osvaldo in bed, in the background. Osvaldo is a young boy of an indeterminate age, as pale as a white mushroom, semi-paralyzed and immobile. He is dressed in a strange black costume with a cowl over his head, giving him the appearance of a midget monk. He is staring at a wooden reel used to wind or unwind cotton or wool which is spinning around on the bed. The camera tracks closer to him. Over the reel, hanging from the ceiling, there is a small, spherical object which turns against the motion of the reel.*

164. LS: *Gelsomina between the two little girls. The older of the two pulls Gelsomina by the hand. In the background, the floor is covered with stored potatoes; propped on a table against the back wall is a painting with a religious theme.*

LITTLE GIRL: Go on, make him laugh!
GELSOMINA: But who is he?

165. MCU: *the first little girl, looking out of frame at Osvaldo.*

LITTLE GIRL: He's Osvaldo . . . he's my cousin, he's sick.

166. MS: *Osvaldo, his face half-hidden behind the blanket.*

LITTLE GIRL (*off*): He always stays inside here.

167. MS: *the second little girl.*

SECOND LITTLE GIRL: They don't want anyone to come to see him. You make him laugh!

168. LS: *Gelsomina, as the first little girl runs around a chair and the second stands behind her.*

GELSOMINA: But what should I do . . . ?

LITTLE GIRL: Do what you were doing earlier. . . . What you were
doing earlier.

*Gelsomina moves around the chair, mimicking a bird, as the first little
girl sits on the chair and hides her face in her hands.*

GELSOMINA (*whistling*): The little bird, the little bird . . .

169. MS: *the second little girl, who spins around and claps her hands.*

170. MS: *Osvaldo, staring in amazement at Gelsomina out of frame. He suddenly turns his head.*

171. *As in 168. The little boy with the black cape enters the room.*

SECOND LITTLE GIRL (*turning to him*): Natalino! Natalino!

*Gelsomina stops her routine and, with a fascinated stare, she walks to the
foreground toward Osvaldo (who is out of frame), to come into* MS.

172. MCU: *Osvaldo, staring at Gelsomina out of frame.*

173. MCU: *Gelsomina, entranced by the vision of Osvaldo. In the extreme left
background, a door opens, and an aggressive old nun appears and starts
shouting, picking up a cane from the table.*

OLD NUN: You're nothing but a pack of scoundrels!

174. MS: *the two little girls.*

OLD NUN (*off*): *I'll give your legs a whipping! ... Go on, quick, get
out, get out ... go on and get out of here!*

*The two girls and the little boy run out of the room, the camera tracking
after them.*

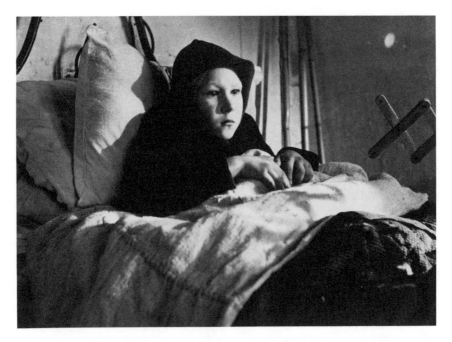

175. LS: *Gelsomina in the left foreground waving good-bye to Osvaldo out of frame, and the old nun in the right background, behind Gelsomina.*

OLD NUN: And you . . . who let you come up here? Get out immediately!

Gelsomina runs past the nun and out the door.

176. MS: *the kitchen door from another room. The Mother-in-Law walks from the kitchen through the door, carrying a plate of macaroni. There she halts (MS) and leans against the doorframe, looking toward Zampanò, out of frame to the left, and then, standing, she begins to eat.*

177. MCU: *Zampanò sitting and eating.*

178. MCU: *Mother-in-Law eating and wiping her brow.*

179. *As in 177.*

     ZAMPANÒ: Do you eat standing up like a horse?

180. *As in 178.*

     MOTHER-IN-LAW (*speaking between bites*): I always eat on my
     feet. . . . Who else takes care of the house if I don't? I've had two
     husbands and they're both dead. . . . I've gotten up for three nights at
     one o'clock to cook. Do you think I'm tired? . . . If it took my fancy, I
     could dance for the entire night. . . . We older women are better than
     young girls, we are.

181. *As in 177.*

     ZAMPANÒ: And why don't you get married again?

182. *As in 180.*

     MOTHER-IN-LAW: What? Yet another husband? I'm enough to give
     orders in this house.

183. *As in 181.*

     ZAMPANÒ: Why? Is that all a husband is good for, to give orders?

184. *As in 182.*

     MOTHER-IN-LAW: Why? . . . Aren't I made of flesh and blood? Every-
     body likes sweets, don't they?

185. *As in 183.*

186. *As in 184. Mother-in-Law turns toward someone in the kitchen, out of
     frame.*

     MOTHER-IN-LAW: Hey, you! What're you doing there? Get moving! I'll
     give you a kick, I will!

187. *As in 185. Zampanò has put the plate on a table next to him.*

188. *As in 186.*

> MOTHER-IN-LAW: My first husband was big and tall like you. I kept all
> his clothes . . .

189. *As in 187.*

> MOTHER-IN-LAW (*off*): . . . they don't fit anyone.

> *Zampanò turns to the kitchen door, out of frame on the right.*

190. MS: *Gelsomina, framed by the door. She walks from the kitchen to the
room where Zampanò is, and the camera pans left to follow her as she
approaches him.*

> GELSOMINA: Zampanò . . . Zampanò . . . upstairs . . .

> *The camera frames them in* MS *as Gelsomina senses the presence of the
Mother-in-Law and stands behind Zampanò with an embarrassed
expression.*

191. *As in 188. Mother-in-Law nodding to Gelsomina out of frame as she says:*

> MOTHER-IN-LAW: Now I'll bring something for you, too. (*She leaves
> the room and goes back into the kitchen.*)

192. MS: *Gelsomina and Zampanò.*

> GELSOMINA (*continuing excitedly*): There's a little boy with a head like
> this . . . he's all . . .

193. MS: *Mother-in-Law leaves the kitchen with a plate of macaroni and enters
the room where Zampanò and Gelsomina are waiting.*

> MOTHER-IN-LAW (*to Gelsomina*): Here, eat . . . (*Camera tracks left on
> her as she hands the pasta to Gelsomina and addresses Zampanò,*

framing them all in MS.) Why don't you help me bring up a demijohn
of wine, since there's no more left over here.

ZAMPANÒ (*standing up*): Ah, say . . . are those clothes really no use to
anyone?

MOTHER-IN-LAW: And who'd they fit? I told you, there aren't many
men like you in the world . . .

ZAMPANÒ (*as they stand by the cellar door on the left*): Is there a hat?
Because . . . I could really use a hat.

194. MS: *Gelsomina nodding in agreement and wearing a funny smile.*

195. MS: *Mother-in-Law and Zampanò, standing by the cellar door.*

MOTHER-IN-LAW: Sure, come on. Come and see for yourself.

*As the Mother-in-Law goes down the stairs to the cellar, Zampanò fol-
lows her, but then momentarily turns around to exchange a wink with
Gelsomina, doing so with an air of self-satisfied complicity.*

196. MS: *Gelsomina winking back at Zampanò; then, taking Zampanò's seat by
the table, Gelsomina begins to eat her macaroni, still smiling, but a
sudden thought transforms her expression as she suddenly becomes conscious of what is happening between the two in the cellar. Gelsomina
stands up and looks (out of frame) toward the cellar door.*

197. LS: *the automobile of the newlyweds with guests waving good-bye as it
drives away quickly down a lonely country road. Dissolve.*[11]

198. ELS: *the deserted tables in the farmyard after the departure of most of
the wedding guests. A couple is dancing to the music of the song, "It's
Bajon's Fault," played by a young man on an accordion.*

199. MS: *Gelsomina's back. She is looking out the stable window at what is
taking place in the farmyard. Then she turns around and looks inside
toward Zampanò (out of frame).*

200. LS: *Zampanò, wearing his new hat, sitting on the straw as he tries on his
new clothes.*

201. *As in 199. Gelsomina now wearing a distressed expression. Camera pans slightly on her as she moves to the left, holding a piece of bread, and sits down.*

202. LS: *Zampanò standing up.*

203. MS: *Gelsomina still sitting on the straw, her eyes downcast for a few moments, as she unconsciously recalls in her melancholy mood the melody she once heard under the eaves of a building while it was raining. She begins to hum it softly, almost without realizing it. Then she becomes aware of what she is doing; completely absorbed by the music, she addresses Zampanò as she rises to her feet.*

GELSOMINA: Do you remember it . . . how beautiful it was, Zampanò?
   (*Standing, she hums the tune again and exits frame right.*)

204. MS: *Zampanò, in profile, stands on one leg and puts on his new trousers. Gelsomina enters frame from the left foreground.*

GELSOMINA (*humming the tune again*): . . . that day, under the rain, from that window? (*While humming, Gelsomina walks toward the right background so as to reach a LS, then turns toward Zampanò, who has turned his back to the camera and now stands in the left foreground.*) Why don't you teach me to play the trumpet, Zampanò? I learn fast. (*She walks toward Zampanò in the foreground.*) What did Rosa do? Did she work like me?

Zampanò walks toward the background and makes a half-turn toward her. He is extremely proud of his new clothes.

ZAMPANÒ: Well, how do I look? Huh? (*While adjusting his hat, he mutters:*) Women!

Gelsomina stares at him in silence and she flashes a brief smile which disappears immediately, giving place to an outburst of tears as she walks away from Zampanò, almost too embarrassed to show her emotions.

ZAMPANÒ (*complainingly*): You can't smoke in here! (*Zampanò, in the right foreground, turns to the left and looks at Gelsomina leaning against the wall in the left background, finally noticing her distress. He walks toward her as he says:*) Now what the hell's the matter with you?

*Camera follows Gelsomina (*LS*) hastily moving left, as if trying to escape from Zampanò, who is dropped from the frame.*

GELSOMINA: Nothing!
ZAMPANÒ (*off*): Then why are you crying?
GELSOMINA: Because I feel like it! (*As she walks left, she falls into a hole.*) Ehi, ehi!

205. MS: *Zampanò walks left toward the hole and looks down.*

206. *Overhead* LS *of Gelsomina from Zampanò's* POV.

ZAMPANÒ (*off*): Come on, climb out.
GELSOMINA: No!

207. MCU: *Zampanò grins and carelessly puts his unlit cigarette behind his ear.*

ZAMPANÒ: Come on, climb out of there. Do you want to stay there all night?

208. *As in 206. Gelsomina looks up at Zampanò.*

GELSOMINA: Yes, all night!

209. MS: *Zampanò turns, walks away to the right, and takes off his jacket, preparing to go to bed. Dissolve.*

210. LS: *the hole. After daybreak, Gelsomina crawls slowly out, then she continues to crawl on all fours over the straw-covered ground until she reaches the sleeping Zampanò. Camera tracks slightly right and forward*

so as to follow her, then stops and frames her kneeling by Zampanò, back to camera. They are in LS.

211. MCU: *Zampanò sleeping on his back.*

212. MCU: *Gelsomina.*

   GELSOMINA: Hey! I'm leaving! I'm going back home, because I'm really fed up!

213. LS: *Zampanò, sleeping, with Gelsomina on her hands and knees beside him, her back to the camera. Gelsomina then stands up and walks right, and continues her conversation seriously.*

   GELSOMINA: It's not because of the job . . . I could like the work. I like being a performer. (*Gelsomina kneels on the other side of Zampanò, pointing angrily.*) It's you I don't like! (*Poking Zampanò in the ribs, Gelsomina rudely awakens him.*)
   ZAMPANÒ: Huh? What is it?
   GELSOMINA: (*standing up and walking right away from him*): I'm leaving!

214. *As in 211. Zampanò awakens with a grunt.*

215. MCU: *Gelsomina, now angry.*

   GELSOMINA: I'm going back home!

216. *As in 214. Zampanò turns over to go back to sleep.*

   ZAMPANÒ: Ah, cut it out, you idiot!

217. MCU: *Gelsomina turns and walks toward the door of the stable in the far distant background. Camera remains stationary.*

   GELSOMINA: And I'm leaving you my shoes . . . and my overcoat. I'm leaving you everything!

218. LS: *the exterior of the stable. Gelsomina stoops as she emerges through a small opening in the stable wall, stops outside, and takes off her shoes. The farmyard is deserted. Camera tracks slightly right as Gelsomina heads toward the rear of the van in the right foreground. She reaches it and camera frames her in* MS. *She throws the shoes inside the van. She removes her army surplus overcoat and puts her old, tattered cape on. She is muttering angrily to herself.*

GELSOMINA (*very vexed and distressed*): Everyday. Everything. I tell him. But him, no! (*She grabs her old canvas tennis shoes, bangs one against the other, then walks right, past the van, toward the farmhouse. Camera tracks on her as she leaves and frames her in* LS *as she stops by a barbed-wire fence and turns toward the stable out of frame.*)

GELSOMINA (*yelling*): I'm leaving!

Camera remains stationary in an ELS *of the deserted countryside, the fence running along the right side of frame toward the distant horizon and the farmhouse visible in the far distance as Gelsomina walks away toward the background.*

219. MCU *of Gelsomina seen from the right and from high angle. Camera tracks on her walking away toward the left beside the fence. She blows her nose and waves to the right of frame. Dissolve.*

220. LS: *Gelsomina walking into frame from the right along a deserted country road. She stops, turns around, then heads toward the side of the road and sits by a grassy ridge. Sound-over of a processional theme.*

221. MS: *Gelsomina, seated. A little hole in the ridge can be seen on her right side. Suddenly, she turns toward it, reaches inside, and takes out a small insect, placing it on the back of her left hand. As it flies back to the hole, she picks it up again, places it on the back of her left hand, and gently blows it away into the wind. She smiles contentedly. She pulls her cape around her. Then her expression changes abruptly to a sad frown until she hears the sound of the approaching music. She turns to left of frame. Sound-over: processional music in a different arrangement. Suddenly Gelsomina turns to right of frame.*

222. LS: *a small band of three musicians is marching in single file from right to left along the top of the ridge toward Gelsomina, who is still seated on the same spot in the center of the frame. She rises to her feet as they march by. At first motionless, the camera then follows them to the left, leaving Gelsomina out of frame.*

223. MS: *Gelsomina's left profile from high angle as she walks down the road by the ridge. She looks toward the musicians out of frame in amazement. She is attracted by this sudden and festive apparition, and forgets her own melancholy as she follows them down the road.*

224. LS: *the three musicians, now in the center of the road, from Gelsomina's POV.*

225. *As in 223. Gelsomina clownishly dances along with a smile.*

226. ELS: *the three musicians still seen from rear, marching along, followed closely by Gelsomina, toward an intersection in the far background, where a horse-drawn cart and two white oxen are passing by. Dissolve.*

227. ELS: *a religious procession descending a narrow road just outside a small town. Sound-over of the processional music, now played in a slower and more solemn arrangement. Dissolve.*

228. MS: *a crucifix carried along in the procession, which has now reached the center of the town.*

229. LS: *a high angle on a group of children dressed in white and escorted by two nuns. Camera tilts slightly upward to an ELS to reveal the entire procession—choirboys, altarboys, priests, supplicants, and spectators.*

230. MS: *a frowning priest blessing the crowd.*

231. MCU: *Gelsomina, genuflecting and making the sign of the cross in the midst of a crowd of spectators. She looks upward.*

232. MS: *a crucifix being carried along in the procession.*

233. LS: *the procession, followed by a stray dog.*

234. MS: *people crowding against the window of a butcher shop, seen from inside the shop. A pig carcass can be seen hanging in the right foreground. Gelsomina bumps against the window, looks inside, smiles, and passes on in the rush of the crowd, exiting frame right. Camera tracks across the interior of the butcher shop to reach the door and frames Gelsomina outside (LS). Then, as she tries to enter the door, coming to a MS, a man stops her and turns her around back toward the crowd.*[12]

235. MCU: *Gelsomina, being jostled by the crowd.*

236. MCU: *the crowd. Gelsomina, in the middle of the crowd, enters frame from the right and backs around a corner into a side street, only to be confronted by an onrushing stream of more excited spectators heading her way. She ducks to the left to avoid them as the camera tracks to follow*

her, framing her in MCU *as she leans against a wall upon which is affixed a poster labeled "Immaculate Madonna." She looks upward ecstatically.*

237. MS: *an icon of the Madonna and Child, being carried in the procession.*

238. LS: *the icon and the crowd passing below shot from a balcony overhead. Camera tracks slightly left as to follow their movement.*

239. MS: *lanterns being carried toward the town cathedral in the background, its façade decorated with hundreds of small lights.*

240. *The procession, figures framed in* MS.

241. ELS: *the front of the cathedral and the procession heading toward it from the balcony. In the left foreground the outside sign of a bar dominates.*

242. *As in 240. The procession enters the cathedral.*

243. LS: *the altar inside the cathedral. Camera tilts up toward the dome. Dissolve.*

244. ELS: *the piazza outside the cathedral at night, crowded with spectators. Camera continues to tilt upward to reveal a high wire suspended across the piazza upon which is balanced a tightwire walker. He is holding a balancing pole and wearing a pair of angel's wings. The crowd applauds as he concludes one of his routines and reaches the end of the wire safely.*

245. *Camera tracks from a* MCU *to a* MS *of the acrobat's partner, a woman who is speaking to the crowd through a loudspeaker mounted on a black car.*

FOOL'S PARTNER And now, the Fool will climb up to perform the most dangerous of his feats. He will eat a plate of spaghetti suspended in space . . .

246. ELS: *the crowd seen from the top of a building.*

FOOL'S PARTNER (*off*): . . . forty meters above the ground. We beg you to observe complete silence . . .

247. MS: *the car, behind which the woman is standing.*

> FOOL'S PARTNER: . . . during the entire performance to come . . . (*The woman tips one of the car's headlights up toward the acrobat, and the camera tilts up to follow the beam of light upward.*) (*off*): . . . since even the slightest distraction could prove fatal.
>
> *Camera stops its tilting up to frame a window crowded with spectators in* LS.

248. MCU: *a high angle on Gelsomina in the crowd, looking upward.*

> FOOL'S PARTNER (*off*): Ladies and gentlemen, I present to you . . .

249. LS: *the acrobat's back as he is starting his new routine.*

FOOL'S PARTNER (*off*): . . . the Fool . . . in his stunt that is unique in all the world!

250. LS: *the spectators'* POV *of the Fool as he advances along the wire carrying a table and two chairs.*

251. LS: *the crowd from the Fool's* POV.

252. MCU: *the Fool's Partner as she addresses the Fool.*

FOOL'S PARTNER: Hey, how are things going up there, are they all right?

253. LS: *the Fool, balancing himself on a chair.*

THE FOOL: Yes, but it's a bit chilly. In fact, I've worked up appetite enough for two people.

254. *As in 248.*

255. ELS: *the Fool, from the audience's* POV.

THE FOOL: Damn this wind, it even blew away my tablecloth!

256. *As in 252.*

FOOL'S PARTNER: What? You sit down at the table without asking us if we would like to join you?

257. LS: *the Fool, from a high angle.*

THE FOOL: There's a place here, and if anyone wants to come up, he's welcome!

258. *As in 254. Gelsomina, now amused.*

259. *As in 257. All of a sudden, the table falls to the ground.*

260. LS: *the Fool from below as he breaks his fall with the pole. The chair falls from underneath him as well.*

261. *As in 258. Gelsomina, now frightened.*

262. LS: *the crowd from the Fool's* POV.

263. LS: *the Fool from the end of the wire, as he twists and turns around and around it, balancing himself with the pole.*

264. ELS: *the crowded piazza from one end of it as the crowd applauds wildly.*

265. *As in 261. Gelsomina applauding.*

266. LS: *the Fool standing on his head on the wire.*

267. *As in 265. Gelsomina applauding and smiling with admiration.*

268. ELS: *the Fool walking backwards on the wire.*

269. LS: *the crowded piazza from an extreme high angle.*

270. LS: *the Fool standing on his platform at the end of the wire and climbing back into the building.*

271. *As in 267.*

272. LS: *the Fool's platform from the spectators'* POV. *Suddenly the lights are extinguished and the façade of the building is darkened.*

273. *Camera tracks right on the Fool's Partner in* MS *as she collects offerings from the crowd.*

FOOL'S PARTNER: Thank you, gentlemen . . . thank you, thank you.

274. MCU: *Gelsomina staring at the crowd with the Fool's face visible directly behind her, as he pushes past her, glances at her, and walks toward the*

left foreground. He exits frame from the left, and the camera reframes on Gelsomina in MCU.

275. MCU: *the Fool walks left to his car and puts his equipment inside it.*

276. MCU: *the Fool's Partner collecting offerings.*

277. MCU: *the Fool, at the wheel of his car.*

THE FOOL: I'll wait for you in the *trattoria*, O.K.?

278. MCU: *the Fool's Partner, as she answers back.*

FOOL'S PARTNER: O.K.

279. *As in 277. The Fool catches sight of Gelsomina, out of frame, while rolling up the car window.*

280. MCU: *Gelsomina, staring at the out-of-frame Fool in amazement and admiration.*

281. *As in 279. The Fool almost breaks into laughter at the sight of Gelsomina's face, still out of frame.*

282. *As in 280.*

283. *As in 277. The Fool starting the engine.*

284. MS: *the car moving through the midst of the crowd.*

THE FOOL: Come on, will you let me by?

Dissolve.

285. ELS: *a small, half-darkened, and deserted square at night. By the monument in the center of the square stand a group of soldiers and Gelsomina, who is marching about. She runs around behind the monument. The men are making fun of her.*

GELSOMINA: Attention, soldiers! . . . One, two . . . one, two.
SOLDIER: You're nuts!
GELSOMINA: One, two, one, two, one, two . . . no . . . no.

286. MS: *Gelsomina drinks at the fountain by the monument.*

287. ELS: *the square. Two soldiers are about to leave.*

SOLDIER: Ciao, Mario . . . I'm leaving, hey. Say hello to (*mumbling a name*) for me. Ciao, Mario.

Gelsomina (LS) enters frame right from behind the monument and mumbles to herself.

GELSOMINA: No! I'm not coming anymore! I'm not coming with you anymore! I'm not coming! No! No! No!

One of the men comes up behind her, flips her cape over her head, and causes her to stumble to the ground.

288. MS: *Gelsomina in the middle of frame as she uncovers her head and looks upward. Camera tilts up so as to follow her movement. Sound of church bells. In the far distance, Zampanò's motorcycle is visible as it drives toward the foreground. Gelsomina looks downward and then upward again toward the approaching motorcycle. After having tilted down and up, camera pans slightly right at first, following her movement and showing Gelsomina in the foreground and the approaching motorcycle in the background. Then camera pans left to follow the motorcycle until it reaches the square. As soon as the motorcycle halts, camera frames it in a LS, leaving Gelsomina out of frame.*

289. MCU: *Gelsomina, staring apprehensively up at the motorcycle out of frame.*

290. MS: *Zampanò gets off the motorcycle seat and turns off the engine. He looks at Gelsomina angrily, and as he takes off the scarf that is half-covering his face, he orders:*

ZAMPANÒ: Get in!

291. *As in 289. Gelsomina stares at Zampanò in despair, standing up and backing away from him. Camera tracks on her (MS) as she moves back and then left.*

GELSOMINA: I don't want to come with you anymore. . . . I don't want to come anymore . . .

292. MS *of Zampanò.*

GELSOMINA (*off*): No, never! No! No!

293. LS: *Gelsomina by a shop shutter.*

294. *As in 292.*

ZAMPANÒ (*angrily*): I said to get in!

295. *As in 293.*

GELSOMINA: No! No! There! (*She kicks a scrap of paper toward Zampanò in a futile act of self-defense.*)

296. *As in 294. Zampanò stares at Gelsomina and then exits frame from the right.*

ZAMPANÒ: Come here!

297. *As in 295. Zampanò enters frame from left foreground and walks menacingly toward Gelsomina. Camera tracks left on Gelsomina as she tries to escape from Zampanò; he traps her in a little alley on the left.*

GELSOMINA: No! No! No! (*He slaps her.*) Ay! Ay!

Camera tracks slightly backward.

ZAMPANÒ: Now move . . .

Camera tracks on Gelsomina as he pushes her left toward the motorcycle and then into the rear of the van. They are now in LS.

ZAMPANÒ: Come on . . . and keep your mouth shut! (*Camera tracks on Zampanò* [MS] *as he walks around the van and stops to address the onlookers.*) Does anybody have any objections? Ah, I thought not!

298. ELS: *the square. Zampanò gets on the motorcycle, starts the engine, and drives away. Camera pans on the motorcycle as it moves to the fore-ground at first, then circles the monument and drives off into the distance down the deserted city street. Fade out.*

299. MCU: *Gelsomina inside the van, awakened by the braying of a donkey.*

300. LS: *the rear of the van, in front of which the donkey is standing. Gelsomina climbs out of the van and stares at the donkey. Then she walks away from the van toward camera, looking around her. As she moves left, camera tracks on her* (MS). *A man holding a child in his arms greets her as she passes by his caravan.*

MAN: Good morning.

Gelsomina (MS) *nods back at him, then turns her head toward the right of frame.*

301. MS: *the side of a caravan, the window of which frames a woman working inside.*

302. MS: *Gelsomina, walking slowly left. Camera tracks on her. Gelsomina spots a woman sitting in the background with a dog on her lap.*

WOMAN: Good morning.

Camera continues to track on Gelsomina as she walks left toward a circus tent, suddenly attracted by the sound of a violin.

303. MCU: *Gelsomina looking inside the circus tent over one of the tent ropes.*

304. LS: *the Fool, perched on the back of a chair in the middle of the circus ring and playing a miniature violin.*

305. *As in 303. Gelsomina enraptured by the music.*

306. MCU: *the Fool's left profile, as he plays. His cigarette is stuck between the violin's pegs. He stops playing and puffs the cigarette, then nods toward Gelsomina, finally noticing her out of frame.*

307. *As in 305. Gelsomina smiling. At the sound of Zampanò whistling, Gelsomina suddenly turns around with a start.*

308. MS: *Zampanò is standing on the stairway of the left side of a caravan. Two people are seated inside the open caravan.*

ZAMPANÒ: Hey! . . . Come on over here. Come on, move!

309. MS: *Gelsomina first looks toward Zampanò out of frame, then turns away.*

310. LS: *Gelsomina in the left background facing Zampanò (MS) whose back is to the camera in the right foreground. As Gelsomina approaches the caravan, camera tracks on Zampanò, who is taking a seat with the other two people inside it.*

ZAMPANÒ: There she is!

Camera halts in a MS of the right side of the caravan as Gelsomina joins them.

CIRCUS OWNER'S WIFE (*with a pronounced Venetian accent*): Come on, come on over. Have a seat.

ZAMPANÒ: Say hello to the owner's wife.

GELSOMINA: It's a pleasure.

OWNER'S WIFE: A pleasure.

ZAMPANÒ: Signor Giraffa.[13]

GIRAFFA (*the owner, also with a pronounced Venetian accent*): It's a pleasure.

ZAMPANÒ: I've taught this girl everything, I have. Cigarette?

311. MS: *the owner's wife seated behind a table.*

OWNER'S WIFE: Would you like a cup of coffee?

312. MCU: *Gelsomina shakes her head negatively.*

313. MS: *Zampanò and Giraffa, as Zampanò lights a cigarette.*

ZAMPANÒ: Go on, take it, go on. . . . When I took her on . . .

314. LS: *The inside of a caravan where a woman is sewing and a young girl is cleaning vegetables.*

ZAMPANÒ (*off*): . . . she didn't even have any shoes.

315. MCU: *Gelsomina, stirring her coffee, her eyes downcast.*

ZAMPANÒ (*off*): She's not like us who've traveled all over the world.

316. *The open caravan, on which they are seated, in* MS. *Giraffa suddenly leaps to his feet and shouts:*

GIRAFFA: Damn this wind! Nazareno! Watch the tent, it's blowing away! (*Giraffa goes down one step and turns toward Zampanò.*) I warn you I don't pay. I don't pay anything to anybody. I leave you all the tips. The other performers also work that way. They make the rounds with the plate and are very satisfied like that.

OWNER'S WIFE: That's right.

ZAMPANÒ: That's perfect! We haven't ever argued, have we?

GIRAFFA: Then you can even start tonight. You have the girl for going around the audience. . . . We've got a deal! (*The two men shake hands, then they part.*) Damn this wind!

GELSOMINA: (*standing to the rear of the caravan by the owner's wife who is still sitting with her*): Where are we?

OWNER'S WIFE (*pointing*): In Rome. That's St. Paul's.[14]

GELSOMINA: And will we stay with the circus, too? (*Gelsomina walks away from the caravan toward the tent in the left background.*)

317. LS: *Giraffa and Zampanò by the entrance of the tent, from inside. Camera tracks on them as they move left inside and frames them in* MCU *when they stop. Gelsomina enters the tent from another entrance in the background and follows them.*

ZAMPANÒ: Ah, this tent feels pretty sturdy . . .

GIRAFFA: Come on, come on in.

ZAMPANÒ: Say, about how many people can fit inside here?

GIRAFFA: Oh, four hundred seats . . . and then more standing up.

318. MCU: *the Fool as he turns toward them out of frame, playing his violin.*[15]

319. MS: *Giraffa and Zampanò, as Zampanò tips his hat.*

ZAMPANÒ: Hello.

320. MCU: *the Fool, as he stops playing.*

THE FOOL: Ahhhhhhhh! Ahhhhhhh! Ahhhhhhh!

321. LS: *the Fool jumps off the chair and runs toward the camera, stopping in* MS.

THE FOOL (*with a Tuscan accent*): Look who's here! "Lifle."

322. MCU: *Zampanò frowns at the Fool out of frame.*

323. MS: *the Fool. Camera tracks slightly right as he walks toward Zampanò and Giraffa.*

THE FOOL: Ah, you did very well in taking Zampanò on. In a circus you need animals.

324. MCU: *the Fool with Giraffa beside him, while Gelsomina is visible in the background.*

THE FOOL: I'm only joking, you know I'm always joking. Do you want a cigarette?

325. MCU *of Zampanò.*

THE FOOL (*off*): Ah, you already have one. I really must admit . . .

326. *As in 324. The Fool turns to Giraffa.*

THE FOOL: . . . he is a great artist, and what a variety in his repertoire! You should do . . . Ah! (*He turns to Zampanò out of frame.*) That's it! The routine with the chain.

327. *As in 325.*

THE FOOL (*off*): It's been a long while since you've done that one.
ZAMPANÒ: (*as he brushes aside the Fool's hand holding a cigarette*): Listen! Let me give you some friendly advice. Don't ever, ever speak to me . . .

328. MCU: *Gelsomina, biting her nails with an apprehensive expression.*

ZAMPANÒ (*off*): . . . otherwise it's going to end very badly.

329. MS: *Giraffa in the center of frame, the Fool on his left side, and Zampanò on his right, his back to the camera; Gelsomina is standing behind them in the background.*

ZAMPANÒ: Clear?

THE FOOL: But . . .

Camera tracks on Zampanò as he moves right and leaves the others out of frame.

THE FOOL (*off*): I . . . I was only joking. Why are you taking it so badly? (*The Fool snickers.*)

Zampanò stops and turns around to face the Fool, out of frame.

ZAMPANÒ (*menacingly*): I told you, O.K.?

Zampanò snaps his finger at Gelsomina, out of frame, and leaves the tent. Gelsomina walks into frame from the left, and turns toward the Fool, who is out of frame.

330. MCU: *the Fool, as he bids Gelsomina good-bye.*

THE FOOL: Madame!

331. LS: *Gelsomina bumps into the door with a thud. Then she leaves. Dissolve.*

332. LS: *a low angle shot of the Fool twirling around on a trapeze at the top of the circus tent.*

333. MCU: *Gelsomina on the left, Giraffa on the right looking up at the trapeze; Zampanò stands behind them in the center of frame. Zampanò and Gelsomina are wearing their costumes and Giraffa is made up as a clown.*

334. MS: *two performers with a donkey stare upward, fearing a fall from the trapeze.*

335. *As in 332. Camera tilts down with the Fool as he falls from the wire.*

336. MS: *the Fool landing safely on the donkey, which is standing in the center of the circus ring. The Fool is wearing the same pair of angel's wings that he wore earlier on the high wire over the square when Gelsomina first saw him. The crowd applauds.*

337. *As in 333. Gelsomina and Giraffa applaud.*

338. MS: *the Fool on the donkey as he tips his hat to the crowd and accepts their applause.*

339. *As in 337. Gelsomina excitedly turns to Zampanò, who is frowning. Then, she turns away from him and stops clapping because of his displeasure.*

340. MS: *the Fool, now playing his miniature violin, riding the donkey left-ward around the circus ring.*

341. *As in 339.*

342. *As in 340. Camera follows the Fool as he exits the ring, passing in front of Zampanò and Gelsomina as she is applauding and he is frowning.*

343. MCU: *Zampanò, adjusting his chain. Gelsomina stands behind him, her back to the camera. Suddenly the Fool turns to Zampanò and says over his shoulder:*

THE FOOL: Go get 'em, "lifle"! (*The Fool then rushes away, exiting frame from the left.*)

344. MS: *the Fool rushes to the circus ring for an encore. Camera pans on him and finally frames him in a* MCU *as he halts and takes a bow with his hat.*

345. *As in 343. Zampanò, muttering to himself.*

ZAMPANÒ: A great man!

346. MS: *the Fool and two clowns turn around in a circle as they exchange*

each other's hats. As they finish the routine, camera pans on the Fool as he leaves the ring, waving his hat to the crowd.

347. MS: *Zampanò, as the Fool backs into the frame from the left in the background.*

   THE FOOL (*to Gelsomina, who is standing behind Zampanò*): Don't worry, everything will go badly!

348. MS: *Giraffa, addressing the audience with a microphone. Gelsomina and Zampanò are standing behind him.*

   GIRAFFA: And now, ladies and gentlemen, we shall turn to a number from the Giraffa Circus show: Zampanò . . .

349. MS: *Zampanò's left profile, smiling as he prepares to enter the ring. Gelsomina stands beside him, looking at him and smiling. Zampanò crosses the frame and exits left.*

   GIRAFFA (*off*): . . . or, the man with the lungs of steel!

350. MCU *of Zampanò. Camera pans on him as he enters the ring, followed by Gelsomina; then camera frames them in* LS *as Zampanò removes his cloak with a flourish and hands it to Gelsomina. He then begins his usual spiel.*

   ZAMPANÒ: Ladies and gentlemen, here before you I am holding a chain more than a half centimeter thick.

351. MS: *Giraffa watching the routine out of frame as the Fool walks up behind him. Camera follows the Fool as he slowly moves to take a seat in the audience.*

   ZAMPANÒ (*off*): It's made of pig iron and is stronger than steel. You will observe me pass the chain around my chest and fasten it tightly with this hook. With only . . .

352. MS: *Zampanò, performing, as Gelsomina stands near him.*

   ZAMPANÒ: . . . the expansion of my pectoral muscles—that is, my chest—I shall shatter the hook. Now, somebody among you might claim that the hook is sawed in the middle. Just a moment, check with your own eyes. (*Zampanò hands the chain to Gelsomina.*) Signorina Gelsomina, if you please.

   Camera pans on Gelsomina as she moves left to show the chain to the crowd, leaving Zampanò out of frame.

   THE FOOL (*off, clapping his hands and shouting in the audience*): Bravo! Bravo!

353. MCU: *Zampanò, showing the piece of cloth to the crowd.*

THE FOOL (*off*): Bravissimo! Encore! Encore!

354. MS: *Gelsomina, back to the camera, which pans on her as she continues showing the chain to the audience, until she reaches the Fool seated in the front row.*

THE FOOL: Terrific! Bravo!

355. MCU: *Gelsomina, right of frame, and the Fool, left of frame.*

THE FOOL: Very good! Yes! Yes!

356. *As in 353.*

ZAMPANÒ: This piece of cloth is not meant to protect me . . . (*Zampanò pauses in his spiel because of the Fool's comic antics.*) . . . but it is used to spare you the sight of blood in case . . .

357. MCU: *the Fool, facetiously testing the strength of the chain and grunting loudly, while Gelsomina stands beside him with a smile.*

ZAMPANÒ (*off*): . . . the hook cuts my flesh.

The Fool's antics continue to accompany Zampanò's routine, and the audience laughs.

358. MCU *of Zampanò. Camera pans left as he goes toward the Fool and takes the chain away from him. Then it pans right as he returns to the center of the ring, while Gelsomina is putting the strap of her drum over her head in the background.*

ZAMPANÒ: I won't tell you that you need the strength of two yokes of oxen here—you probably aren't all professors—but even the least intelligent person can see that three things are required: sound lungs, ribs of steel, . . .

359. MS: *the Fool in the audience.*

ZAMPANÒ (*off*): . . . and superhuman strength.

360. MCU: *Giraffa, as he whispers to the Fool, out of frame.*

GIRAFFA: Get out of there!

361. *As in 359. The Fool gestures placatingly to Giraffa.*

ZAMPANÒ (*off*): If there are any squeamish people in the audience, I advise you not to look . . .

362. MS: *Zampanò wraps the chain around his chest.*

ZAMPANÒ: The drum will roll three times. (*Camera tilts on Zampanò as he kneels and prepares to start his routine.*) Signorina Gelsomina, if you please.

Zampanò inflates his lungs, as Gelsomina, behind him to frame right, begins to roll the drum.

363. MS: *the Fool stands up, taking off his hat.*

THE FOOL: Zampanò!

364. MCU *of Zampanò (as at end of 362).*

THE FOOL (*off*): Please excuse me!

365. MCU *of the Fool.*

THE FOOL: But you're wanted on the telephone!

366. MCU: *Zampanò frowns angrily at the Fool, out of frame, then, with a grimace, he strains to break the chain to the roll of the drum. Sound of laughter over.*

367. MCU *of the Fool. Camera pans left as he leaves his seat.*

368. *As in 366. Zampanò finally shatters the chain with a grunt.*

369. MS: *Giraffa, standing by the exit as the Fool walks by.*

> GIRAFFA (*looking at the Fool*): That bastard! (*He then speaks to several children about to perform.*) Hurry up! It's your turn now!

370. LS: *the Fool at frame left as he leaves the tent.*

371. MS: *Giraffa and Zampanò, as the latter leaves the ring.*

> GIRAFFA: There, there, calm down, Zampanò. Now let me talk to that good-for-nothing!
> ZAMPANÒ: Where is he? I'll kill him! (*He pushes aside one of the circus hands trying to restrain him.*) I'll kill him!

372. LS: *a high angle of the Fool running away from the tent.*

373. MS: *Zampanò grapples with two circus hands. As Zampanò and the two men leave frame from the left, Gelsomina appears from behind Giraffa who stands in MS by a pole.*

374. LS: *Zampanò, struggling with the circus hands. Camera pans right as he runs from the tent.*

> ZAMPANÒ: Where are you? Where are you, you swine?

Camera stays motionless as Zampanò runs toward the foreground and pans right as he ascends stairs and addresses a man who is sitting in an open caravan.

> ZAMPANÒ: Is that swine hiding here somewhere?
> MAN: I haven't seen him.

Camera pans left as Zampanò descends the stairs of the caravan and approaches the foreground.

ZAMPANÒ (*shouting*): Where are you, you coward? Where are you? (*He moves quickly away from camera, halts, falls on his hands and knees, and searches under the caravan for the Fool.*) I'll make you never want to laugh again! (*He stands up, saying in disgust:*) What a great man! (*Then he turns around toward the tent, adjusting his cape.*) Dissolve.

375. LS: *Gelsomina approaches, carrying a pail of water. It is night, and she is outside Zampanò's van. Camera first tracks back, then pans slightly right on Gelsomina as she reaches Zampanò (MS) by the van. Zampanò washes his face from a washbasin which Gelsomina is filling, then dries his face.*

GELSOMINA: But why does he have it in for you, that guy?
ZAMPANÒ: How do I know?
GELSOMINA: What . . . ?

ZAMPANÒ: Nothing! I didn't do anything to him. . . . It's him who does nothing but tease me. (*Zampanò walks left, drying himself.*) But there'll come a day when he'll pay for everything.

GELSOMINA: But who is he?

ZAMPANÒ: He's the bastard son of a gypsy, that's who he is!

GELSOMINA: Have you known him for a long time?

ZAMPANÒ: Even too long!

GELSOMINA (*with the basin in her hands*): He also knew Rosa, didn't he?

ZAMPANÒ: Listen, he doesn't know anything, either about Rosa or about me. Nothing . . . but I don't want to hear anymore said about him. . . . Now you come to bed!

Zampanò climbs into the van and out of frame, as the camera tracks left slightly on Gelsomina. All of a sudden in the silence of the night from the other side of the circus tent, the tender sound of a violin can be heard playing Gelsomina's theme. She pours the water into a nearby bucket and turns toward the sound and the camera.

376. MS: *Gelsomina, back to the camera, as she walks around the deserted circus tent. The Fool is visible beside his car in the distant background.*

377. MS: *the Fool, seated on the running board of the left side of the car. With a smile, he motions to Gelsomina to remain silent and to go away.*

378. MS: *Gelsomina, responding with a smile. Then, she turns and walks away.*

379. *As in 377.*

380. LS: *Gelsomina walking away.*

381. LS: *Gelsomina, from inside the van, with Zampanò in the extreme foreground asleep. Gelsomina climbs into the van, kneels beside Zampanò, and stares at him. Fade out.*

382. *Fade in.* MS: *the Fool, wearing a staved-in top hat, jumps up in the air in the center of the circus ring. It is the following day.*

383. LS: *Gelsomina, carrying a pail of water in front of Giraffa's caravan. Camera tracks backward on her as she reaches Giraffa seated on the bleachers and frames her in* MS. *The Fool enters the frame with a leap from the left foreground. He is wearing a pair of dark glasses.*

THE FOOL (*examining Gelsomina's face and holding her chin*): Hey, still here? Look how she walks . . . heh, heh. What did I tell you? She has exactly the face we need. Don't you see? (*The Fool then takes the trombone from Giraffa and hands it to Gelsomina.*) Take this. Come on, come on, come on, come on, come on.

Camera tracks slightly left on them as they move away from Giraffa toward the center of the circus ring.

THE FOOL: Put the bucket down, for heaven's sake. Here you are! I've always done this number when I have had a girl with me.

As they reach the center of the ring, camera pauses and frames them in MS. *He puts the top hat on Gelsomina's head. A little girl approaches them from the rear.*

LITTLE GIRL: Good, Gelsomina, work with us, work with us!
THE FOOL (*to the little girl*): Go away! Go away! (*To Gelsomina.*) Come on, try to play, try!

Gelsomina blows into the trombone. An off-key sound issues forth, and she smiles.

THE FOOL: Ohhh! Terrific! Do you realize that you have a real talent for this? Now, try to understand very carefully. I play the violin.

Camera tracks slightly left as the Fool, playing his miniature violin, walks away from Gelsomina, who is now out of frame.

THE FOOL: And when you hear that I do like that, you come up behind me—real silent and quiet from over there—and play the trombone just like you did.

384. MCU: *Gelsomina, looking at the Fool out of frame. She smiles and nods that she understands.*

THE FOOL (*off*): Did you understand me? Now, let's try it.

Gelsomina's smile changes to an anxious expression at the Fool's suggestion.

GELSOMINA: I can't.

385. MS: *the Fool's right profile, as he is about to start playing.*

THE FOOL: Why not?

386. *As in 384.*

GELSOMINA: Zampanò doesn't want me to.

387. MCU *of the Fool.*

THE FOOL (*with an ironic, victimized tone*): Did you hear that? There you are. Then you say that it's my fault!

388. LS: *Giraffa on the bleachers.*

GIRAFFA: Where is Zampanò? Go over there, go call him so I can talk to him.

Camera tracks slightly backward as Giraffa climbs down from the bleachers and walks toward Gelsomina; the camera frames Giraffa in MS with Gelsomina in the left foreground facing him.

GELSOMINA: He's not there. He went to town.
GIRAFFA: O.K. I'll talk to him later! What are you afraid of, he won't bite you! . . . We're all one big happy family here, we all work together. . . . Everything you learn is all profit, isn't it? (*Giraffa takes the top hat, which Gelsomina has just removed, and replaces it on Gelsomina's head.*)

389. *As in 387.*

> THE FOOL (*didactically*): Now, remember this; when I reach this spot
> here . . . (*The Fool points to the proper position with the violin bow.*)

390. MCU: *Gelsomina in the left of frame, with Giraffa standing behind her
in MS.*

> THE FOOL (*off*): Did you understand?

> *Gelsomina nods at him and smiles.*

> THE FOOL (*off*): Did you really understand?

391. MCU: *the Fool turns and walks left to reach a LS.*

> THE FOOL: Now, get ready. Ladies and gentlemen, I am now going to
> play a very, very sad tune for you.

> (*The Fool begins to play Gelsomina's theme with his back to the camera.
> A few circus employees watch him.*)

392. *As in 390.*

393. LS: *the Fool, who stops playing, turns around with his hands on his hips
in disgust over Gelsomina's failure to follow his directions.*

394. *As in 392.*

> GIRAFFA (*nudging Gelsomina with his cane*): He told you: play!

> *Gelsomina blows one loud note.*

395. *As in 393.*

> A BOY (*in the background*): Earlier, stupid!
> THE FOOL: Terrific!

396. *As in 394. Gelsomina smiles at first at the Fool's sarcastic praise.*

THE FOOL (*off*): Very good!

Gelsomina's smile turns into a distressed expression.

THE FOOL (*off*): It's clear that staying with Zampanò even makes you intelligent!

397. *As in 395.*

THE FOOL: Don't wait for me to finish; you've got to interrupt me! (*The Fool becomes angry and begins to gesticulate with his hands.*) And then I told you to come over here to play, over here where I'm standing, you fool! Now, let's try again. (*The Fool turns around as he starts playing his violin again.*) Come on!

398. *As in 396. Giraffa prompts Gelsomina with his cane. She smiles, more confident now, and she strides forward and out of frame from the left foreground.*

399. *As in 397. Gelsomina enters frame from right foreground; as Gelsomina approches the Fool, she plays a single out-of-key note on the instrument.*

THE FOOL (*suddenly turning around*): Excellent!

400. MCU: *Gelsomina, who turns toward camera, smiling with satisfaction, while the Fool stands beside her in MS. During the following speech, Gelsomina repeatedly turns from the Fool to Giraffa out of frame.*

THE FOOL: Terrific! Now, Gelsomina, we'll do this three times, and after that I'll make a circle around the ring, and you come up behind me playing along with me. Do you understand? (*Gelsomina nods.*) Look at what you have to do. You have to put one finger here and another there, and then all you need to do is to blow. Just try it. (*As Gelsomina blows a few notes, they both move away into the background, marching.*)

401. MCU: *Giraffa is in the right foreground, looking at the routine out of frame. Zampanò approaches the circus ring from the background; Giraffa turns to his left toward Zampanò.*

402. LS: *the Fool, closely followed by Gelsomina. Camera pans left on them as they parade around the circus ring playing their instruments. Camera halts as they bump into Giraffa and Zampanò, who angrily jerks the trombone away from Gelsomina.*

GIRAFFA: What's the matter, Zampanò? She's working. I told her to.
ZAMPANÒ: She works only with me!

As Zampanò says this, the Fool plays two notes in pizzicato on his violin, twirling around.

403. MCU: *the Fool, his back to the camera, staring at Zampanò (MS), his face to camera.*

THE FOOL: Zum, zum!

404. MCU: *Gelsomina in right foreground. Giraffa stands behind her in MS. Gelsomina looks worried, as Giraffa speaks to Zampanò, out of frame.*

GIRAFFA: Excuse me, but I don't understand you. I looked for you, you were in town, otherwise I would have told you first. What's wrong with that? We all work together here.

405. *As in 403.*

ZAMPANÒ: With that guy there, she doesn't work!
THE FOOL (*turning his face toward the camera*): Zum, zum! (*He plucks the violin again, and Zampanò furiously grabs him by the collar.*)

ZAMPANÒ: Listen, knock it off, you!
THE FOOL (*removing his dark glasses and moving away from Zampanò toward the background*): Ayi! I don't speak to you. You told me yourself that I shouldn't speak to you, and I don't!

406. *As in 404. Gelsomina stares at Zampanò at first, but as Giraffa taps her arm, she turns to go away.*

GIRAFFA: Gelsomina, go over there with my wife, and then I'll talk to him.

407. MS: *Zampanò's right profile, with the Fool in the background looking at him and walking away.*

ZAMPANÒ (*angrily to Gelsomina*): You stay here! I'll tell her what she has to do! And if I say that she doesn't work with that tramp . . .

408. *As at the end of 406. Gelsomina puts on her top hat.*

ZAMPANÒ (*off*): . . . she doesn't work with him!
GIRAFFA: But why, Zampanò?

409. *As in 407.*

ZAMPANÒ: Because I want it that way, because I want it that way!

The Fool picks up a bucket full of water and throws it at Zampanò, drenching him. Zampanò turns to the Fool, throws his hat at him, and, as the Fool races around a caravan on the left, the camera pans quickly left and then right on the Fool running away.

410. *As in 408.*

GELSOMINA: Zampanò! Zampanò!

411. LS: *Zampanò chasing the Fool up the bleachers and over the fence, as two circus hands pursue them.*

GIRAFFA (*off*): Let the Fool alone! Goffredo! Nazareno! Stop them before they kill each other!

412. LS: *Zampanò leaping down from the fence, with the Fool escaping in the distance.*

GIRAFFA (*off*): Run, quick, Paolo!

413. LS: *one of the circus hands, back in the circus ring.*

GIRAFFA (*off*): Quick—he's an animal!

Camera pans left as the circus hand races around the fence, passing the spot where Giraffa and Gelsomina·are standing.

GIRAFFA: Damn these gypsy tramps!
YOUNG MAN: Zampanò! He has a knife!

Giraffa exits frame, running after the employee. A woman from the background reaches out to comfort Gelsomina, who is whimpering.

AIDA: Don't worry, don't worry, Gelsomina.

414. ELS: *a number of men are running across a field after Zampanò and the Fool. A bar is in the extreme background.*

AIDA (*off*): Now they'll stop them. Blessed Virgin Mary!

415. LS: *the front door of the bar from inside as the Fool rushes into the room. Camera pans on him (MS) as he goes left to a back door, then right again, picking up a chair and throwing it at Zampanò, who has appeared in the doorway.*

416. LS: *Zampanò with a knife. As the chair falls to the floor in front of him, three circus hands enter in pursuit. He rushes forward to attack the Fool, and the circus hands tackle him from behind.*

ZAMPANÒ (*grunting*): No! No!

417. MS: *the Fool, entering the bathroom.*

THE FOOL: Hey, be careful!

418. MS: *Zampanò grappling with the two men.*

THE FOOL (*off*): He has a knife!

Zampanò pushes one of the men away from him onto a nearby table.

419. MS: *the Fool closes the bathroom door behind him.*

420. MS: *Zampanò pushes the second man away and then, backing away, threatens them with his knife.*

ZAMPANÒ: I'll kill the first man who comes near me! (*Zampanò then exits frame from left foreground.*)

421. MCU: *Zampanò at the bathroom door, his back to camera. First he tries*

to open the locked door. When this is unsuccessful, he tries several times to break it down with his shoulder.

ZAMPANÒ (*in a menacing tone*): Open the door! Come out here, you
  dirty coward!

422. MS *of the two circus employees.*

423. *As in 421.*

ZAMPANÒ: Open up! Open up!

424. *As in 422. Behind the two circus hands a crowd is already gathering outside the door. Two* carabinieri[16] *block the door, then one comes inside to investigate.*

ONE OF THE CARABINIERI: Get back, get back! What's going on here?
ONE OF THE CIRCUS HANDS: Nothing! Nothing!
ONE OF THE CARABINIERI (*to Zampanò out of frame*): Hey, you!

425. *As in 423. Zampanò turns around angrily, staring out of frame at the officer.*

ONE OF THE CARABINIERI (*off*): Throw down that knife!

Zampanò's angry expression turns to fear. Dissolve.

426. MS *of Giraffa. Camera tracks on him as he walks right, disturbed by Zampanò's arrest. He reaches his wife and Gelsomina, handing his wife a coat. Camera frames the three in* MS. *Gelsomina is visibly distressed and wrings her hands.*

GIRAFFA: No one has ever caused the Giraffa Circus to look so bad.
  (*Giraffa turns away and, followed by his wife, walks toward the back-
    ground, passing Aida, who moves to take his place in the foreground.*)
GELSOMINA (*turning toward Giraffa*): But it was the Fool's fault!
GIRAFFA (*turning slightly toward Gelsomina as he walks away*): I've
  never had anything to do with the law.

AIDA (*stopping beside Gelsomina*): And where are you going to go now?

GIRAFFA'S WIFE (*in the background*): Then stay with us . . . when he gets out, he'll come looking for you.

AIDA: Oh, come on! (*Camera tracks on them as they walk right.*) Leave him behind, for heaven's sake! It's better to lose him than to find him, a guy like that!

427. MS *of Giraffa's wife as she is packing up, aided by a young girl in foreground; the caravan is behind them; a woman is standing on its patio.*

GIRAFFA'S WIFE: But what can you do, all alone? At least here with us, a crust of bread is a sure thing.

428. MS *of Gelsomina and Aida.*

GELSOMINA (*anxiously*): But . . . the motorcycle?

429. *As in 427. Giraffa enters the patio of the caravan in the background.*

GIRAFFA'S WIFE: We'll bring it to the *carabinieri,* and they'll take care of giving it to him.

430. *As in 428.*

THE WOMAN ON THE CARAVAN (*off*): Gelsomina! Come with us!

GELSOMINA (*apprehensively*): And where will I sleep?

Camera tracks right on them, as Aida leads Gelsomina to her caravan and frames them in LS *as they stand by the steps, their backs to the camera.*

AIDA: With me. Come and I'll show you. There's room for two people in my room.

GIRAFFA (*off*): Get moving. . . . Go on, let's get started.

431. *As in 427. Giraffa climbs down the steps of his caravan to join his wife and the young girl.*

GIRAFFA: . . . since there's everything to disassemble and at four o'clock, the truck will be here! (*To Gelsomina out of frame.*) And you, you do whatever you want; if you want to come, come . . .

432. MS: *Gelsomina looks distressfully at Giraffa out of frame.*

GIRAFFA (*off*): . . . if you want to wait for him, wait for him!

433. MS: *Giraffa, addressing Gelsomina angrily out of frame; camera tracks on him as he moves left, leaving the others out of frame.*

GIRAFFA: But he won't work with us anymore. Neither him nor the other one, never again! (*He looks upward.*) Unhitch that tent!

434. LS: *the top of the tent, from Giraffa's* POV. *Camera tilts downward as the tent collapses. The circus hands run to fold it up. Fade out.*

435. *Fade in.* MCU: *Gelsomina, lying in the van at night.*

THE FOOL (*off*): Gelsomina . . . Gelsomina . . .

At the sound of the Fool's whistling, Gelsomina looks up in surprise, turns around, and spots a flashlight in the background.

436. MS: *Gelsomina raises the blanket over her eyes to escape the glare of the flashlight.*

437. MCU: *the Fool lowers the flashlight with a grin.*

THE FOOL: Were you sleeping?

438. MS: *Gelsomina shakes her head.*

439. *As in 437. The Fool makes a face.*

THE FOOL: What an animal stink there is in here!

440. *As in 438.*

THE FOOL (*off*): How can you stand to stay inside?

441. *As in 439.*

THE FOOL (*rolling a cigarette*): Zampanò is still in jail; maybe they'll let him out tomorrow.
GELSOMINA (*off*): Tomorrow?
THE FOOL: Well, it's possible.

442. *As in 440.*

GELSOMINA (*looking down*): It was your fault, since Zampanò never did you any harm. (*She raises her eyebrows.*) So why did they let you out?

443. *As in 441.*

THE FOOL: Well, from a certain point of view, the fault might perhaps be mine, but he was holding the knife. (*He finishes rolling his cigarette and places it between his lips, motioning to Gelsomina.*) Come on . . . climb down!

444. LS: *the Fool, from inside the van, as he opens its door; Gelsomina kneels in profile in the right foreground.*

THE FOOL: Get out! Oh, it'll do him good to be in jail for a while. He's got so many years left to live! (*He moves away from the van.*) I'm the one who'll die early.

Gelsomina finally climbs out of the van, and follows the Fool as he moves toward the bleachers in the far background. Camera remains motionless, finally framing them in LS.

THE FOOL: Oh, what a beautiful breeze! Let's sit down here together for a while. . . . Mmmmmm! What a beautiful negligee you have on! . . . Sit down!

Gelsomina is wearing a blanket on her shoulders that reaches down to her feet.

THE FOOL: Come on, sit down!

445. MS: *the Fool and Gelsomina, sitting side by side on the bleachers. The Fool looks at her with a mixture of amusement and tenderness. She makes a funny face.*

THE FOOL: What a funny face you have! . . . But are you sure you're a woman? . . . You look like an artichoke!

Gelsomina frowns and turns to walk away from him. Camera pans slightly left to follow her, leaving the Fool out of frame.

GELSOMINA (*seriously*): I don't know if I'll stay with Zampanò.

446. MS *of the Fool.*

447. MS *of Gelsomina.*

GELSOMINA: The others asked me to go with them.

448. *As in 446. The Fool stares at Gelsomina out of frame.*

THE FOOL (*ironically*): It's a good time to drop him, isn't it? (*Then the Fool breaks out into a laugh and stretches out upon a bleacher bench. Camera pans slightly left, so as to frame him in LS.*) Ha, ha, ha, ha, ha ha, ha, ha! Can you imagine the expression he'll wear tomorrow when he gets out and finds nobody around any longer!

449. *As in 447.*

THE FOOL (*off*): That's it, you should do it! (*He laughs again.*)

450. MCU: *the Fool, puffing his cigarette while lying on the bench.*

THE FOOL: What an animal! (*He turns to Gelsomina out of frame.*) I really don't have anything against him, it's only that when I look at him, I feel like teasing him. (*He laughs again and puffs his cigarette.*)

451. *As in 449.*

    THE FOOL (*off*): I don't know why . . . (*He laughs again.*)

452. LS: *the Fool, at first still lying on the bench and then sitting upright in* MS.

    THE FOOL: . . . I swear to you I don't know why, . . . (*Camera tilts upward to frame him in* MCU.) . . . something just makes me act like that. But how did you . . .

453. *As in 451.*

    THE FOOL (*off*): . . . manage to land up with Zampanò?

    GELSOMINA (*her eyes downcast and shrugging her shoulders*): He gave ten thousand lire to my mother . . .

454. *As at the end of 452.*

    THE FOOL (*feigning amazement*): Nooooooo! That much?

455. *As in 451.*

    GELSOMINA (*muttering softly*): I have four sisters, all of them younger . . .

456. *As in 454.*

    THE FOOL: Do you care for him?

457. *As in 455.*

    GELSOMINA (*raising her eyes and looking surprised as if the thought had never occurred to her*): Me . . . ?
    THE FOOL (*off*): Yes, you . . .

458. *As in 456.*

THE FOOL: Who else?

459. *As in 457.*

THE FOOL (*off*): You could have run away, couldn't you?

Gelsomina lowers her eyes with a frown.

GELSOMINA (*almost crying*): I tried . . . no use . . .

460. *As in 458.*

THE FOOL (*irritated*): Sometimes you really make me angry. What do you mean, "no use"? If you don't want to stay with him, go off with the others, why don't you?

461. *As in 459.*

GELSOMINA (*sobbing and finally crying*): If I go with them, it's the same . . . if I stay with Zampanò, it's the same. . . . What difference does it make if I go with them? . . . I'm no use to anybody, there! Ugh! (*Gelsomina turns away from camera and walks toward the bleachers, taking a seat.*) I'm fed up with living!

462. MCU: *Gelsomina in the left foreground, crying; the Fool is seated behind her.*

THE FOOL (*leaning toward her*): Do you know how to cook?
GELSOMINA (*sniffling*): Huh?
THE FOOL: I asked you if you knew how to cook . . .
GELSOMINA: No.
THE FOOL: Well . . . well, what do you know how to do? Can you sing? Can you dance?
GELSOMINA: A little bit . . .

THE FOOL: Maybe . . . you like to make love? Do you? Well, what *do* you like, then? (*He stares at her implacably.*) And you're even ugly!

GELSOMINA: What am I doing in this world?

The Fool moves toward Gelsomina; camera tracks slightly right to a MCU *of the two on the bleachers from a slightly higher angle.*

THE FOOL: Tell me. What if I asked you to come away with me? I'd teach you to walk on the high wire, up there in the air with all the lights turned on you. I have a car, we'd always travel around, we'd have a great time. Would you like that? Huh? Ha! Ha! And instead, nothing doing! Your role in life is to stay with your Zampanò, doing all those stupid little routines and taking a bunch of licks on your back like a jackass! . . . Well, life is like that. But, . . . say, Zampanò wouldn't keep you around if you weren't good for something. Say, what did he do that time you escaped?

GELSOMINA: So many slaps . . .

THE FOOL: But why didn't he let you run away? . . . I don't understand it. I wouldn't keep you with me for even a day. Who knows, maybe . . . (*The Fool has a sudden inspiration.*) . . . maybe he cares for you.

GELSOMINA (*raising her eyes toward him*): Zampanò? . . . Me?

THE FOOL: Yes . . . and why not? He's just like a dog. Have you ever seen dogs who look at you as if they want to say something but, instead, only bark?

GELSOMINA: Poor guy . . . huh?

THE FOOL: Ha, ha . . . but you're right—poor guy!

(*Camera moves slightly right with him as he stands up, leaving Gelsomina out of frame. Now sad and deep in thought, the Fool turns toward Gelsomina.*) But if you don't stay with him, who will?

463. MCU: *Gelsomina, staring at the Fool, out of frame.*

THE FOOL (*off*): I'm not educated . . .

464. MS: *the Fool, back to the camera.*

THE FOOL: . . . but I read a few books. You may not believe it, but everything that exists in the world has some purpose. (*The Fool walks away from camera, then turns around to look at Gelsomina out of frame.*) Here . . . take . . . that pebble there, for instance.
GELSOMINA (*off*): Which pebble?
THE FOOL: Oh . . . this one, any one of them . . . (*The Fool reaches down to pick up a pebble.*) Well . . . even this serves some purpose . . .

465. *As in 463.*

THE FOOL (*off*): . . . even this little pebble.

466. MS *of the Fool.*

GELSOMINA (*off*): And what purpose does it serve?
THE FOOL: It . . . but how do I know? (*The Fool approaches the foreground, shrugging his shoulders*). If I knew, do you know who I'd be?
GELSOMINA (*off*): Who?
THE FOOL: God Almighty who knows everything. When you're born, when you'll die. Who else could know that? No . . . I don't know what purpose this pebble serves, but it must serve some purpose. Because if it is useless, then everything is useless . . . (*The Fool tosses the pebble into the air and catches it again.*) . . . even the stars. . . . At least that's what I think. (*He points to Gelsomina.*) And even you . . . even you serve some purpose . . . (*Camera tilts down as the Fool sits by Gelsomina, framing them both in a* MCU.) . . . with that artichoke head of yours.

Gelsomina reaches for the pebble and smiles.

467. MCU: *Gelsomina, holding and observing the pebble and nodding in agreement. She turns to the Fool, out of frame, looks at the pebble again, stands up, walks a few steps away from him, and then makes a right turn, looking at him. Camera tilts up, then pans left and right slightly so as to follow her.*

GELSOMINA: I'll . . . one of these days, I'll take some matches, and I'll burn everything, mattresses . . .

468. MS *of the Fool laughing.*

> GELSOMINA (*off*): . . . blankets, everything.

469. MS: *the Fool in the foreground, his back to the camera, as he looks at Gelsomina standing in the background.*

> GELSOMINA: That way he'll learn. I never said I didn't want to go with him. He paid ten thousand lire, and I set to work. And he gave me slaps. (*The Fool laughs as Gelsomina gets more and more excited in her speech and walks up and down.*) Is this how you act? He doesn't think! (*She touches her temple.*) And I tell him so, but him—nothing doing. And what good does it do then? I'll even put poison in his soup! Oh no? And I'll burn everything, everything. . . . If I don't stay with him, who will? Right?

470. MCU *of the Fool.*

THE FOOL (*gently*): Then they told you to stay with them? Did they?

471. MS: *Gelsomina, enraptured, as she stares at the pebble.*

472. *As in 470.*

THE FOOL (*whistling and snapping his fingers*): Eh!

473. *As in 471. The Fool enters frame from the left.*

THE FOOL: Wake up! I asked you if they told you to stay with them?

Gelsomina nods.

THE FOOL: And . . . didn't you hear anything about me?
GELSOMINA (*her eyes downcast*): They said they didn't want you working here anymore. (*She raises her eyes again.*) Neither you nor
   Zampanò.
THE FOOL (*feigning a lack of concern*): Huh! . . . Imagine how that
   upsets me! And who wants to stay here anyway? (*Camera follows the
   Fool as he walks away from Gelsomina and crosses behind her, making
   a half-turn to the right.*) Wherever I go, I make a pile of money! It's
   them who need me, I don't need anybody! Me . . . today I'm here,
   tomorrow, who knows? The less I stay in one place, the better I like it,
   because people bore me immediately, there you have it! And . . . I'm
   leaving on my own.

Gelsomina walks from the foreground toward the Fool.

THE FOOL: I'm like that, what can you do? I don't have either a home or
   a roof over my head!
GELSOMINA: But why did you say earlier that you'll die soon?

Camera tracks toward them.

THE FOOL: Oh! . . . That's an idea I've always had in my head. (*The Fool makes a half-circle around Gelsomina.*) With this kind of profession, what can you expect? (*On the rear of the van, the Fool simulates with his hand and his voice a man walking and then falling into empty space.*) Plum, plum, plum, plum, plum, plum, plum, pata, pum, fete. I'll break my neck one day or another, and nobody will ever look for me again.

474. MCU *of Gelsomina.*

GELSOMINA (*pityingly*): What about your mother?

475. MCU: *the Fool, leaning against the rear of the van.*

THE FOOL (*evading the question*): So, what're you going to do? Wait for him . . .

476. *As in 474. Gelsomina lowering her eyes.*

THE FOOL (*off*): . . . or go off with the others?

477. *As in 475.*

THE FOOL: Come on, climb on . . .

478. MS: *the Fool and Gelsomina. He reaches for her to push her into the van.*

THE FOOL: I'll drive the motorcycle in front of the *carabinieri* barracks so he'll find you when they let him out, O.K.?

The Fool closes the gate of the van behind Gelsomina, and he exits frame left as he turns around the van. Camera frames Gelsomina in MS as she stares at the pebble.

THE FOOL (*off*): Oh . . . will this dinosaur move?

Out of frame, he starts the engine with a laugh. Gelsomina nods while she continues to stare at the pebble with a smile, as the van drives away. Dissolve.

479. LS: *a deserted city street with a large, plain apartment building, typical of low-income housing, in the background. The van moves toward foreground past the building; as it makes a half-turn, camera tracks to follow it and then holds on it as it halts by a sidewalk. The Fool gets off and walks left toward a nearby telephone pole.*

> THE FOOL (*whistling*): What a machine! . . . Come on, come on, get out!

480. MS: *the Fool, leaning against the telephone pole.*

> THE FOOL: There it is . . . the barracks.

481. MCU: *Gelsomina smiling and then lowering her eyes.*

482. *As in 480. Camera pans as the Fool moves right and forward.*

> THE FOOL: Well . . . (*He makes a farewell gesture.*) Ciao!

483. *As in 481.*

> THE FOOL (*off*): Good-bye . . .
> GELSOMINA: Are you leaving?

484. *As at end of 482.*

> THE FOOL: Yes, I am. But . . . would you really like to come with me?

485. *As in 483.*

> THE FOOL (*off, chuckling*): Huh? . . .

Gelsomina lowers her eyes without making a reply.

486. *As in 484.*

> THE FOOL: Well . . . but I already told you I don't have any intention of taking on a girl, since one really wouldn't be any use to me.

487. *As in 485. Gelsomina now with her head bowed in disappointment.*

488. *As in 486. The Fool unfastens the little chain he wears around his neck.*

489. *As in 487. The Fool's arms enter frame from the left and fasten the chain around her neck, while he is humming Gelsomina's name.*

> THE FOOL (*off*): Here, this will be . . .

> *Gelsomina touches the chain.*

490. MCU *of the Fool.*

> THE FOOL (*awkwardly*): . . . a little souvenir . . . bye!

> *The Fool waves, turns around and walks away into the distance, singing Gelsomina's name.*

> THE FOOL: Gelsomina, Gelsomina, Tarirarirarira.

491. *As in 489.*

> THE FOOL (*off*): Ciao!

> *She looks up, smiles affectionately, and waves.*

492. LS *of the Fool.*

> THE FOOL: Ciao! (*Camera pans to the right on him as he walks away whistling into the distance. He turns again toward Gelsomina.*) Good-bye, Gelsomina!

493. *As at the end of 491. Gelsomina waving good-bye to the Fool, out of frame, with tears in her eyes.*

494. ELS: *the Fool walking away.*

495. MCU: *Gelsomina clasps her chain in her hands and bows her head. Dissolve.*

496. LS: *the van from the rear. The van is still parked by the sidewalk. A stray passerby stares at Gelsomina, seated on the curb.*

497. LS: *Zampanò exits the barracks up a driveway and then stops to look around for Gelsomina.*

GELSOMINA (*off*): Zampanò?

498. MS: *Gelsomina from Zampanò's POV as she stands up by the motorcycle.*

GELSOMINA: I'm over here.

499. MS: *Zampanò with a sullen, dejected expression, puffing a cigarette.*

500. MS: *Gelsomina with a pixie smile.*

GELSOMINA: They told me I could go and work with them . . .

501. *As in 499. Zampanò, looking down.*

GELSOMINA (*off*): . . . but I . . .
ZAMPANò: You could have gone!

502. MS: *Gelsomina, looking down at the pebble she is still clutching tightly in her hand. She smiles, more confident now.*

503. LS: *Gelsomina and Zampanò to the right of the van. Gelsomina goes to the back of the van and pulls Zampanò's jacket out for him. Then she returns to Zampanò and helps him put it on. Dissolve.*

504. MS: *Zampanò, back to the camera, driving the motorcycle down a road. Dissolve.*

505. ELS: *seashore at daybreak from the moving motorcycle.*[17]

506. MS *of Gelsomina, curled up in the rear of the van. She has her eyes half closed, as if dozing, completely absorbed in thought. A tin pan falling on her head brings her back to reality.*

507. LS: *the van, as it comes to a halt beside the road. Overcome by an intense sense of excitement, Gelsomina climbs out of the van and, as she touches the ground, she races away from the van to the right a short distance along the coastal road. Camera follows. Then she stops and runs back to the van. Camera tracks left to her and Zampanò in LS, then pans on Gelsomina, leaving Zampanò out of frame, as she races toward the sea. Camera then halts and frames her in ELS.*

508. MCU: *Gelsomina in right profile. She remains motionless and still with her gaze fixed upon the expanse of sparkling water.*

509. MS: *Zampanò reaches the water, removes his shoes, and rolls up his pants.*

510. MS: *Gelsomina, back to the camera, still gazing at the sea.*

511. MS: *Zampanò, back to the camera, still rolling up his pants.*

GELSOMINA (*off*): Which way is my home?

    ZAMPANÒ (*standing up and pointing to his left*): Over there. (*Camera pans left on him as he slowly enters the water; he stops when the water comes up to his calves.*)

512. MCU: *Gelsomina in right profile. The camera has changed position to reveal a few houses on the horizon.*

GELSOMINA (*contentedly*): Before, I wanted only to go back there. . . .

(*She turns her back to the camera.*) Now, it's not so important to me anymore. . . .

513. LS: *Zampanò turns to face the camera and begins to wade toward the shore.*

GELSOMINA (*off*): Now it seems that my home is with you.
ZAMPANÒ (*calmly but sarcastically as he walks toward the shore*): Is that a fact? A terrific discovery! With the hunger you suffered at your house . . . (*Camera tracks slightly backward and then pans slightly right to frame Zampanò in* MS, *as he is walking back to the shore.*)

514. *As in 512.*

ZAMPANÒ (*off*): . . . you have to make an effort to stay with me!

Camera remains motionless at first as Gelsomina walks angrily away from the sea into LS *range.*

GELSOMINA (*turning to Zampanò*): You're an animal! (*She taps her head.*) You don't think! (*Gelsomina kicks some sand toward him in disgust.*)

515. LS: *Zampanò, back to the camera, as he, having left the water, sits down on the shore, and puts his shoes and socks back on.*

ZAMPANÒ: You really had to tighten your belt, didn't you?

516. LS: *Gelsomina, climbing up the sandy ridge and heading toward the motorcycle in the distance.*

GELSOMINA: Never!

Dissolve.

517. MS: *Zampanò, driving the motorcycle, with a nun on his right and Gelsomina on his left. Camera tracks backward to follow the forward movement of his motorcycle. It is winter now.*

ZAMPANÒ (*to the nun*): There's a storm brewing. What's the nearest
 town?

NUN (*shouting in order to be heard over the engine noise*): It's Magliana,
 eighteen kilometers from here, but you have to go across the
 mountains.[18]

ZAMPANÒ: We won't make it. Not enough gas.

NUN: Here's the convent.

Dissolve.

518. LS: *the convent. Camera tracks left and forward, from the* POV *of the
 motorcycle riders, finally revealing two nuns working in front of the
 doorway. The engine backfires as it comes to a noisy halt.*

519. MS: *the motorcycle. The nun climbs down from the left side.*

NUN (*to Zampanò*): Wait a minute.

*Camera tracks slightly left on the nun, leaving the others out of frame, as
she reaches another nun who enters frame from the left. They are now
both in* MS.

NUN: Mother Superior! I have the oil here! . . . (*She whispers in the
 other nun's ear.*) This man wants to know if he can stay here tonight.

520. MS: *the motorcycle, as Zampanò stands nearby and Gelsomina holds the
 handlebars.*

ZAMPANÒ: Excuse me, Mother Superior, we don't have much gas left.
 (*He glances at his pocket watch.*) It's getting dark and the town is still
 far away . . . and my wife here doesn't feel too well.

521. MS: *the two nuns, looking right at Zampanò out of frame.*

NUN (*to the Mother Superior*): They could sleep in the barn.

MOTHER SUPERIOR (*nodding affirmatively*): All right, just for tonight!

NUN: She said yes. (*Camera follows the nun, leaving the Mother Supe-*

rior out of frame, as the nun walks toward Zampanò and Gelsomina;
the three are framed in MS.) You can stay. You can sleep over there in
the granary.

ZAMPANÒ: Thank you, thank you so much, Mother Superior.

The nun leaves from left of frame.

ZAMPANÒ: And may God always be praised!

Zampanò exits frame from the right.

ZAMPANÒ (*off, to Gelsomina who climbs inside the van*): Go on, hurry
up, pull out the covers!

522. MS: *the nun, as the Mother Superior turns her back to camera and goes*
inside the convent. Dissolve.

523. LS: *Zampanò and Gelsomina, eating by the side of the convent. The nun*
runs into frame from the left, holding a kettle.

NUN: I've found a little bit more!
ZAMPANÒ (*doffing his hat*): Ah, thank you, it's good!

524. MCU: *the nun, spooning out more soup with a smile.*

NUN (*to Gelsomina*): And you . . .

525. MS *of Zampanò and Gelsomina.*

NUN (*off*): . . . don't you want a little bit more?

Gelsomina refuses politely.

ZAMPANÒ (*abruptly*): Go on, take it!

Gelsomina extends her messtin toward the nun out of frame and receives
more soup.

526. MCU: *the nun, with an innocent smile.*

   NUN: But . . .

527. *As in 525.*

   NUN (*off*): . . . does she work with you too?
   ZAMPANÒ (*raising his eyes with an air of self-importance*): Well, she
      helps me a bit, plays the drum . . . the trumpet. Show the sister how
      you play the trumpet!

   Gelsomina puts down her messtin and rises.

528. LS: *Zampanò, the nun, and Gelsomina. Camera tracks right on
   Gelsomina as she rushes enthusiastically to the van, leaving the others
   out of frame. She takes out the trumpet and returns, as the camera tracks
   on her and then frames them all in* LS *again.*

529. MS: *Zampanò, his mouth full, motions for her to begin playing.*

530. MS: *Gelsomina in left profile at first, as she starts playing; then she turns
   her back to camera, as she plays her theme.*

531. *As in 529. Zampanò looking up toward the nun, out of frame, with a
   puzzled expression.*

532. LS *of the three. Gelsomina continues playing.*

533. MS: *Gelsomina, back to the camera. She is still playing. As she turns, she
   is seen first in right profile, then facing forward and lowering the instrument; by the end, a shadow of unhappiness colors her expression.*

534. MS: *the nun, enraptured by the music.*

   NUN: Beautiful! . . .

535. MS: *Gelsomina smiles bashfully and curtsies.*

536. MS: *the nun. Camera tracks on her as she moves forward toward Gelsomina, with Zampanò visible in the background, still seated by the wall.*

NUN: . . . how well you play!

ZAMPANÒ: Well, enough of that! (*He turns to Gelsomina out of frame as he stands up and takes a few steps toward the foreground.*) Here, wash this stuff!

NUN (*as she takes a few steps toward the background and Zampanò*): Give it to me. I'll wash it myself.

Camera remains motionless and frames them in MS.

ZAMPANÒ: Nooooo! That's her job!

NUN (*grabbing the dirty messtins*): No, no, we'll do it together. How clever she is! How well she plays! (*She turns to Gelsomina, out of frame.*) What do you call that song?

GELSOMINA (*off*): I don't know.

Zampanò, standing behind the nun, glances left.

537. LS: *another nun chopping firewood.*

ZAMPANÒ (*off*): Hey! . . . What are you doing, sister?

538. MS: *Zampanò looking to his right.*

> ZAMPANÒ: No, sister . . . give that to me. This is not the kind of work
>   for you. (*Camera pans slightly right on Zampanò as he walks toward
>   the nun who is working, then remains stationary and frames them in
>   LS.*) Give it here, come on!
> NUN: Nonsense. I always do it.
> ZAMPANÒ (*taking the ax from the nun*): I'll cut you enough wood for the
>   entire winter. Leave it!
> NUN: Oh, my goodness!

539. MCU: *Gelsomina, her back to camera, and the nun, facing the camera.*

NUN (*pointing to left of frame*): Do you always sleep inside there?

*Camera moves slightly left to follow Gelsomina as she faces the camera
and takes a few steps toward the van to replace the trumpet inside.*

> GELSOMINA: Yes . . . but there's lots of room . . . I have pots, a lamp
>   . . . everything just like in a house . . .
> NUN: How nice!

*Camera tracks right as they move away from the van and down a sloping
driveway. Tracking backward as they move along a path, camera frames
them in MS.*

> NUN: And do you like it, always going around from one place to another?
> GELSOMINA: His work is like that.
> NUN: Well, even we travel around. We change convents every two years.
>   This is already my second.

GELSOMINA: Why?

NUN: That way we won't become too attached to the things of this world. You become fond of where you live, don't you? You even become fond of a plant. And then you run the risk of forgetting the most important thing of all, which is God. (*The nun makes a half-turn, laughing, and the camera tracks to follow them as they go back to the convent.*) We both travel around. You follow your husband and I follow mine.[19]

Gelsomina makes a half-turn and then faces the camera, as Zampanò can be seen working in the distant background.

GELSOMINA: Well, that's right . . . to each his own. (*Gelsomina is struck and delighted by this comparison.*)

NUN: Would you like to visit the whole convent? I'll go with you. (*Camera tracks on them as the nun leads Gelsomina up the slope toward the convent.*) It's a very old convent, you know, it's more than a thousand years old.

Dissolve.

540. LS: *Zampanò and Gelsomina inside the barn. It is night. Zampanò is lying on the floor, left of frame, smoking a cigarette. Gelsomina is kneeling by a wall in the back of the room. Then she stands up, approaches Zampanò, and looks thoughtfully in his direction.*

GELSOMINA: Zampanò!

541. MS: *Zampanò, sullenly puffing his cigarette.*

542. *As in 540.*

GELSOMINA: But why do you keep me with you? . . . I'm not pretty. I don't know how to cook. I don't know how to do anything. Huh?

543. *As in 541.*

ZAMPANÒ: What the hell do you want? Now . . . go to sleep, go on. What a potato-head you are! (*He removes his cap and begins to pull up the hood of his sweater.*)

544. MS: *Gelsomina, curling up under the cover of her makeshift bed, beside which lie her trumpet and a burning candle.*

545. MS: *Zampanò; he now wears both hood and cap on his head.*

546. *As in 544.*

GELSOMINA (*whispering*): It's raining . . . it's nice here.

547. MS: *Zampanò in the foreground, with Gelsomina in LS in the background by the wall.*

GELSOMINA: Zampanò . . .

ZAMPANÒ: Huh?
GELSOMINA: Would you mind if I died?
ZAMPANÒ: Why? Do you want to die?
GELSOMINA: Once I felt like really dying . . . better than living with that guy, I told myself. (*She sits up with a smile.*) Now, I'd even marry you . . . since we have to stay together all the time . . . if even a pebble serves some purpose . . .

548. MCU: *Gelsomina, tapping her head.*

GELSOMINA: . . . you have to think about things like that. But you never think about anything!

549. MS *of Zampanò.*

ZAMPANÒ (*brusquely*): There's nothing to think about here.

550. *As in 548.*

GELSOMINA: But there is . . .

551. *As in 549. Zampanò raises his head from the pillow.*

ZAMPANÒ (*angrily*): And what should I think about?

552. *As in 550.*

553. *As in 551. Zampanò turns his back on Gelsomina.*

> ZAMPANÒ: Come on, tell me. Will you stop it with all these stupid
> questions? Go to bed, I'm sleepy.

554. MS: *Zampanò in foreground, facing forward; Gelsomina in LS in back-*
> *ground lies back down on her bed.*

> GELSOMINA: Zampanò, do you care for me a little? (*Receiving no re-*
> *sponse, Gelsomina sits up again, picks up the trumpet, and plays a few*
> *notes of her theme.*)

> ZAMPANÒ (*irritated*): Will you knock it off?

> *Gelsomina quickly puts her trumpet away and goes to sleep. Fade out.*

555. *Fade in. LS: a high angle on the inside of the barn. It is the dead of*
> *night. Gelsomina is still sleeping in the same spot, while Zampanò's bed*
> *is deserted. Suddenly a clap of thunder awakens Gelsomina. Outside it is*
> *pouring rain. She gets up and reaches Zampanò's deserted bed. A light-*
> *ning bolt suddenly illuminates her; a shawl covers her head.*

> GELSOMINA: Zampanò!

556. LS: *Zampanò stands before the iron grating covering a little chapel.*

557. LS: *a high angle of Gelsomina as she walks toward Zampanò. Camera*
> *pans on her as she moves right.*

> GELSOMINA: Zampanò!

558. MCU *of Zampanò. He is trying to insert his huge hand through the iron*
> *grating without success.*

> GELSOMINA (*off*): Zampanò!

Zampanò turns left to face her out of frame.

559. LS: *Gelsomina approaches the foreground.*

560. *As in 556. Zampanò climbs down a few steps.*

ZAMPANÒ: Hey! . . .

561. MCU: *Gelsomina, confused and staring at Zampanò.*

ZAMPANÒ (*off*): There are some silver hearts . . .

562. CU *of Zampanò.*

ZAMPANÒ: . . . nailed up on that wall.[20] My hands are . . .

563. CU: *Gelsomina, wearing an innocent smile.*

ZAMPANÒ (*off*): . . . too large. See if you can reach them.

564. *As in 562.*

ZAMPANÒ: You try. . . . Come on.

GELSOMINA (*off, horrified by the thought of stealing from a convent shrine*): No! . . . No!

565. MCU *of Gelsomina.*

GELSOMINA: What are you trying to do?

566. MCU *of Zampanò.*

ZAMPANÒ (*angrily slapping her, out of frame*): What do you mean "No"? Who're you saying "No" to?

567. MCU: *Gelsomina, who falls back, covering her face with her shawl and bumping against the wall.*

GELSOMINA (*crying*): No! No!

568. *As in 564. Zampanò moves back against the wall as camera frames him in a* MS.

GELSOMINA (*off*): You shouldn't do it!
ZAMPANÒ: Shut up! Shut up!

569. LS: *Gelsomina, against the wall, in the shadows. She turns around toward the wall and kneels. The camera tilts down to follow her. Then, in tears, she turns to her right toward Zampanò, out of frame. A clap of thunder on the sound track. Fade out.*

570. *Fade in.* LS: *the front of the convent at daybreak. Zampanò* (LS) *stands in the foreground with the Mother Superior, their backs to camera, in front of the motorcycle. In the center-left of frame, there stands a crucifix. In the distant background, Gelsomina is leaving the convent with two nuns. Sound of church bells.*

ZAMPANÒ: Thank you, thank you . . .
NUN: God be praised! Have a good trip!
ZAMPANÒ: Thank you, arrivederci! (*He bows obsequiously to the nun.*)
    Gelsomina! (*He puts his hat on and prepares to leave.*)
NUN (*rushing toward Gelsomina from the exit*): Have a good trip! Wait
    a moment!

571. MCU: *Gelsomina, a handkerchief to her face, and the nun, her back to camera.*

NUN: What's the matter?
GELSOMINA (*sobbing*): Nothing!

572. *Reverse angle of 571, now Gelsomina has her back to camera.*

NUN: Do you want to stay here? I'll speak to the Mother Superior.

Gelsomina shakes her head.

573. *As in 571. Camera pans right to follow Gelsomina, who leaves the nun (out of frame) and joins Zampanò by the motorcycle. Camera frames them in* LS.

> ZAMPANÒ (*in the middle of the frame*): Sisters. (*He turns to Gelsomina and hands her a paper sack of food.*) Take this, put it away. (*He speaks to the nuns once again.*) Many thanks for your generosity and your hospitality. Sincere thanks . . . from a humble performer!

> *A nun enters frame from the left foreground, as he is about to climb onto the motorcycle.*

> ZAMPANÒ (*to Gelsomina*): Push!

> *As the nun waves good-bye, Zampanò starts the engine and Gelsomina pushes the van.*

574. MCU: *Gelsomina, smiling and crying at the same time; she waves.*

575. MS: *the nun as she waves good-bye with a very worried expression.*

576. MS: *the rear of the van as Gelsomina hops into it. She turns around to wave to the nun.*

577. LS: *the nun, standing by the crucifix. Camera tracks away from her, assuming Gelsomina's* POV.

578. MS: *Gelsomina, waving good-bye and crying. Dissolve.*

> *The next three shots are deep-focus tracking shots of landscapes from the* POV *of the moving van.*

579. ELS *of a herd of horses grazing. Dissolve.*

580. ELS *of a small lake seen from a mountain road. Dissolve.*

581. ELS: *countryside, crossed by a road on which the Fool's car has broken down. Camera stops tracking as the motorcycle comes to a halt.*

582. MS: *Gelsomina, sitting up in the van and looking outside.*

583. LS: *the van. Zampanò slowly and menacingly climbs off the motorcycle. Gelsomina cautiously appears from the rear of the van.*

584. LS: *the Fool's car, with the Fool in the extreme left background, fixing a flat tire.*

585. MS: *the Fool carrying an inner tube toward his car. As he looks up and spots Zampanò out of frame, he stops. An expression of instinctive alarm appears upon his face.*

586. MS: *Zampanò, with Gelsomina standing in the background.*

587. MS: *the Fool, whistling, attempts to disguise his fear with his habitual provocative informality.*

THE FOOL: Hey! "Lifle"! Come to give me a hand, have you? (*Camera tracks on him* [MS] *as he walks right toward his car, smiling, waving at Gelsomina.*) Gelsomina! (*The Fool hums her name in his usual manner. Camera tilts down as he kneels on the ground with the patched inner tube beside the car, then halts as he rubs his hands and continues his work as if nothing was happening. Whistling.*) I'll help you one day or another, too.

Zampanò's legs enter frame from the right and, as the Fool reaches for a can of rubber cement on the ground, Zampanò kicks it under the car.

588. MCU: *the Fool, from higher angle, as he glances up toward Zampanò, out of frame, and smiles, pretending he is in no danger.*

THE FOOL (*with a joking rebuke*): Now, now, now, now, "Lifle."

589. MS: *the Fool and Zampanò's legs. The Fool suddenly grabs the crank and jumps to his feet. Camera tilts up to follow his movement. With the unexpected quickness of a bull, Zampanò seizes the Fool's arms, stopping the crank in mid-air, and pushes the Fool toward the automobile's hood.*

590. MCU: *the Fool, back to camera, and Zampanò, facing the camera, as they struggle. Zampanò presses the Fool's back against the hood.*

591. MCU: *the Fool, still holding the crank, struggling. Zampanò's arms hold him down.*

   ZAMPANÒ (*off*): Throw it down!

592. CU: *Zampanò, struggling.*

   ZAMPANÒ: Throw it down!

593. *As in 591. The Fool drops the crank and struggles helplessly.*

594. MCU: *Zampanò, chuckling.*

   GELSOMINA (*off*): Zampanò! That's enough! That's enough!
   ZAMPANÒ (*to the Fool*): Tease me now! Tease me now! (*Zampanò pulls the Fool up by his coat and then punches him twice with his fist.*)

595. MCU: *the Fool falls back against the hood, striking his head.*

596. LS: *Gelsomina in front of the van.*

   GELSOMINA: Zampanò! Enough! That's enough! No!

597. MCU: *Zampanò, again hitting the Fool, whose back is to the camera.*

598. *As in 595.*

   THE FOOL (*looking up at Zampanò, out of frame*): You don't really want to kill me, do you?

599. MCU: *Zampanò turning away from camera, with the Fool in the extreme foreground, lying on the hood and kicking at Zampanò. Then the Fool stands on his feet and Zampanò hits him again.*

600. CU: *right profile of the Fool, as he bumps his head again on the car.*

601. LS: *Gelsomina running toward the two men and finally halting. Zampanò enters frame from left foreground. Camera frames them in* MCU.

GELSOMINA: Enough! Enough!
ZAMPANÒ (*to the Fool*): That's a present from "Lifle"!

602. CU: *the Fool in agony.*

GELSOMINA (*off*): That's enough! Come away. Come away, for God's sake!

603. MS: *Zampanò, as Gelsomina pushes him away from the Fool, now out of frame.*

ZAMPANÒ: And the next time, it'll be worse!

GELSOMINA: Let's go! Let's go!
THE FOOL (*off*): Worse than this?

604. MCU *of the Fool. Camera tracks backward and then left, as the Fool realizes that his watch is broken while wiping the blood away from his face.*

THE FOOL (*staggering away*): Hey! You broke my watch!

605. LS: *Gelsomina looks back at the Fool while Zampanò continues toward the van.*

606. LS: *the Fool, staggering toward the side of the road. Camera tracks left to follow him.*

607. MCU *of Gelsomina.*

608. LS: *the Fool, first holding his head while falling to his knees, and then collapsing.*

609. LS: *Gelsomina, as at end of 605. She runs toward the Fool, out of frame, and leaves the frame from the right foreground.*

610. LS: *the Fool, lying on the ground. Gelsomina rushes into frame from the left foreground and toward him. She kneels by his side and then turns to call out to Zampanò, out of frame.*

GELSOMINA: Zampanò! Run! Hurry!

611. MCU: *Zampanò, lighting his cigarette.*

GELSOMINA (*off*): He's hurt! He's hurt!

Zampanò walks toward Gelsomina, out of frame, leaving frame from the right foreground.

612. LS: *Gelsomina by the Fool. Zampanò enters frame from left foreground.*

GELSOMINA: He's hurt!
ZAMPANÒ: Hey! (*He kicks the Fool's foot.*)

613. MCU: *the Fool, gasping in pain on the grass.*

GELSOMINA (*off*): He's dying!

614. MCU: *Gelsomina in terror.*

615. MS: *Zampanò's torso. He kneels beside the Fool.*

GELSOMINA (*off*): He's dying!
ZAMPANÒ: Come on, get up—don't act like a clown!

616. MCU: *the Fool, dying, as Zampanò turns him over.*

GELSOMINA (*off*): He's dying! He's dying!

617. MS: *Zampanò tries to revive the Fool.*

GELSOMINA (*off*): He's dying!

618. MCU: *Gelsomina, her fists pressed to her cheeks, sobbing in terror.*

619. MS: *Zampanò, turning toward Gelsomina, out of frame.*

ZAMPANÒ (*angrily*): Will you knock it off? (*He addresses the Fool.*)
Hey, you! (*Zampanò pulls up the Fool's hand and suddenly realizes that
it is completely limp. He drops the hand.*)
GELSOMINA (*off*): No! No! No!

620. MCU *of the dead Fool.*

621. MCU: *Gelsomina, in total despair, her hands on her face.*

ZAMPANÒ (*off*): Shut up!
GELSOMINA: No! No! No!

622. MCU: *Zampanò, both angry and desperate.*

ZAMPANÒ: Shut up! Will you shut up?
GELSOMINA (*off*): No! No! No! No!

Zampanò stands up.

623. MCU: *Zampanò in the left of frame. Camera pans slightly left and then right to follow him.*

ZAMPANÒ: Now they'll arrest me! (*Then camera frames him in* MS *as he walks away in total confusion. Camera remains motionless as Zampanò returns toward the foreground, looking helplessly in every direction.*)

624. MCU: *the Fool's legs. Zampanò reaches to seize them from right of frame and then drags him away. Camera pans to follow the Fool's body as it is dragged away to the right of frame. The Fool's arms are outstretched.*

625. MCU: *Gelsomina stares out of frame at the body.*

626. MS: *at ground level, of the Fool on his back. Zampanò lifts the body onto his shoulders. Camera follows this upward movement. Then Zampanò heads toward the background.*

627. *As in 625.*

628. LS: *Zampanò beneath a bridge, carrying the Fool's body.*

629. *As in 627. Gelsomina trembling and sobbing.*

630. LS: *Zampanò climbs back up the embankment without the body of the Fool. Camera pans right and then tilts up to follow him as he comes up the embankment and reaches the Fool's car. Camera pans left to follow Zampanò in* LS *from a low angle as he pushes the car onto the bridge.*

631. MCU: *Zampanò, back to camera, entering frame from left and looking behind him to make sure no one sees him as he pushes the car from the*

*side. Camera pans slightly left to follow him as he moves to the front
bumper and begins to tip the car over the side of the bridge.*

632. LS: *the car, falling over the bridge. Camera tilts down to follow its
movement. The car bursts into flames with an eerie, almost unreal sound.*

633. LS: *Gelsomina, curled up on the ground. Camera moves slightly to the
right as Zampanò rushes into the frame from the left foreground, drags
Gelsomina up by the arm, and pulls her toward the van in the distance.
Dissolve.*

*The next five shots are tracking shots of various landscapes as fall be-
comes winter. The sound of the motorcycle is continuous over these shots.*

634. ELS *of a valley from a mountain road. Dissolve.*

635. LS *of a wood from the road-level. Dissolve.*

636. LS *of leafless trees. Dissolve.*

637. ELS *of a town, built into a hillside. Dissolve.*

638. ELS *of a snowy field. Dissolve.*

639. MS: *Zampanò, as he walks around in the midst of a circle of spectators
in the dead of winter. He is wearing his leather jacket to protect himself
from the cold and is finishing his usual spiel. Camera pans to follow his
circular movement.*

ZAMPANÒ: If there are any squeamish people in the audience, I'd advise
them not to look. The hook can rip into my flesh and some blood might
spill. The drum will roll three times.

640. LS: *Zampanò, about to start his routine. Gelsomina stands beside him
wearing her bowler hat and holding her drum.*

ZAMPANÒ: If you please, Signorina Gelsomina . . . (*Zampanò gets on*

his knees and flexes his chest to shatter the chain. Now impatiently.)
Signorina Gelsomina!

641. MS: *Gelsomina in profile, standing motionless, as if traumatized, with
her gaze fixed upon empty space.*

ZAMPANÒ (*off*): Signorina Gelsomina . . .

642. MS: *Zampanò in profile as he flexes his muscles to shatter the chain.*

ZAMPANÒ (*angrily*): . . . the drum . . .

643. MS: *Gelsomina turns to Zampanò.*

GELSOMINA (*whimpering*): The Fool is hurt!

644. MCU: *Zampanò looking at Gelsomina, out of frame.*

GELSOMINA (*off*): Zampanò!

645. MCU: *Gelsomina, still whimpering like a puppy.*

GELSOMINA: Zampanò! The Fool is hurt!

Dissolve.

646. ELS: *a road to the mountains in the dead of winter. Zampanò's motorcycle
drives down the road as the camera tracks behind it. Dissolve.*

647. MS: *the right side of Zampanò's van as it travels down the road. There is
a strange owl painted on the canvas. Dissolve.*

648. MS: *section of a snow-covered hillside. The camera pans right to reach
Zampanò's motorcycle driving down the road toward the right foreground
and frames it in LS as it comes to a halt. Zampanò gets off and walks
around to the rear of the van.*

649. MS: *Zampanò from inside the van as he enters frame from the left and peers inside.*

ZAMPANÒ (*to Gelsomina inside the van, out of frame*): What's gotten into you? What's the matter? (*He takes off his hat in desperation and scratches his head.*) Will you get it through your head that nobody saw us. Nobody's looking for us. Nobody's even thinking about us. . . . I'm hungry. You stay here, I'll do it! (*He picks up pots and pans, then turns away and looks around for a place to build a fire.*)

650. MS: *Gelsomina, curled up inside the van, sobbing.*

651. LS: *Zampanò puts down the pots and pans and places a tripod on the ground. Camera tracks right as he walks to right of frame so as to reach a clump of snow.*

652. LS: *Zampanò, as he scoops up some snow for cooking water.*

653. ELS: *the van. Gelsomina appears from behind it.*

654. *As in 652. Zampanò looks up and spots Gelsomina, out of frame.*

655. LS: *Zampanò stands up.*

ZAMPANÒ (*anxiously*): Hey!

656. MS: *Gelsomina, her back to the camera, walks, bewildered, down the road.*

ZAMPANÒ (*off*): Where are you going?

657. *As in 655. Camera tracks backward at first and then right to follow Zampanò as he runs after Gelsomina.*

ZAMPANÒ: Hey! Now, where are you going? Hey! (*He reaches Gelsomina and seizes her coat sleeves.*)

658. MS: *Zampanò, his back to camera, and Gelsomina, as he turns her toward him.*

ZAMPANÒ: Now, where are you trying to go, huh?

659. MCU: *Zampanò, staring at Gelsomina, out of frame.*

660. MS: *Gelsomina, whimpering. Camera pans right so as to follow her as she walks back to the van.*

661. MCU: *Zampanò, staring at Gelsomina as she moves away.*

ZAMPANÒ: Hey! Do you want to go home? Hey!

662. LS: *Gelsomina makes a half turn toward Zampanò, out of frame, and shakes her head. Then she walks toward the van in the background. Dissolve.*

663. ELS: *a road in the woods. The camera tracks forward as if from the motorcycle seat. Dissolve.*

664. LS: *the van, with a campfire burning nearby. Zampanò walks from the campfire to the van.*

665. MS: *Zampanò, from inside the van, as he opens the flaps and peers inside. He is unshaven and haggard, obviously exhausted and worried over Gelsomina's erratic behavior.*

ZAMPANÒ: Come on! (*Gelsomina, out of frame, whimpers like a puppy.*) Eat something!

666. MS: *Gelsomina, lying under the covers and whimpering.*

667. *As in 665.*

ZAMPANÒ (*angrily*): But stop crying! Stop it! (*He turns away; the flaps close. He reopens them.*) Stop it! I can't stand it anymore! . . . It's cold now. I'm going to sleep.

668. MS: *Gelsomina, jumping up in bed with a terrified look.*

GELSOMINA: No!

669. MCU *of Zampanò.*

670. *As in 668.*

GELSOMINA: You can't come in! . . . You can't come in!

671. *As in 667.*

ZAMPANÒ: Be quiet! . . . I'll sleep outside. (*He pulls the flaps shut.*)

672. *As in 670. Gelsomina crawls back underneath the covers. Fade out.*

673. *Fade in.* ELS: *snow-covered fields. The road can be seen in the left foreground, while the van (LS) is parked by an abandoned building. Zampanò walks from the van to the building.*[21]

674. MS: *Zampanò, kneeling by the campfire to fan its flames. Suddenly he looks up to the right.*

675. LS *of the van in the left foreground, against a snow-patched landscape. Gelsomina climbs out of the van, trailing an overcoat behind her. Camera tracks slightly right to follow her, back to camera, as she gazes toward the horizon.*

676. *As in 674.*

677. LS: *Gelsomina, looking around and then approaching the foreground. Her face has lost the tragic expression that has marked it from the day of the crime; her features are calmer now, stretched out into a kind of vague smile.*

678. MCU: *Zampanò standing up, from Gelsomina's* POV.

679. MCU: *Gelsomina, from Zampanò's* POV.

GELSOMINA (*in a subdued tone*): It's nice here.

680. MS: *Zampanò, from Gelsomina's* POV.

ZAMPANÒ: It's cold. . . . Sit over there. . . . Take a bit of sun.

681. MS: *Gelsomina, from Zampanò's* POV. *Camera pans right to follow her as she walks to a wall, then turns around and stands against it.*

682. MS: *Zampanò, also standing by a wall.*

683. MS: *Gelsomina, standing by the wall. Now she seems calm and tranquil. She places the coat on the ground. Camera tilts down as she sits, then tracks slightly backward, so as to frame her in* LS *against the wall.*

684. MS *of Zampanò. Camera tilts down as he kneels by the fire.*

685. MS *of Gelsomina. She looks around as if seeing everything for the first time. She softly caresses her overcoat and her bangs. She turns right toward Zampanò, out of frame, as he speaks.*

686. MS: *Zampanò, by the fire.*

ZAMPANÒ: Let's eat some soup, O.K.? (*He tastes the soup.*) It's lacking something . . .

687. LS: *Zampanò, kneeling in front of the fire. Gelsomina, in the left foreground, gets up and goes over to the fire to assist Zampanò.*

GELSOMINA: Leave it. I'll do it.

688. *As in 686.*

ZAMPANÒ (*obviously relieved*): Finally! For ten days, you haven't moved, do you know that?

689. MCU: *Gelsomina, from Zampanò's* POV.

690. MS: *Zampanò, sitting against the wall, with a landscape visible over his shoulder.*

ZAMPANÒ: I didn't want to kill him. I only punched him two times . . . and there was nothing wrong with him . . . just a little bit of blood from his nose . . . then I walk off and he falls down. (*He becomes more and more excited.*) But should I spend the rest of my life in jail for a couple of punches? I just want to be left alone to work in peace! . . . I've got the right to make a living, don't I?

691. MS: *Gelsomina ladles some soup into a messtin. She hands it to Zampanò, out of frame.*

692. *As in 690. Zampanò takes the soup from left of frame.*

693. MS: *Gelsomina, tasting her soup.*

694. *As in 692. Zampanò, sighing in relief.*

ZAMPANÒ (*taking off his hat*): Much better! Now we can leave. There's a fair here in town.

695. *As in 693.*

ZAMPANÒ (*off*): It's just a few kilometers away. Afterwards, we'll go there and earn a real pile of money!

Gelsomina suddenly begins to whimper.

ZAMPANÒ (*apprehensively*): Now what's the matter?

696. *As in 694.*

ZAMPANÒ (*aggressively*): What's the matter with you?

697. *As in 695.*

GELSOMINA (*anguished*): The Fool . . . is . . . hurt!

698. *As in 696. Zampanò stops eating.*

699. *As in 697. Gelsomina whimpering once again as she wipes the tears from her eyes and turns to Zampanò, out of frame.*

700. LS: *Zampanò, seated against the wall and looking toward Gelsomina in the left foreground.*

ZAMPANÒ: Hey! (*He crawls toward Gelsomina and shakes her knee.*) I'll take you home. . . . Do you want me to take you back to your mother? Huh? . . . Hey! . . . Don't you want me to take you back to your mother?

701. MS: *Gelsomina, staring into empty space.*

GELSOMINA (*pensively*): If I don't stay with you, who will?

702. MCU: *Zampanò finally loses his temper in desperation.*

ZAMPANÒ: I just can't go on like this! I've got to earn my living! You're sick! . . . You're sick up here. (*Zampanò furiously strikes his forehead.*)

703. *As in 701. Gelsomina now stares toward Zampanò, out of frame.*

704. LS: *Zampanò in right background, Gelsomina in left foreground. She lies down and covers herself.*

ZAMPANÒ: Go back inside there. What are you doing? It's cold! (*Zampanò crawls back to the wall and sits against it.*) Come on, get in, come on!
GELSOMINA (*trembling*): You killed him . . . ! It's nice here in the sun.

705. MS: *Gelsomina lying by her section of the wall.*

GELSOMINA: I wanted to run away. He told me to stay with you. (*She closes her eyes.*) We need a little more wood here. The fire is dying out.

Dissolve.

706. LS *of the two. Zampanò is seated in the same spot, facing the smoldering fire. Gelsomina is still lying asleep, by the wall of the abandoned building.*

707. MCU: *Zampanò, puffing his cigarette, this time wearing a new expression—hard and determined.*

708. LS *of the two. As Zampanò gets to his feet, camera pans on him walking toward the right foreground and reaching the rear of the van. Camera frames Zampanò's back in* MS *as he retrieves Gelsomina's possessions and a blanket from the van. Camera pans left as he walks toward the still-sleeping Gelsomina and frames him in* LS *as he covers her with the blanket, kneels and slips some money under her pillow. Then camera pans right as he gathers up the pots, the bowls, and the tripod from the fire; it pans left as Zampanò goes and takes a last look at Gelsomina, framing his back in* MS.

709. MS: *Gelsomina, sleeping, from Zampanò's* POV.

710. LS: *Zampanò looks toward the van, which dominates the right foreground of the frame. Gelsomina's trumpet is visible inside the van. He rushes toward the van, places everything inside, and is about to lower the canvas flap when he notices the trumpet. He momentarily hesitates but then he takes the instrument, looks at it as if absorbed in thought, and then goes over to place it tenderly near Gelsomina. Then he heads toward the van and reaches to close the flap. Sound-over of Gelsomina's theme.*

711. LS: *the van, as Zampanò closes the rear flap, puts on his hat, and passes around the van to the motorcycle. He pushes the motorcycle without starting the engine.*

712. LS: *Gelsomina, curled up under the covers, from Zampanò's* POV. *Her trumpet is lying beside her. Camera tracks right.*

713. MS: *Zampanò, in profile, as he glances back toward Gelsomina, out of frame, while pushing the motorcycle. Camera tracks to follow him.*

714. LS: *Gelsomina from Zampanò's* POV.

715. MS *of Zampanò. Camera remains motionless as he hops on the seat while the motorcycle and van are rolling down the road.*

716. ELS *of the still-sleeping Gelsomina, from the van. Sound-over of the roar of the motorcycle's engine, now starting.*

717. LS: *the van, driving away in the distance, on a deserted road. Fade out.*

718. *Fade in.* MS: *the front of an old convertible into which are packed the "artists" of a small circus. A dwarf is shouting through a megaphone to people along the road; an enormous fat man and a brunette woman are seated behind him and the driver. The fat man is clashing a pair of cymbals and the woman is beating a large drum. Camera tracks backward as car moves forward.*

719. MS: *the left side of the convertible. Camera tracks left to follow the car, and then halts as the car, followed by a crowd of children, makes a right turn toward the entrance of a circus. The dwarf addresses the crowd, advertising the evening show of the Medini Circus. His words are almost inaudible over the noise of the cymbals, the drums, and the screaming children.*

> DWARF: Everybody come to the circus! . . . Everybody come to the circus! . . . This evening—a great spectacle—fifty lire, you'll die laughing! . . . Everybody come to the circus!

720. LS: *the rear of a caravan. Zampanò can be seen seated inside. The convertible enters frame from the left foreground. As the car stops and people start getting out, Zampanò climbs out of the caravan.*

VOICES OF THE PEOPLE GETTING OUT OF THE CAR: Now . . .
   children, knock it off! Go away . . . go to the beach . . . go home . . .
   we'll see you tonight at the show!

*Camera pans right, halts, then pans left to follow Zampanò who, putting
his jacket on and buttoning his shirt, walks around the car and toward the
foreground.*

BRUNETTE: Hey! Where are you going?
ZAMPANÒ: I'm going to take a walk.
BRUNETTE: Do you want me to come with you?
ZAMPANÒ: No, I'm coming right back.

Zampanò exits frame from the left foreground, leaving the woman in MS
by the car. Dissolve.

721. MCU: *Zampanò in profile lighting a cigarette. Camera tracks to follow
   him as he walks left and approaches a sidewalk ice-cream vendor. He
   walks around the vendor and faces the camera, which frames him in* MS.

ZAMPANÒ: A thirty-lire cone of vanilla. . . . A bit of lemon, too.

Camera tracks on Zampanò, framing his back in MS, *as he walks to the
left as soon as he receives his ice-cream cone. He swallows most of the
cone in one gulp, then continues chewing at it. A woman's voice (off) is
singing Gelsomina's theme. Zampanò turns around toward the camera,
puzzled. The woman's voice stops abruptly. He begins to walk again.
Woman's voice (off) resumes singing Gelsomina's theme. Zampanò first
turns left, then right, looking for the source of the music.*

722. LS: *a young woman hanging her laundry out to dry in an open yard.
   Three children in the background are dancing in a circle, holding each
   other's hands; a fourth child is seated behind them, watching.*

723. MS: *Zampanò slowly approaches the foreground, walking behind a
   barbed wire fence. He stops and looks over the barbed wire, puffing his*

*cigarette and resting his right hand on the wire. The young woman (off)
is singing Gelsomina's theme.*

ZAMPANÒ: Hey!

724. LS: *young woman, back to camera, picking up a basket of laundry. She
turns around to the left.*

ZAMPANÒ (*off*): Hey, you! . . . Where did you . . .

725. *As in 723.*

ZAMPANÒ: . . . learn that song?
YOUNG WOMAN (*off*): What song?
ZAMPANÒ: That . . . that one, the one you were singing just now.

726. *As in 724.*

YOUNG WOMAN: Ah . . . this one? (*She sings Gelsomina's theme once
again.*)

727. *As in 725.*

ZAMPANÒ: That's the one.

728. LS *of the young woman (as in 726), as she walks toward the foreground.
Camera then frames her in MS as she puts down the basket of laundry.*

YOUNG WOMAN: Oh, a girl who was here a long time ago used to sing it.
ZAMPANÒ (*off*): But how long ago?
YOUNG WOMAN: Oh, a long time ago . . . four, five years . . . she
always used to play this song with a trumpet . . . and so, it stuck in my
mind . . . (*She hangs the laundry up on the line, remaining half-hidden
behind it as it blows in the wind.*)

729. *As in 727.*

ZAMPANÒ: And where is she now?

730. MS: *the young woman, at first behind the laundry (as at the end of 728);
then, she walks left into view and speaks to Zampanò, out of frame.*

> YOUNG WOMAN: She's dead, poor thing. . . . But . . . but you must be
> one of the people from the circus! She was also like you; she was a
> vagabond. . . . (*The young woman walks right, behind the laundry,
> once again.*) Nobody knew her here. Nobody knew anything about
> her . . .

731. *As in 729. Camera moves closer to Zampanò as the woman continues her
tale.*

> YOUNG WOMAN (*off*): . . . she never spoke . . . she seemed crazy. . . .
> My father found her one evening on the beach . . . she was sick, poor
> thing. She had a fever.

732. *The laundry nearly fills the frame. As it blows in the wind, we see the
children playing. The young woman is almost entirely concealed.*

> YOUNG WOMAN: We brought her inside the house, but she didn't explain
> anything . . . she cried . . . she didn't eat anything . . .

733. MCU: *Zampanò, his eyes downcast.*

> YOUNG WOMAN (*off*): When she was a little better, she used to sit
> outside there in the sun. . . . She would thank us and play her
> trumpet . . .

734. MS: *the young woman, hanging up more laundry.*

> YOUNG WOMAN: Then, one morning she didn't wake up. . . . The
> mayor took care of everything, he wrote around to see who she was,
> but . . . if you want to go to the Mayor's . . . ?

735. *As in 733. Zampanò lost in thought. He turns around and is about to walk
away, but then he turns back again to the young woman, out of frame,
and, as if in a trance, he waves good-bye. Dissolve.*

736. LS: *a high angle of the fat man shouting in a megaphone in front of the Medini Circus. Camera pans right so as to frame the inside of the open circus ring. In* ELS, *an acrobat is performing on a trapeze, and the brunette woman is dancing around in the middle of the ring. As soon as the acrobat completes his routine and the crowd applauds, the ringmaster enters the ring, dressed in a tuxedo.*

> RINGMASTER: And now, Zampanò is here for you! The man with the lungs of steel. Afterwards, there'll be a comic sketch that will make you die laughing!

737. LS: *the ringmaster, as he prompts the band, out of frame.*

> RINGMASTER: Let's go!

Camera pans right so as to follow Zampanò as he enters the ring and walks around it. Zampanò wears his usual performing costume for the chain routine; he removes his cape. Camera follows him as he paces back and forth in the ring; he seems almost oblivious of the audience. His voice is listless and lacks expression as he begins his spiel, making a full turn around the ring. Camera pans 360 degrees to follow him and halts as he stops in front of the performers' entrance to the ring.

> ZAMPANÒ: Ladies and gentlemen, here is a chain and a hook a half-centimeter thick made of pig iron, stronger than steel. With the simple expansion of my pectoral muscles—that is to say, my chest—I shall shatter this hook. (*Zampanò stops and kneels to the ground. Camera frames him in* LS. *He looks worn-out and visibly aged.*) This piece of cloth is not meant to protect me but to spare the public the sight of blood if the hook tears my flesh. If anybody in the audience is squeamish, it's better not to watch. (*He gestures to the band.*) If you please!

738. ELS: *the circus ring from a high angle; Zampanò is kneeling in the middle of the ring. Sound-over: a drum roll. Dissolve.*

739. LS: *the interior of an* osteria.[22] *Zampanò is seated at a table in the right*

foreground, visibly drunk. The owner of the establishment stands behind him and is trying to persuade him to stop drinking and leave.

OWNER: Come on, that's enough drinking now. . . . Come on, it's late. . . . Let's go to bed!

ZAMPANÒ (*pushing him away*): Leave me alone!

OWNER: Now, let's go to bed . . . move, come on . . .

ZAMPANÒ (*angrily pushing Owner away*): Leave me alone, will you?

OWNER: Come on, be good, don't drink any more. (*He taps Zampanò's right shoulder.*) Look. I'll help you outside myself. (*He signals to someone to come over to help him.*) I'll take you over to Amilcare's whose wine is better than mine. Get up, come on. Let's go! (*Zampanò stands up and gulps down the last drop of wine from a carafe. The owner begins to pull him toward the exit.*) And stop drinking. Come on, come with me. Listen to me, let's go . . .

ZAMPANÒ: I can walk by myself! I can walk by myself!

OWNER: O.K., I understand, I understand! Now, let's go . . . !

ZAMPANÒ: Let me alone, and get your hands off me!

OWNER (*as they walk toward the background*): The bill please . . . over there.

CUSTOMER: Throw him into the ocean, go on . . . !

Zampanò (LS) *angrily kicks the chair out from under the customer and grapples drunkenly with him until the owner separates the two men.*

CUSTOMER: Hey, what'd you want? Get out of here! . . . Beat it!

Zampanò then sits on a bench behind him to the right of frame, and the owner calls for help.

OWNER: Oho! . . . Let those guys alone! . . . Boy, are you nuts? (*He speaks to some other customers, who help him push Zampanò to the exit.*) Give me a hand here!

ZAMPANÒ: Come out in the open, and I'll show you who you are and who I am. You have some guts! The guts of a coward! Leave me alone!

740. LS: *the door of the* osteria *from the square outside, as Zampanò is forced outdoors.*

ZAMPANÒ: Let me go . . . let me go, I told you!

OWNER (*to the two men who are scuffling with Zampanò*): You guys go away! . . . Go away!

Camera remains motionless as they move toward the foreground.

ZAMPANÒ (*scuffling with the others*): Let me go! Let me go! You're really brave! (*Zampanò knocks one man to the ground, then in turn is pulled down and kicked.*) One at a time!

OWNER: Leave him alone!

The man with whom Zampanò was scuffling inside the osteria *now comes out the door and enters the fray.*

CUSTOMER (*to Zampanò*): You're disgusting! . . . You're pathetic!

Zampanò, on his feet, escapes the Owner's grasp and rushes to grapple with the man. All three men now begin to attack him, while the Owner continues without success to pull Zampanò away from them. Zampanò falls, and as one of the men kicks him in the side, the Owner—while helping Zampanò to his feet—addresses his attackers:

OWNER: What are you doing? . . . Taking advantage of a drunk!

The attackers leave Zampanò and the Owner, to head back toward the osteria, *while the Owner pushes Zampanò away from them toward the foreground.*

ZAMPANÒ: Leave me alone! . . . Let me go . . . ! (*In a fit of anger, Zampanò strikes the Owner.*)

OWNER: What are you doing? Are you going to fight with me, too? Don't you recognize me?

ZAMPANÒ: I don't have any friends!

OWNER (*walking away from Zampanò, between the trolley tracks, toward the background*): O.K., I'll leave you alone. Then you can do what you want!

Camera tracks slightly right to follow Zampanò (LS), *as he kicks over an empty tin drum and staggers, mumbling to himself.*

ZAMPANÒ: Ah, yes . . . I don't want any friends!

OWNER: Oh, sure . . . break everything!

ZAMPANÒ (*mumbling*): Friend . . . ! Why . . . why don't you all come out and face me here right now?

OWNER (*in the far distance*): Ah, you miserable . . .

ZAMPANÒ: Come on right now! . . . I'll crush you all! (*He kicks another tin drum.*) I . . . I'll crush you! (*He picks up the drum, and holding it over his head, throws it toward the foreground out of frame.*) Cowards . . . ! I don't need . . . I don't need anybody! (*He staggers toward the foreground and leans against a trolley pole. Camera frames him in* MS.) I . . . I want to be alone . . . alone.

Dissolve.

741. LS: *a deserted beach at night as the white-capped waves break upon the sand.*

742. *Camera tracks Zampanò in* MS *as he staggers to the right along the beach. The circus caravans are visible in the distant background on the top of a sandy ridge. Zampanò rubs his eyes with his fists; as he turns toward camera, we see that his face is battered.*

743. MS: *Zampanò, his back to camera, walking toward the waves in the background so as to reach a* LS. *He stops and leans over, taking up a handful of sea water and splashing it on his face. Then he turns around and staggers back up the shore toward the receding camera, and collapses on the sand in the foreground.*

744. MCU: *Zampanò, exhausted and bruised from his earlier scuffle outside the* osteria. *He breathes heavily and slowly for some time, remaining motionless, staring into space. The profound silence is broken only by the sound of the backwash of the ocean waves. Zampanò slowly looks upward toward the stars. Then, in desperation, he looks around him. He begins to sob and tremble. He stares back toward the sea and breaks into tears.*

745. LS: *Zampanò, prostrate on the beach, clutching the sand in desperation as he weeps. The camera pulls away from Zampanò until it reaches an* ELS *from an extreme high angle; the sound of Gelsomina's theme builds in crescendo.*[23] *Fade out.*

The End.

Notes on the Continuity Script

1. Ten thousand lire, at either the exchange rate in 1954 or that of today, is a very small sum indeed.
2. In the shooting script (hereafter SS), the major part of the second sequence is omitted from the final version of the film. It treats Gelsomina's unsuccessful attempt to return home. The omitted sequence also provides the reader of the continuity script with a sample of Fellini's poetic and somewhat vague style in his shooting scripts. Much of his script is changed radically or revised on an improvisational basis during the actual shooting of any given scene. Obviously the visual elements of film also interest Fellini more than complex dialogue.

Exterior. A café on a state road. The dawn of day. Day is beginning to break. Zampanò's motorcycle arrives in front of a small trucker's café and stops near a public fountain. Two or three trucks are parked in the space in front of the café, whose metal shutter is only half open. Zampanò dismounts wearily from the motorcycle. He slowly unwinds the thick woolen scarf that is wrapped around his neck up to his nose; he approaches the little fountain, leans over, drinks, and washes his face while puffing hard. Straightening up again, he dries himself off with a handkerchief; it seems as if he has almost forgotten about Gelsomina. He looks at the café; he moves toward it; then the thought of Gelsomina comes to his

*mind again and makes him curious. He approaches the rear of his vehicle
and looks inside.*

*Interior. The van. The dawn of day. Half-buried under the rags, rumpled
up like a kitten, Gelsomina is staring at him through half-closed, sleep-
filled eyes.*

*Exterior. The café on the state road. The dawn of day. Zampanò stares at
Gelsomina for a moment in silence. Then he quickly says:*
ZAMPANÒ: Come on, get out!
*Gelsomina appears at the opening of the van and looks around. Her binge
has worn off and with it, her euphoria, as well as the precise memory of
what has occurred. She is frightened and terrified. Zampanò addresses
her:*
ZAMPANÒ: Hey, wake up! Will you wake up?
*He grabs her by the arm and pulls her to the ground. He pushes her
toward the fountain, abruptly but also, in his own manner, awkwardly
cordial and just a bit impatiently.*
ZAMPANÒ: Wash your face, it'll do you good!
*Tottering and still groggy, Gelsomina leans over the fountain as Zampanò
grasps her head and pushes it under the water, holding her under it by
force even though Gelsomina, half suffocating, struggles and flaps her
arms about. Zampanò laughs.*
ZAMPANÒ: Wake up! This'll wake you up!
*He releases her. Gelsomina is dripping wet, coughing, and out of breath.
Zampanò tosses his scarf inside the van and motions to Gelsomina to
follow him toward the café.*
ZAMPANÒ: Come on, pull yourself together!
*Gelsomina dries herself as best she can; she follows him mechanically,
dripping and looking foolish again. Zampanò enters the café; Gelsomina
stops at the doorway, held back by a wild fear typical of stray dogs.
Zampanò calls her from inside, somewhat impatiently:*
ZAMPANÒ: (*off*): Come on, move it!
Gelsomina goes inside.

*Interior. The café. The dawn of day. The interior of the small café is dimly
lit. There are a few truck drivers and a few workers. At one of the tables, a*

*man is sleeping with his head resting on his arms. The others are standing
up along the bar. Zampanò turns to the sleepy girl serving the clients and
says with his usual instinctive tone of pretentious grandeur and superficial
cordiality:*

ZAMPANÒ: Two coffees! With grappa!

*And he leans on the counter, looking around, without paying any attention
whatsoever to Gelsomina. Gelsomina is extremely disoriented and frightened. She looks at Zampanò, then at this unusual place. For a moment, by
chance, her eyes meet those of Zampanò. Submissively, she asks:*

GELSOMINA: Where is this place?

*Zampanò is distracted by the cups the girl places before him; he takes one,
points with his chin at the other, saying curtly to Gelsomina:*

ZAMPANÒ: Take it!

*And he begins to sip his coffee, looking into space. Gelsomina dares not
take the cup; but her courage then returns, and she drinks her coffee
in silence. Zampanò has already finished; he goes to the register, pays,
and heads, swaying, toward the exit; he makes a sign with his hand to
Gelsomina, without even turning around.*

ZAMPANÒ: Come on!

Gelsomina quickly sets the cup down and follows him. Zampanò leaves.

*Exterior. The café on the state road. The dawn of day. Zampanò goes out,
followed by Gelsomina; he heads for the van, looking around for something. He stops in front of a trucker and asks:*

ZAMPANÒ: Where is the gas station?

TRUCK DRIVER: Up the road. A hundred meters.

*Zampanò nods and turns toward the van. Gelsomina slowly follows him
and stops some distance away. Zampanò turns toward her, as if he were
waiting for her. Gelsomina does not move; she is upset, she wants to say
something but does not dare. Then she decides to do so.*

GELSOMINA: Maybe I'll go back.

Zampanò stares at her in silence. Gelsomina continues:

GELSOMINA: Don't go to any trouble. I'll walk back.

*Zampanò experiences a moment of anger, but he is still friendly. He slaps
his forehead, as if to indicate that Gelsomina is crazy.*

ZAMPANÒ: Hey! (*Then, summarily and more aggressively.*) Come on, get
moving!

Since Gelsomina has not budged, Zampanò takes a step toward her, gives
her two slaps on the behind, and saying more imperiously but with the tone
of a person who gives little importance to what is happening:
ZAMPANÒ: Get moving!
He pushes her toward the van and grasps the motorcycle by the handlebars
without climbing on; he turns to Gelsomina and says curtly:
ZAMPANÒ: Get moving! Push from behind. I ran out of gas. (*Then, more*
violently.) Come on, push!
Gelsomina does not have the courage to rebel. She puts her hands on the
rear of the motorcycle, plants her feet, and pushes. The vehicle moves.
Zampanò and Gelsomina begin moving along down the road, pushing the
motorcycle.

3. Italians quite frequently give their last names first when asked to identify
    themselves.

4. Zampanò's entire comic routine is based upon the mispronunciation of
    various words: "lung rady" for "young lady," "lifle" for "rifle," "hinting"
    for "hunting." This kind of word game is typical of children's play and may
    be compared to what is known as "pig Latin" among American children.
    We have attempted to render this in our translation of the original Italian
    screenplay.

5. In the SS, the comic routine is somewhat clearer, since some of the
    important dialogue from the SS was omitted in the final version:

    ZAMPANÒ (*continuing to yell*): Very good, "lung rady" Gelsomina!
    You've recited the lines about the game birds so well that now I'll make a
    mistake and, instead of shooting at the quail, I shall have to shoot at you!
    GELSOMINA: But where are those ducks?
    Zampanò turns around slowly. With the rifle in his hand, he pretends to
    take aim at an imaginary game bird.
    ZAMPANÒ: O.K. Since there aren't any ducks, you play the duck and I'll
    play the hunter. (*By now, Zampanò has Gelsomina in his sights while she*
    has begun to skip around in a circle.) If you don't stand still, how can I
    shoot at you?
    Gelsomina becomes even more excited, but the expectation of the imminent

*shot frightens her. At a certain point, she stops, plugs her ears, and even
before Zampanò fires, she falls upon the ground. Zampanò shoots: the rifle
explodes with a cloud of smoke. Zampanò falls down because of the recoil.
A gunshot. Laughter. He gets up and with a clownish pose complains.*
ZAMPANÒ: This isn't a duck, it's a jackass!

6. A *trattoria* is generally a popular, low-priced, and family-run restaurant
    without pretensions, serving local specialities to local people.

7. In the SS, the man's name is Medini (the same name Fellini gives to the
    circus for which Zampanò works at the end of the film).

8. In the SS, shot 91 occurs in an entirely different location and at a different
    restaurant.

9. The SS here reveals that the director first had in mind for Gelsomina's
    theme a tune from the distant past, not the enormously popular melody that
    Nino Rota composed especially for the film:

    *Exterior. Town square. Day. Pouring rain. The day is almost over, and
    everything is gray and bleak in the semi-deserted street of the town that
    Zampanò and Gelsomina have reached. The subdued sound of a radio off-
    camera (a seventeenth-century tune). Zampanò and Gelsomina are stand-
    ing up against the wall of a house, protected by the eave of a roof. They do
    not speak to each other; they both stare into empty space. It is cold; both
    have raised the collars of their overcoats. On the other side of the street,
    in the corridor of a small workshop, a mechanic is putting the finishing
    touches on a repair job to the engine of the motorcycle. Gelsomina's face
    expresses a desolation that is growing more and more profound. A window
    on the other side of the street is lit. Inside, nothing can be discerned; from
    time to time, a woman's profile can be seen moving calmly about the room,
    from inside which the soft sound of a radio can be heard. Gelsomina stares
    at the window. The mechanic stands up and calls loudly to Zampanò across
    the street:*
    MECHANIC: All fixed!
    *Zampanò moves away from the wall, but Gelsomina does not follow him.
    She seems not to have understood that they must leave once again. Only*

Zampanò's movement has aroused her. She suddenly announces with tears in her eyes and her voice suffocated by an infinite anguish:

GELSOMINA: I'm going back!

Zampanò stops to look at her. He does not understand. Still more laboriously, Gelsomina declares:

GELSOMINA: I'm going back home!

Zampanò looks at her for a moment in threatening silence. He does not answer her. He crosses the street, reaching the motorcycle; when he is on the other side of the street, he says decisively, without shouting, but in a strong voice:

ZAMPANÒ: Get moving!

Gelsomina remains flattened against the wall for a few more minutes, mute from her anguish; then she knows nothing else to do but to cross the street in her turn, under the rain, joining Zampanò. Dissolve.

10. This is the first line of a song popular when the film was released.

11. In the SS, Fellini had originally included an interesting sequence in which Gelsomina speaks of dying and compares herself to some of the farm animals she encounters:

Interior. The stable. Night. The huge stable is dimly illuminated by a single reddish light. The animals are lined up, some standing, others lying down, chewing their cuds. The sound of a radio and the cries of young people filter in from outside. Gelsomina is curled up on a pile of hay, and she is speaking with an old farmhand who is lying on a kind of platform made of planks, midway between the floor and the roof. He is a man who is already completely gray, with twinkling eyes and a sharp-featured, wrinkled face. As Gelsomina points at the animals, one by one, he names them.

FARMHAND: That's Colomba.

GELSOMINA: And that one over there?

FARMHAND: That's Bellavita.

GELSOMINA: And that one, why is he shivering? What's wrong?

FARMHAND: That's Caporale. He always shivers at night.

GELSOMINA (*shocked*): Why? Is he afraid?

FARMHAND: He's crazy. He sees spirits. When night comes, he begins to shiver.

GELSOMINA (*impressed*): He's crazy! (*Gelsomina gets up, carefully approaches the animal, and observes it; instinctively, she attempts to imitate its expression with her face and its trembling with her body.*) What an expression! How he trembles! He trembles so much! (*She goes back to her place and continues:*) And during the day, does he shiver?

FARMHAND: No. During the day, no. He works. (*He stretches out to sleep.*) Now, I'm going to sleep.

GELSOMINA (*after a pause*): I'm also afraid at night. Sometimes. Aren't you?

The farmhand snickers silently.

GELSOMINA: I feel like dying. What am I doing in the world? I'm a bit . . . (*She touches her forehead with her finger. A calm snore issues forth from the left. Gelsomina gets up to look.*) (*in a low voice*): Mister! (*Silence. Gelsomina climbs up the rungs of a little ladder and finds herself face to face with the farmhand, who is already sleeping soundly. Gelsomina observes him and says to herself with an air of sincere, affectionate surprise:*) Who would have thought it? Now he looks just like a baked apple! (*She remains there staring at him for a moment, then climbs down the ladder. She is alone in the half-dark stable. Only the noise of the animals chewing their cuds or breathing can be heard. A deep sense of discomfort darkens Gelsomina's mood.*) We all grow old. Who knows how we die . . . and after that . . . who knows after that? (*Then Gelsomina is drawn to the "crazy" ox. She slowly approaches him and stares into his eyes; she looks in the direction of the ox's glance, as if she hopes to see what the ox "sees"; she is a bit afraid. In a tone midway between aggressive and maternal, she asks the ox softly:*) But what's the matter? What are you staring at? (*She touches her forehead, as if to tell him that he is crazy.*) But you . . . huh? (*She does not realize that Zampanò has entered the stable and is looking at her with a suspicious curiosity. Only now does Gelsomina see him. Pointing to the ox, she says to him in a natural tone:*) He's crazy . . . he sees spirits. (*She comes toward Zampanò; she continues to speak, very excited, full of desire to begin her story.*) He works during the day . . . when night comes, he begins to shiver. He shivers all over. Like this. (*She imitates the ox's shivering in a clownish manner; her taste for comic imitation overcomes her and inspires her to clownish exaggeration and to laughter.*) His tail shivers . . . his horns shiver—tac, tac, tac— his horns bang against each other. (*Gelsomina laughs and falls back down upon the hay. Zampanò makes no reply; he is seated upon the hay, laying down a large bundle which he has taken from inside his jacket. Gelsomina asks him abruptly:)* Do you believe in spirits?

Zampanò still makes no reply; he is untying his jacket.

GELSOMINA: Zampanò!

Zampanò notices that his pockets are stuffed, and he'takes some cakes out of them which he observes with curiosity; then he laughs to himself.

GELSOMINA: Zampanò! Do you believe in spirits?

Zampanò shrugs his shoulders with annoyance; he puts the cakes in Gelsomina's hands, remarking:

ZAMPANÒ: Go over there . . . eat, go on!

Unconsciously, Gelsomina seeks to draw his attention, to succeed in speaking with him in some fashion. She takes a morsel of cake and declares with excitement:

GELSOMINA: Now you watch, Zampanò! (*She tosses the morsel of cake into the air and swallows it as it falls; she laughs and then she asks:*) But don't you ever see your poor, dead parents in your dreams? Are your father and mother still alive?

Zampanò is completely absorbed in unwrapping the bundle: a jacket and a hat are inside. Gelsomina's question has the power to attract his attention for a brief moment.

ZAMPANÒ: No!

Unconsciously delighted in having come upon a topic for conversation, Gelsomina insists with sincere interest:

GELSOMINA: How long is it that they've been dead?

Zampanò makes a vague gesture; he does not reply immediately. He spreads the jacket out, presses it and examines it; then he says softly:

ZAMPANÒ: My father was better than I was. Bigger. He did the sword ladder, three coils of the chains, death-defying leaps on trains. He fell down seven meters. Bleeding from the mouth, he was dead. I picked him up myself. Spirits are just nonsense. (*He gets up on his feet with his jacket in his hand and makes a gesture as if he were counting money.*) That's all that matters. When you croak, you croak!

12. In the SS, it is Christmas time and the description of the shop that Gelsomina passes is entirely different:

Some shopwindows are still open: Gelsomina stops in front of an enormous appliance store whose large plate-glass windows, illuminated by neon lights in an eerie fashion, display dozens of white, sinister, and very mysterious electrical devices. Cotton puffs representing snow, silver-colored decorations, and a little Christmas tree flashing on and off render the whole picture even more squalid. Gelsomina stares ecstatically; then she continues on her way.

13. In the SS, the circus owner's name is Colombaioni, not Giraffa.

14. St. Paul's Outside-the-Walls, one of the four major basilicas in Rome.

15. In the SS, the Fool is playing the seventeenth-century melody (see note 9) rather than what eventually became Gelsomina's theme, Rota's original composition.

16. The *carabinieri* are a national paramilitary police force in Italy. Originally, they carried carbines (hence their name) and served the House of Savoy as their royal police force. Like regular military troops, they are housed in special barracks and are drafted into service.

17. In the SS, there is an interesting routine which is never performed in the final film. Since the routine treats the question of how men should treat women, it is of interest to an analysis of Zampanò's character:

A town square. Day. It is market time with the usual confusion in a little square where such a market is taking place. In a corner of the square, Zampanò and Gelsomina are doing their routines. With a rope in his hand, Zampanò is tying up Gelsomina, who is seated on a stool.
ZAMPANÒ (*with the air of a confidence man*): Attention, please! Now I'll show you the only way to treat women when you love and really care for them. (*Zampanò makes a gesture with his fingers under Gelsomina's throat as if to say he would gladly cut it. Some people in the audience laugh. Even Zampanò laughs. Zampanò continues tying up Gelsomina.*) When a woman takes a man, ladies and gentlemen, she ties him up for his entire life. In order to get almost even, the man should tie up the woman at least

fifteen times a day, just like I'm doing now, and the woman should be satisfied that her husband treats her like I'm treating her, but I'm coming immediately to the point: I'd like to find the one woman who loves her husband and really cares for him—raise your hand, please! (*Zampanò turns toward the audience. They are all laughing.*) You saw how nobody raised her hand? (*He points toward Gelsomina.*) And now see how she's tied up—to untie all these knots will take some doing, I think, and I'll show you in a moment how the young lady will get out of her chains, but we're not through yet . . . (*Zampanò grabs the sabers.*) . . . a barrier of sabers will be formed around her body. (*Zampanò places the sabers around Gelsomina.*) And now see how she's tied up! These sabers will jump out one at a time with any movement of her body. The danger of this act lies in the exit from the sabers! They have sharp points, one prick under the breast or under the neck is enough to be fatal . . . and I would end up in jail. Yes, ladies and gentlemen. If you will allow me, before I begin I shall go around the crowd, and if you think that this act is worth five or ten lire . . . thanks if you can, and if you can't, thanks just the same. (*Zampanò begins his round. He turns to Gelsomina.*) Meanwhile, the young lady is comfortable. Isn't that right?
Everybody laughs.
GELSOMINA: Yes, Mr. Zampanò!
Dissolve.

18. No town named "Magliana" is listed in either the classic *Enciclopedia Treccani* (Rome: Istituto dell'enciclopedia italiana, 1929–1937), or the *Grande Dizionario Enciclopedico UTET* (Turin: UTET, 1969). However, both reference works list several towns named "Magliano" in the provinces of Grosseto, Rieti, and Rome. Thus, in the entire film only the earlier reference to St. Paul's Cathedral in Rome (see note 14) is a verifiable geographical location.

19. Nuns are often referred to as "brides of Christ," thereby making possible the nun's humorous remark.

20. It is common practice in Italy and other Latin countries to place *ex votos,* or tokens of appreciation for answered prayers, on chapel altars. They may

even be made of precious metals (as are the silver hearts Zampanò is attempting to steal) when the person making the offering is wealthy.

21. In the SS, Fellini specifies that the abandoned building should be a chapel, but this is not evident from the structure actually used in the film.

22. An *osteria* is a tavern or wine-shop which may also function as a restaurant or *trattoria*.

23. Fellini's description of the last sequence from the SS is of interest to anyone who has seen the powerful closing scene of the final film:

Exterior. The beach. Night. Zampanò staggers across the dark and deserted beach, heading toward the sea. He enters the water with his shoes and pants on, stopping when the water reaches almost up to his calves. He leans over, takes several handfuls of water, and throws them on his face and head two or three times, wheezing and panting like an ox. Dripping in this manner, he goes slowly back up the beach. He lets himself collapse upon the sand. He continues to pant and slowly dries off his face with his sleeve and the hem of his jacket. And he remains motionless in this fashion, with his gaze staring out into empty space. Around him there reigns a profound silence. The sound of the backwash of the waves fills the night. Zampanò's heavy breathing subsides little by little. A kind of ponderous calm replaces the excitement of his drunkenness. He looks slowly around. He sees nothing but the darkness, and in the darkness the white crests of the waves on the breakers. Now, Zampanò is almost no longer breathing. Desperate, he is becoming aware of the confusing terror which has mysteriously disturbed him during the entire day. He slowly raises his gaze up, toward the sky. There is no moon. The sky glimmers with stars. Zampanò stares up for a long while with the terrified fear of a brute who for the first time views the firmament. Once again, he turns his gaze toward the sea. A sob arises in his breast and causes him to shake all over. Zampanò weeps. The End.

Contexts

The Making of
La Strada

ecause Fellini considers *La Strada* his most typical work, he has discussed it at length on a number of occasions, but never more cogently than in a recent book that looks back on the work twenty-five years after its appearance. His remarks underline the poetic quality of the film. In a special issue of the Italian film journal *Cinema,* a number of Fellini's collaborators on *La Strada* reminisced about how the film came to be made and their specific contributions to it. The two brief but enlightening statements by Tullio Pinelli and Ennio Flaiano reveal the complicated process by which Fellini and his writers create a script and a story. Moraldo Rossi, the assistant director,

provides an account of a drive in the country that eventually resulted in one of the most celebrated incidents of *La Strada*—the mysterious appearance of a riderless horse (shot 122) as Gelsomina waits dejectedly for Zampanò. The description by the production director, Luigi Giacosi, of the difficulties encountered during the production of the film should remind us that on-location work is far from simple, seldom less complicated than constructing sets in a studio. Finally, Giulietta Masina's discussion of her acting style and her understanding of the character of Gelsomina offers interesting insights into the interpretation of this key character.

The Genesis of *La Strada*

Federico Fellini

How may one describe how the idea of a film is born? When and from where does it come, and what are the often disconnected and concealed paths over which it travels?

Twenty-five years have passed since I shot *La Strada,* and it is difficult for me to remember.[1] Once it is finished, a film seems to leave me forever, taking everything else along with it, the memories included. If I have ever declared, for instance, that a film may be born out of a meaningless detail such as, for example, the impression of a color, the memory either of a glance or of a tune that rings in your ear obsessively and constantly for days on end, or, as you remind me, that *La Dolce Vita* first came to me in the apparition of a woman wearing a dress that made her look like a vegetable, walking down the Via Veneto on a sunlit morning—if I say such things, I am not totally convinced that I am sincere, and when a journalist friend repeats them back to me, I feel ridiculous. I do not believe there are many people in the world who consider their lives unfulfilled because I do not know how to articulate the relationship between this dress and that film I later made. But perhaps my impatience with this kind of inquiry arises from the fact that very often the original causes of the creative process, especially when too clearly identified and isolated as authoritative proofs for semiological speculation, can suddenly become improbable, at times even a bit comic, unbearably ostentatious, simply false, or, last but not least, endowed with a deep and embarrassing gratuitousness.

Why do I make that film, that very film, instead of another one? I do not wish to know why. The reasons are obscure, inexplicable, and confused. The only reason one can honestly cite is the signature on a contract: I sign, take the advance, and then, since I do not want to give it back, I must make the film. And I try to make it as it seems to me the film wishes itself to be made.

At the beginning of *La Strada*'s creation, there merely existed a confused feeling of the film, a suspended note that aroused in me an undefined sense of melan-

From Federico Fellini, *Fare un film* (Turin: Einaudi, 1980), pp. 57–60. Translated by Peter Bondanella and Manuela Gieri.
1. Fellini's statement about the making of *La strada* was originally published in 1979.

choly, a sense of guilt as pervasive as a shadow, vague and consuming, composed of memories and forebodings. This feeling insistently suggested the journey of two creatures who remain together because of fate, without even knowing why. The story was born very easily: the characters appeared spontaneously, dragging others behind them, as if the film had been ready for a long time and needed only to be rediscovered. What made me rediscover it, then? First of all, I think it was Giulietta. For some time, I had been thinking of a film for Giulietta. As an actress, she seems to me particularly capable of expressing spontaneously the amazements of a clown. There you have it—Giulietta is really an actress-clown, a true female clown. This definition, so illustrious to me, irritates actors who perhaps view it as something reductive, undignified, even coarse. They are incorrect: the clownish artistry of an actor, in my opinion, is his most precious quality, the sign of an aristocratic calling to dramatic art.

So, then, Gelsomina appeared to me in the guise of a clown, and immediately beside her, as a contrast, there appeared a massive and dark shadow, Zampanò. And, naturally, the road, the circus with its colorful rags, its menacing and heartbreaking music, its cruel fairy-tale atmosphere. I have spoken about the circus so many times that it would be impudent of me to insist upon it anymore.

When I mentioned to [Tullio] Pinelli what, even if still confused, the film might be, his ears turned red with amazement, and soon afterwards he told me that during his summer vacation, while he was riding horseback on his boundless estate in the Tuscan countryside, he, too, had imagined stories of vagabond characters along dusty roads and ancient little villages; a picaresque tale of gypsies and acrobats. We talked excitedly for the entire afternoon; it was as if Gelsomina and Zampanò were recounting to us the story of their wanderings, their encounters, their lives.

The countryside, the villages, the valleys of their travels were for me those of the Appennine Mountains between Tuscany and Romagna. In the winter, when I was a boy, the hog castrators would come down from those lead-colored mountains with their sharpened knives hanging from their waists, just as in Breughel's paintings, heralded by the terrified squeals of the pigs who heard them arrive from the depths of their sties.

For a time, I must have kept a notebook in which I wrote down everything that seemed to me to have some relevance to the film, remarks or notes something more or less like this: "In a miraculous silence, it snows on the sea. Unintelligible compositions of clouds. In the clear night, the singing of a nightingale fills the sky and then stops abruptly. The little goblins of an August midday annoying those trying to fall asleep open-mouthed under the oaks. . . ." The first notes about the film were of this type. But what did they mean? What kind of a film was it? In Gambettola, there was a little boy, the son of farmers, who used to tell us that when the ox bellowed in the stable, he would see a huge piece of red lasagna come out of the wall, a sort of very long carpet floating in the air that would cross his head under his left eye and vanish, little by little, in the sun's reflection. This little boy used to say that once he even saw two large spheres of dark silver come off the belltower while the clock struck two, and they passed through his head. He was a strange child, and Gelsomina had to be a bit like that.

If I were even more shameless than I am, I could point out other reasons, perhaps deeper roots, that certainly gave life to the characters and the narration of their story in my fantasy: remorseful feelings, nostalgia, regrets, the fairy tale of a betrayed innocence, the melancholy hope for a pure world made up of trustworthy relationships, and the impossibility and the betrayal of all this; in short, all the confused, obscure sense of guilt that has been nourished, increased, and administered with tireless care by Catholic blackmail. But in order to go back to these roots, one would need the assistance of a psychoanalyst of great genius.

I think I made the film because I fell in love with that *bambina-vecchina*[2] who is both a little crazy and a little saintly; with that ruffled, funny, clumsy, and very tender clown whom I called Gelsomina, who even now manages to bend my mind with melancholy whenever I hear the music of her trumpet.

2. Our translation has left Fellini's rather poetic phrase in the original Italian: it means "child-old woman," underlining Gelsomina's ageless qualities.

The History of
a Collaboration:
A Complementary Diversity

Tullio Pinelli

As happens every autumn, I was returning from Piedmont. I had walked around villages during market days; I had seen the arrivals and the departures of the pedlars' carts and had examined them closely as well; I had listened to stories of mysterious murders along the broad roads, recounted with the same aura of legend as if they had taken place in the Far West, instead of on the state highways around Turin. As soon as I saw Fellini in Rome, I told him: "I've got an idea for a movie." "Me, too," he answered.

He had had the same idea, though in a less dramatic, more lighthearted tone.

This occurred three years ago; *La Strada* is being shot only now. The creation of the story idea took us a long time; from the very start, the film took on for the both of us the quality of a onerous commitment. We spent nearly four months just in the writing of the screenplay and the dialogue. Of course, we had not been impressed merely by the peculiar exterior aspects of that environment; on the contrary, what especially struck us was the possibility of a story that could respond to our much more intimate needs. In *La Strada,* we told the story of the encounter between two creatures who have nothing in common; the durability of their life together, apparently absurd and without meaning, through adventures and encounters that would normally lead them to separate from one another; until the discovery of the almost imperceptible transformation that one produced upon the other, according to a providential plan.

This sense of the supernatural in everyday life—together with the joy of living—are the most important points of contact I have with Fellini, and upon which our longlasting friendship and collaboration have been based. For the rest, I do not think that two people more different one from the other exist, but that diversity is nevertheless a successful and complementary one. It often happens either while working or talking that we reach the same conclusion or have the same intuition almost at the same instant.

From *Cinema* 7 (1954):449. Translated by Peter Bondanella and Manuela Gieri.

This, as I said, is what happened with the idea for *La Strada*. . . . This easy and rapid understanding is not the result of habit. It occurred right from the very start of our relationship. I must confess I knew nothing about Fellini before meeting him. I just ran into him briefly once in a studio, and that was it. One day, we met again while reading the opposite sides of the same newspaper hanging outside a newspaper stand. We spent the afternoon talking; and soon we began to divide up the works we had been commissioned to work on. It was still the time of the "discovery" of the cinema; in 1946, Italy was yet to be discovered or, to put it more accurately, to be rediscovered, in that exciting atmosphere which the aftermath of the war had created and which everyone still remembers. Thus we soon found ourselves associated in adventures meant to strengthen a friendship or to create one.

I Spoke Badly of *La Strada*

Ennio Flaiano

I believe that very few films have required as much patience and faith as *La Strada*. I knew Fellini and Pinelli's story idea since its very first formulation in 1951, and when I was finally asked to collaborate on the screenplay in 1953, I found myself compelled to play the role of devil's advocate. For three months, I spoke badly of *La Strada:* this, in short, was the nature of my participation. I denounced a certain vague atmosphere, certain affected habits of its characters; I insisted that, in order for the fairy tale, which was even too beautiful, to come down to earth, its symbolism should melt into the narration.

I traveled over many roads in Lazio with Fellini and Pinelli, visited small circuses, talked to vagabond artists—and what unexpected encounters!—while taking notes about characters, farces, confidence games, jokes, and defining the secondary characters, becoming more and more convinced that the film was to be found in the streets, and precisely there it had to be looked for.

The credit for *La Strada* goes to its authors, Fellini and Pinelli. It is unnecessary to add that it mostly goes to Fellini who, after the struggle over the screenplay, then found himself alone to master the elements, the characters, the intentions of the story in order to make out of all that a film, and above all to find a balance between the real world of the road and the poetic world of his hypotheses. It must have been difficult to realize a project which, if handled by someone else, might have turned out simply pretentious. . . .

My role in this story has thus been that of having helped and perhaps even having compelled Fellini and Pinelli, out of their indignation, to take the entire thing very seriously. For after the happy joint adventure of *I Vitelloni,* we had the problem of not disappointing each other too much.

From *Cinema* 7 (1954):449. Translated by Peter Bondanella and Manuela Gieri.

Fellini and the Phantom Horse

Moraldo Rossi

I n the spring of 1952, one night while we were driving down one of those fast, narrow streets that gently leads from the growing division between the Cassia and the Flaminia roads into the Roman countryside, Federico Fellini was telling me about his film, *La Strada*. . . .

It was a suggestive atmosphere that nourished the imagination and enlivened Fellini's fantastic world.

Our drive was interrupted by an abrupt stop. Federico unsuccessfully tried to back up, but the street was too narrow. Once the car was finally in reverse, we then went backward up the street for almost twenty meters until we reached a large tree, which seemed to overshadow everything around us, considering how very dark it was. Meanwhile, he was telling me about a strange horse that had been fully illuminated by our headlights a few moments earlier: a lonely, dark silhouette that was slowly limping along in the fields. And he had noticed that its body was strangely spotted by large marks, like those from a serious disease. It had been a striking vision; but then, not even the shadow of the "horse" could be seen, no matter how much we insistently illuminated the entire area. That phantom animal seemed to have been truly swallowed up by the darkness.

Later on, Federico continued telling me about his film. I think I began that very night to have certain positive feelings about *La Strada*, the wide ranges of that poetic world flowing out from the happy blending of both realistic and fantastic elements.

Two years had to pass before reaching the day of the first take on that very laborious film and, after the successful parenthesis of *I Vitelloni*, we began the shooting of *La Strada* in an ancient and half-ruined convent in Bagnoregio. Three tiny nuns who looked as old as the place in which they were living—last survivors of a richer and more numerous progeny of Poor Clares—were keeping alive there that feeble breath of life.

Within the remote walls of the monastery, full of vivid memories, in the nar-

From *Cinema* 7 (1954):454. Translated by Peter Bondanella and Manuela Gieri.

rowness of the little cloisters and along the mysterious corridors, Fellini continued to discover his world over and over again, giving everything more meaning with the perseverance and courage of an explorer; there Fellini dematerialized his characters and formalized them, while trying to maintain the balance with reality with the patience of a monk, watching over the smallest detail with extreme care, himself playing the actors' roles, collecting and then conveying Masina's impassioned possibilities as a mime, and smoothing over some characteristics of Quinn's vigorous acting style, which would have otherwise seemed a bit strange. . . .

Later on, during the projection, I saw the convent sequence and noted the positive results of his completed efforts.

In Bagnoregio and the other villages of the Italian province that we visited with Federico during the months of his "wandering," we spent more time than we had planned because of the usual problems one experiences while moving about; then Gelsomina and Zampanò's motorcycle would arrive with us in the squares of all the villages, and there they would put on their routine. Spitting fire and breaking chains made of pig iron, they would give a stirring performance for the crowds of villagers.

And the most sympathetic and curious person in the audience was always, of course, Fellini himself.

The Most Strenuous Film in a Career of Forty-Three Years

Luigi Giacosi

W hen Fellini told me about *La Strada* for the first time, it was probably during the most difficult moment of his entire career. In fact, *The White Sheik* had been released a little earlier, and notwithstanding the undeniable qualities of that film, the producers continued to see Fellini more as a writer of screenplays than as a director.

The *La Strada* project seemed very difficult at first examination because it was, as everyone would agree, an unusual film, totally outside the norm. I proposed *La Strada* to a producer, and I persuaded him so successfully that we made test shots. Because of a number of hitches, the film was unfortunately interrupted further; instead, we realized another courageous project with the same producer, that of *I Vitelloni*.

But Fellini did not abandon the idea of his film.

A new opportunity was, in a certain sense, facilitated by the success of *I Vitelloni:* at any rate, the only studio that had immediately believed in Fellini, following him from the beginning until the very end and indeed—what is even more important—giving him total freedom, was the Ponti-De Laurentiis Studio.

Insofar as the actual shooting was concerned, I must admit that, at least from my point of view, *La Strada* was, without any shadow of a doubt, the most strenuous and troublesome film of my entire lengthy career in the cinema, which began some forty-three years ago. The fact of having to deal with a film shot almost entirely on real exterior locations and, in addition, in the least favorable weather, influenced in a highly negative manner the organization of the production, notwithstanding Fellini's ease in overcoming obstacles, and the tireless dedication of the entire crew, which was always ready to shoot in whatever weather.

Rarely, during my career, have I noticed such a harmony between a director and all the people who rely upon him; indeed, this occurs only in certain exceptional instances. The various components of the crew, from the technicians to the

From *Cinema* 7 (1954):458. Translated by Peter Bondanella and Manuela Gieri.

workers, seemed conscious of their precious collaboration, of the fact that it made possible the birth of an unusual work, and that, because of this, this work was destined to become a great success. . . . *La Strada* was born precisely in such an atmosphere of deep human understanding and of fervid collaboration; its shooting was marked by almost heroic moments and I cannot recall certain episodes without being moved.

For instance, one night we were ready to shoot the scene in which the Fool has to walk a tightrope across the street between two buildings. We had finally located, after many difficulties, a tightwire walker (who would double for Richard Basehart), when an urgent telegram for him suddenly arrived from the studio. I opened it with apprehension: it was his mother-in-law letting him know that his wife had been rushed to the hospital, and was expected to have a baby at any moment. I remembered then that for the entire day, the poor fellow had wandered around, asking when we would finish and when the trains were leaving, because he wanted to join his wife as soon as possible, who was then at the last month of her pregnancy. I read the telegram and kept it in my pocket: for four hours, the acrobat remained there in the air, rehearsing a very difficult scene in which he was risking his life at every moment. And in the meanwhile, a second telegram—this also finding a place in my pocket—announced the birth of a child who was as healthy as his mother. Only on the following morning, in a bar where together with Fellini we all met in order to congratulate him for his cleverness both as an acrobat and as a father, were the two telegrams given to the man who had risked his life the entire night, totally unaware of everything else that was happening. He grabbed them, and after having examined them quickly, put them in his pocket without saying a word: we all felt very uneasy, immediately comparing his anxiety of the previous day to his indifference at the present moment. As for me, when confronted with his cool reaction, I felt the remorse I experienced because of not having told him the entire truth (even if I did so for truly understandable reasons) almost vanish. In an instant, we lost sight of him; then we found him again beside the fountain in the square where he was weeping like a child.

He was soon sent to Rome by car so that he could see his child, whom he was already referring to as the "lawyer."

An "Active" Character: Gelsomina Senses the Life of the Trees

Giulietta Masina

I experienced one of my greatest joys precisely on the road when the children of certain villages, who thought of me as a real acrobat, were crowding half-tenderly and half-teasingly about me. . . . It was a moving experience, especially the performances in the middle of the road with the population of entire villages spontaneously gathering together and with the words and the cries that flew about and which were often not reproduced on the sound track. . . .

Gelsomina's character had both fascinated and frightened me for a very long time. Let me explain myself immediately. Above all, besides my own personal emotional involvement, with Gelsomina I had the responsibility of portraying a typical Italian woman from the lower classes who has to adapt herself to any kind of job in order to survive, and who suffers from hunger, solitude, and a sense of uselessness; but Gelsomina was not a character who could stop at the mere literal expression of these feelings and conditions in life. That is to say, Gelsomina was and is an "active" character. A character, in other words, who never gives up, who is attached to life, I would say, with both hands and feet, and who is engaged in difficult relationships that she does not succeed in resolving. She is carried off in a vagabond kind of work which never gives her the sense of being situated in a specific place and of being normal and human, since every morning the tents are struck and one moves on again; nevertheless, Gelsomina obstinately and stubbornly wants to construct around herself the conditions for a simple and affectionate life without solitude. Besides this, she feels the need to speak with everything and with everyone; she senses the lives of the trees, of the sky, of the wind. Yet all of this is more a lump in the throat than anything else, merely the dream of a harmonious life. On all of this weighs Zampanò's silence, which is her only human presence during her days of grief and who encloses within himself all the desolate distance that often exists between one human being and another. Being together in life and not realizing it, looking at each other as strangers, having an

From *Cinema* 7 (1954): 450–451. Translated by Peter Bondanella and Manuela Gieri.

enormous need for sympathy and companionship, and not knowing where to start—and the weight of those silences, the tentative trials which end clumsily and which are transformed into hatred and rancor.

In my relationship to Zampanò, I always tried by means of a sometimes exaggerated acting style to express the difficulty of communicating with others, which often becomes transformed into an artificial vivacity or into the feeling of not being in the proper place but, rather, being trapped inside a deep sense of embarrassment. Therefore, I often "perform" for Zampanò, even when we are not putting on a show, and I do not feel like myself and am caught up in a sense of great unease. On the other hand, I reacquire the possibility for sincere actions when I no longer have the strength to go on or, when in mourning over the death of the Fool and almost as in a funeral dirge, I close myself up in order to seek a submerged sense of profundity within myself or to voice the emotions of those hundreds of women who have suffered before me.

On the other hand, it seemed to me that in the character of Gelsomina, I also needed to express an aspect of conventional sentimentality and pathos. Let me explain. I think that for a humble fisherman's daughter, the most realistic element of her character is not the tragic, the exemplary, the proud, the bitter, or the conscious elements but, rather, some of the more delicate and superficial aspects. Just as for some young girls, comic strips are an essential basis of their formation, so in some very disadvantaged environments, people's minds are formed from wretched and extremely base relationships, especially for a young girl. Thus, Gelsomina often plays the role of the "wastrel," and she even feels self-pity.

It is evident, then, that both in her relationships with others as well as in her relationship with herself, Gelsomina is never fully adjusted but is full of the inhibitions she suffers, of the things she lacks, and of crises. Therefore, she often attempts to go beyond her boundaries—that is, to imagine herself being "someone else" and to perform even for herself (for example, when she visits the convent, walking behind the nun, Gelsomina begins to walk instinctively like the nun does, or in front of a tree when she poses like the tree and opens her arms as if they were branches).

And Gelsomina constantly seeks, calls out for, and alludes to a loving communion among things and among human beings, but (this is what I felt in her character) she only expresses this "morality" on a latent and uncomplicated level, although living her need for love and unity with everything in a kind of animal-like tenderness, multiplying her gestures (even the absurd ones), squeezing life and tenderness out of every occasion, and relying more upon cries and gestures, which are born from deep within, than upon words.

Of course, this is a path doomed to failure, and Gelsomina soon realizes this. While her head remains dreaming in the clouds, when she happens upon a town and sees a tightrope walker suspended between two buildings who is slowly moving within a golden light, she thinks she is witnessing the concrete realization of all her dreams and that she is seeing, for the first time, a superior species of man who turns his smiling face toward her, finally speaking to her. It is the Fool, but he, too, is an angel destined to fall from grace; he, too, is an illusory figure, since he will die under Zampanò's blows, revealing himself to be extremely fragile and mortal and no more consistent than a dream. But in the meanwhile Gelsomina has learned something, or she thinks she has. The Fool has somehow synthesized this need of hers for love and has informed her that despite everything, she can be content to remain with Zampanò, since Zampanò is also alone and needs her even if he is not aware of it. I had to try to express this moment as a sudden emotional liberation, not as an "understanding" or as an act of taking some sensible and moralistic decision. So I tried an acting style that was both somewhat erratic and excited, as when a cork pops out of a overly compressed bottle, and in the meanwhile, the Fool, who always escapes and who does not wish to give moral lessons, openly laughs at me.

Even today now that I play this role no longer (a role for which I had been waiting for a long time), I retain the image of the Fool in my mind. It still fascinates me, because it represents an extremely sweet punishment for so many weaknesses which I sense are not only mine but also of my generation. He is a romantic character, completely free, very ethereal but at the same time he provides a lesson about life, about concreteness, and about patience and trust. For me, he is really forever just about to descend from his high wire, from his solitary and ethereal security, to speak words of lighthearted courage to me.

The Crisis of
Neo-Realism

L*a Strada* confirmed the Italian cinema's gradual shift away from the documentary style and political content of neo-realism toward a cinema of poetry and personal inspiration, reflecting the very different artistic temperaments of a number of *auteurs*. An influential group of leftist or Marxist critics and film historians in both Italy and France opposed this development, however, advocating a realistic cinema with ideologically motivated themes. The resulting debate over the proper direction for Italian cinema has traditionally been called the "crisis of neo-realism" by film historians.

André Bazin, certainly the most brilliant critic of the mid-1950s, responded sympathetically and enthusiastically to the poetry and philosophical message of *La Strada*. He was also the first to argue that Fellini's leftist opponents were actually proposing a style of socialist realism for the Italian cinema. Guido Aristarco, the editor of Italy's most important Marxist film journal (*Cinema Nuovo*), gives an influential rebuttal to Bazin's defense of Fellini. Between 1955 and 1958, the American film journal *Film Culture* translated and published a number of polemical exchanges between Aristarco and Fellini. They express quite clearly the Marxist critique of Fellini's work. Finally, "Letter to a Marxist Critic" and the interview entitled "The Road Beyond Neo-realism" will provide the reader with the most eloquent defense of his views that Fellini has ever provided.

La Strada

André Bazin

I f Zampanò has a soul . . . .
    The vitality of the Italian cinema is once more confirmed for us by the admirable film of Federico Fellini. It is comforting to recognize that the critics have been almost unanimous in praising it. Perhaps without this support, which has placed snobbism on its side, *La Strada* would have had some difficulty in imposing itself on an inattentive and confused public.

Federico Fellini has here achieved one of those very rare films, of which we forget that they are movies and accept them simply as masterpieces. We remember the discovery of *La Strada* as a great esthetic emotion, an encounter with an unsuspected universe. I mean that it is less a matter of a film's having known how to reach a certain moral and intellectual level than a personal message, for which the cinema certainly appears to be the necessary and natural interpreter, but which would virtually exist before it. It is not a movie which is called *La Strada;* it is *La Strada* which is called a movie. In this sense there comes to mind also the last film of Chaplin's, although in many ways it is quite different. Of *Limelight* too we could say that the cinema was its only adequate incarnation, that it was inconceivable in all other means of expression, and yet everything in it transcended the technique of a particular art form.

Thus *La Strada* confirms in its own way this critical probability, that the cinema has arrived at a stage of its evolution in which the form no longer determines anything, where its language no longer offers any resistance but suggests only as much as any effect of style that the artist might use. Surely it will be said that only the cinema could endow, for example, the extraordinary motorcycle caravan of Zampanò with the force of concrete myth which this object, both unusual and banal, here attains; but we also see very clearly that the film is here neither transforming nor interpreting anything. No lyricism of image or montage attempts to orient our perception; I will even say that there is no mise-en-scène, at least not in cinematic terms. The screen limits itself to showing us the caravan, showing it better and more objectively than could the painter or novelist. I am not

From *Cross Currents* 6, no. 3 (1956):200–203. Reprinted by permission of *Cross Currents*. Translated by Joseph E. Cunneen.

saying the camera has quite plainly photographed it—even the word photography is too much, it has simply shown it to us, or even better, has allowed us to see it. Surely it would be excessive to claim that nothing can be created in terms of the language of film, by its abrasive incidence on the real. Without even considering almost virgin areas like color and the wide screen, the field of tension between technique and the subject treated depends in part on the personality of the director. Orson Welles, for example, always invents through technique. But what we can say with certainty is that from now on progress in the cinema will no longer be necessarily tied to originality of expression, or to the plastic organization of the image, or the images themselves. More exactly, if there is any formal originality about *La Strada,* it consists in always remaining on this side of the cinema. Nothing that Fellini reveals to us owes any supplementary sense to its manner of being shown; nevertheless, this revelation exists only on the screen. It is here that the cinema attains its fullness, which consists in being the art of the real. Surely we understand that Fellini is a great director, but one who does not cheat with reality. Nothing is in the cinema, nothing on the film, in any case, on which he has not previously conferred the fullness of being.

That is why *La Strada* does not at all seem to have departed from Italian neo-realism. But on this subject there is a misunderstanding that needs to be cleared up. In Italy *La Strada* has been received with some reserve by the critical guardians of neo-realist orthodoxy. This criticism is leftist, and in France would be called "Progressist," but these terms are equivocal, for Italian criticism is both more Marxist and more independent. I am thinking of the group around Chiarini and Aristarco in *Cinema Nuovo.* This criticism has again taken up the concept of neo-realism, which was so scorned at one time, and is attempting to define it and orient it. The work of Zavattini is the concrete reference which most conforms to its ideal, although the neo-realism so conceived still remains only a *work in progress,* an investigation which starts out from *données* that have already been acquired and proceeds in a determined direction, but is not a static and already-conquered reality. I do not feel I have the necessary competence to clearly define the evolution of neo-realism, as seen by this Marxist group, but I do not believe I am falsifying its meaning by interpreting it as their substitution for socialist realism, whose theoretical and practical barrenness unfortunately does not need to be demonstrated. In fact, as far as one can define it across the tactical changes of party line in esthetics, socialist realism has never produced anything convincing as such. In painting where its influence is easy to determine, since it opposed the whole modern evolution, the result is known. In literature and in the cinema, the situation is more confused since in these areas we are dealing with arts from which realism has never been eliminated. But if there are good films and good novels which do not contradict the canons of socialist realism, it is still rather doubtful that these rules had any part in their success. On the other hand, we can easily see how they sterilized many other works.

It is true that theories have never given birth to masterpieces and that a creative flowering has a more profound source in history and in men. Italy has had the luck, like Russia around 1925, to find herself in a situation in which a certain cinematographic genius began to spring forth, and this genius was moving in the direction of social progress, and the liberation of men. It is normal and legitimate that the most conscious of the artisans and judges of this important phenomenon concern themselves to prevent it from being broken up; they would like to orient its direction toward the best of the revolutionary development whose cycle was inaugurated by the neo-realism of the immediate postwar period. In the cinema neo-realism can surely be advantageously substituted for socialist realism. The evidence of successful films and their coherence in variety furnish the Marxist esthetician with material for fruitful reflection. If the time comes when this reflection gets ahead of the creative output, then neo-realism will be in danger, but fortunately we have not yet reached that point.

That is why I nevertheless regret the intolerance which this critical group begins to exhibit toward the dissidents of neo-socialist-realism, Rossellini and Fellini (who was Rossellini's assistant and from many points of view remains his disciple). There are some things in Italy which are lamentably like the world of Don Camillo: whoever is anticommunist has to be on the side of the priests. In the face of leftist criticism, the Italian Catholics try to revive neo-realism, whose very ambiguity lends itself to such an experiment. It is unnecessary to go into details in regard to the pitiful results of this Catholic effort. But Rossellini and Fellini are placed, because of this situation, in a very false light. It is true that their recent work could not be understood as social. Besides, as individual citizens, they neither flirt with communism nor cooperate with the Christian Democrats. The result in Rosselini's case is that he is banned on all sides. As for Fellini, the jury is still out, and the success of *La Strada* gives him the advantage of a favorable reception from both sides, but mixed with uneasiness and a definite reticence on the part of the Marxists. Of course these political polarizations play only a complementary role, with greater or less importance depending on the personality of the individual critic. It may even happen that this aspect might be completely ignored, and we have seen Chiari, for example, defend Rossellini's

The Little Flowers of St. Francis, whereas *Cinema Nuovo* was divided on the case of *Senso* made by the communist Visconti. But this context certainly does not contribute to attenuate the hardening of theoretical positions when they lead in the same direction as political mistrust. Thus Fellini is threatened with being evicted from the neo-realist heaven, and cast in the outer darkness already haunted by Rossellini.

Obviously everything depends on the definition that we accept, at the very outset, of neo-realism. But it seems to me that *La Strada* does not contradict *Paisan* or *Open City* in any way, any more than *Bicycle Thief* did. But it is true that Fellini has followed a different road than Zavattini. With Rossellini he has made a choice for a neo-realism of the person. Certainly the first films of Rossellini identified the moral and the social because this coincidence seemed to be the very experience of the Liberation. But *Europe '51* in some sense crossed the social line in order to emerge in the area of a spiritual destiny. What in these works nevertheless remains neo-realism, and can be considered as one of its possible accomplishments, is the esthetic of the mise-en-scène, a direction of the elements of a film which Abbé Ayfre has judiciously described as phenomenological.

We see very well that in *La Strada* nothing is ever revealed to us from the interior of the characters. The point of view of Fellini is the exact contrary of a psychological neo-realism which aims at analysis and ultimately at a description of feelings. Nevertheless, everything can occur in this quasi-Shakespearean world. Gelsomina and the Fool carry with them an aura of the marvelous, which baffles and annoys Zampanò, but this element of wonder is neither supernatural, nor gratuitous, nor even "poetic," it appears simply as a possible quality of nature. Moreover, to return to psychology, the very being of these characters is precisely not to have any, or at least to possess such a rough and primitive psychology that its description would have nothing but a pathological value. But they do have a soul. *La Strada* is nothing but the experience that they have of this fact, and its revelation to our eyes. Gelsomina learns from the Fool that she belongs in the world. She, the idiot, ugly and useless, learns one day from this vaudevillian that she is something besides an outcast; or rather, she learns that she is irreplaceable and that she has a destiny, which is—to be indispensable to Zampanò. The most overwhelming discovery in the film is surely Gelsomina's prostration after the assassination of the Fool by Zampanò. From then on she is haunted by her agony which dwells on that instant in which he, who had virtually given her being, suddenly ceased to exist. Little groans like the cries of mice irresistibly escape from her lips: "The Fool is sick, the Fool is sick." The stupid and stubborn brute who is Zampanò could not have discovered the need he had of Gelsomina through his conscience, and certainly could not sense the eminently spiritual nature of the tie which united them. Terrified by the suffering of the poor girl, at the end of his patience and afraid, he abandons her. But just as the death of the Fool had made life insupportable for Gelsomina, the abandonment and even the death of Gelsomina will little by little reduce this mass of muscles to its spiritual evidence, and Zampanò will end by being crushed by Gelsomina's absence. Not through remorse, or even by love; but through the overwhelming and incomprehensible sorrow which can be the only sensation of his soul, deprived of Gelsomina.

Thus we may consider *La Strada* as a phenomenology of the soul and perhaps even of the Communion of Saints, at least of the interdependence of salvation. With these people who are "poor of spirit" it is impossible to confuse ultimate spiritual realities with those of intelligence or passion, pleasure or beauty. The soul reveals itself there beyond psychological or esthetic categories, and much more clearly because we no longer know how to adorn it with the jewels of conscience. The salt of the tears that Zampanò sheds for the first time in his miserable life on the beach that Gelsomina loved, is the same as that of the infinite sea, which can no longer refresh its sadness here on earth.

Italian Cinema

Guido Aristarco

I n *La Strada* of Federico Fellini we encounter an entirely different conception and understanding of art, an attitude toward it and toward life similar to that prevalent in prewar, and to some extent in contemporary, literature. In this respect Fellini appears anachronistic, tied down as he is to problems and to human dimensions largely already transcended (although they still persist in various domains of culture and art). Along with some of our gifted writers (and Fellini is beyond a doubt a gifted director), he has gathered up and jealously preserved the subtlest poisons of that prewar literature; he carries on the tradition of the poetry of the solitary man, a poetry in which each story, instead of being reflected, lived within the reality of the narrative, is, through a process of individualization, reabsorbed into itself and nullified as an historical entity only to be converted into a symbolic diagram, a legend, a myth.[1]

"We started out with the intention of coming to know and understand reality more profoundly," Pavese once confessed, "and the result is that we are closing ourselves up within a fictitious world inimical to reality. So of course we suffer. In such a climate of unbalance, of moral uncertainty there is bound to come a period of esthetic drought. We remain in, or return to, our adolescence; and in our aimless struggles we invent all sorts of theories, justifications and problems." Fellini, too, tries to find justifications, struggles in his own way, and remains an eternal adolescent, especially in *La Strada,* which he himself describes not by mere coincidence as his most juvenile, most lyrical, most confessional film. He seeks out his own emotions along the treacherous paths of suggestivism and autobiographism and mistakes agitation for an intense need for

From *Film Culture* 1, no. 2 (1955):30–31. Reprinted by permission of *Film Culture* and Guido Aristarco.

1. As editor of the major Marxist cinema journal, *Cinema Nuovo,* Guido Aristarco naturally opposes the "poetry of the solitary man" (what more doctrinaire Marxist critics might have termed "bourgeois individualism") he detects in Fellini's works, not only because of the political implications of such a cinema but also because of the religious connotations in Fellini's early work underlined most especially by the criticism of André Bazin and Geneviève Agel.

poetic expression; transcribing certain memories, contacts, moments, moods of his life—and on a sentimental level at that—is already in his view tantamount to the creation of poetry. His participation in reality is episodic, fragmentary, only sporadically enriched by realistic elements and attitudes; in Fellini we do not have the sense of our actual experiences. Somehow he seems to stop at the "evangelism," the "lyricism," the poetical experiments of wartime humoristic newspapers such as *Marc'Aurelio,* at certain of his own characters and vignettes of that period. . . .

An Interview with Federico Fellini

George Bluestone

Interviewer: I have heard that an unofficial Vatican censor wanted to keep *Le notti di Cabiria* from going to Cannes, but that Cardinal Siri of Genoa was responsible for getting your film approved. Is this true?

Fellini: Where did you hear this?

—I read it. In *Cinema Nuovo* I think.

—Oh, well, if you want to understand my work, don't read *Cinema Nuovo*. They have called *La Strada*—called me—a traitor to neo-realism. In Italy, it is very difficult to find honest, objective criticism about directors. There are too many special interests.

—But there is some truth in the Cardinal Siri story?

—There are certain rumors. They . . . are unimportant.

—Do you find any problem of censorship over here?

—For the film-maker there has always been censorship. In every country. In Italy, if it has not come from the Church, it has come from the bureaucracy. If not from the bureaucracy, then from the communists. But I do think that if a film is a good film, it will find its audience. The trouble with *La Strada* is that the Church seized on it, used it as a flag. The return to spirituality. So *Cinema Nuovo* turned against it. I assure you, if *Cinema Nuovo* had praised it first, the Church might very well have turned against it. It is very hard to see a work for what it is, without prejudice.

—What, then, would you consider a reputable critical analysis of your work?

—Geneviève Agel's book, in French, *Les chemins de Fellini*.[1]

—We hear it said that neo-realism brought the Italian film to world attention, but that now the excitement of the immediate postwar years is over, that the innovations of neo-realism are over, that a vacuum has been created which has left the Italian film confused about where to go. What is your personal reaction to this?

From *Film Culture* 3, no. 3 (1957):3–4. Reprinted by permission of *Film Culture* and George Bluestone.

1. This remark represents one of the few instances in which Fellini has ever recommended a critical interpretation of his work.

—I don't think it is so confused. Remember, after the war our themes were ready-made. Primitive problems: how to survive, war, peace. These problems were topical, immediate, brutal. But today the problems are different. Surely the neo-realists would not hope for the continuation of war and poverty just because it gave them good material. I think the editors of *Cinema Nuovo* are partly responsible for what you call our uncertainty. Instead of realizing that neo-realism was a beginning, they assumed it was an end, a golden age. Some of the neo-realists seem to think that they cannot make a film unless they have a man in old clothes in front of the camera. That is not right. We have not even scratched the surface of Italian life. Who was it—Zavattini?—who said that the film-maker must not try to influence reality by telling a story, that his job is simply to record what passes in front of the camera? Well, no film was ever made that way. Not even by Zavattini.

—Then it is only fair to say that you are optimistic about the future of the Italian film?

—Yes. Neo-realism was only a beginning.

—You feel no uncertainty about the direction of your own work?

—No, not basically. One always has doubts, of course.

—How do the subjects of your films compare with those of the neo-realists, say?

—Well, so far, my films have been mostly autobiographical. They've been based on childhood experiences that made a profound impression on me. When I was twelve, I worked with a traveling circus. I remembered incidents, fragments, and these became *La Strada*. My films are my life. I had no "schools" in mind, no theories when I first began to work.

—Then you would say that essentially you begin a story that has made some impression on you and work out your images and techniques from there?

—Yes, I would say so. . . .

Guido Aristarco Answers Fellini

Guido Aristarco

I was surprised to read the interview Federico Fellini gave to George Bluestone (*Film Culture,* October 1957). First of all, the Cardinal Siri case was not, as Fellini states, merely a matter of unimportant "rumors." In Italy, the case provoked violent reaction, even polemics. *Cinema Nuovo* (no. 107) wrote on the subject: ". . . We take no part in the attack on Fellini which some papers began conducting—not altogether politely—after he, confronted with the perplexing issue of censorship, appealed to the eminent Genovese prelate. We limit ourselves to reporting an opinion expressed on the matter by Alberto Moravia in *Espresso:* 'It means, first of all, that the Italian state is governed by men who, because they are Catholics first and citizens second, do not have the understanding of the State. It means that the real power now is no longer the State's, but is outside of it. It means, finally, that it is useless to have a censorship commission and many other such agencies, since the authorities which must decide on the last appeal are somewhere else. The story of Fellini does but confirm this.'"

What is the trouble between Fellini and *Cinema Nuovo?* We were among the few who defended Fellini; we backed him as far as *I Vitelloni.* But we expressed our doubts regarding *La Strada.* There is one viewpoint, that of Fellini's film, full of mystery, grace—that is, mysticism; then there is another viewpoint, that of *Cinema Nuovo,* holding forth a knowledge of and faith in man, his ability to dominate and modify his world, to solve problems within himself and outside himself—in a word, realism. Was it our purpose, in criticizing *La Strada,* to get Fellini to express a world that does not belong to him? Events and persons that he could not naturally create? It doesn't seem so. But the critic, any critic, has his *ars poetica.* De Sanctis (the great historian of Italian literature) and the great realists are our teachers and inspirers, if we may use the term. In their names and in their teaching we have sought an internal development, a criticism which continues to demand explication—a methodology, a character not cold and self-centered, but militant. Is all this non-objectivity a "prejudice"? Objectivity is a

From *Film Culture* 4, no. 2 (1958):20–21. Reprinted by permission of *Film Culture* and Guido Aristarco.

myth, if we understand it as Fellini and others with him understand it. It is as misleading and false as any other myth. There are, of course, "particular interests," even "political ones," if you wish—but in a large and impartial sense, as in our case.

It is human and unavoidable that Fellini's poetry, which took shape with *La Strada,* should appear to us both limited and irritating, particularly since *Cabiria* and other films affirm the great and uncommon value of this talent. We must not, of course, impose our convictions on the personality of the director, and so we are forced to accept, for the moment, his logic, and comment on this or that isolated sequence as it reflects his talent and direction. Therefore, we don't say, nor have we ever said, that *La Strada* is a badly directed and acted film. We have declared, and do declare, that it is *wrong;* its perspective is wrong. (This personal classification is a relative one, derived from our refusal to support that film's perspective and solution.) Nor should one confuse, as Fellini confuses, the significance which we have attached to "neo-realism" with realism, particularly as elaborated lately in *Cinema Nuovo* reviews. It might be that these reviews (especially of Fellini's films) are somewhat limited by a tone which is, on the whole, negative and perhaps polemic. The intention of these reviews, however, was to contribute to a wider understanding of the director and the overall neo-realistic development, in which, it seems, Fellini takes only a fragmentary part (in his criticism of custom or his use of simple denunciation) but to which, in any case, he is not a "traitor." We have spoken of the vital trend of the Italian postwar cinema as a new civilizing force, a new humanism, but we have always considered it a starting point—not a point of arrival, an "end," a "golden era" beyond which it is not possible to go. We neither conceal nor reject our personal responsibility for the present uncertainty of the Italian cinema (we should have done more and better with greater clarity), but one cannot make us responsible, as Fellini does, for the specific fact that "some of the neo-realists seem to think that they cannot make a film unless they have a man in old clothes in front of the camera." And among the "some," to judge from his films, we must put Fellini himself. It is evident that the flag, the pin-on-the-lapel, of neo-realism is not the rags, at least in the external sense of the word. Fellini remarks, moreover, in his interview that we have not even scratched the surface of Italian life, and he is right. *Cinema Nuovo* has always stressed the need of a progress from chronicle to history, from short story to novel, that is—from neo-realism to realism. From this came our public and private discussions with Zavattini, a genuine exchange of ideas.

We have not agreed with Zavattini—to take one example—on his insistence that the director must not try to influence reality in order to expose it, that his job is merely to register what goes on in front of the camera. This is chronicle, and not history. To this, let us say, Zolaesque method, we have preferred and insisted upon an approach like that of Balzac or Stendhal—a method which would lead us not to neo-realism (naturalism in its various aspects) but to the great, the true and authentic realism.

Confronted with the scattered remnants of the postwar effort which was the crisis of Italian society, we must now understand the crisis of our cinema. We must perceive the reasons behind the decadent suggestions of loneliness, the return to the past, the search for style and expressive moods as seen in some of our "greats" (Visconti, Antonioni, Fellini, Castellani) as well as the simultaneous warmth and color that, in Fellini's case, have ascended into the clouds of mysticism.

But we would like to stress again here that an understanding and acknowledgment of stylistic (and in part, artistic) values do not necessarily indicate agreement and support. Today it is more necessary than ever to get out from under the autobiography, the restricted and subjective view of reality, and onto that road that has been traveled in the literary field in varying degrees by Pavese, Vittorini, and Pratolini.

I wanted to say this to readers of *Film Culture* because, in fact, Federico Fellini has not distinguished the negative critical judgment from the friendship and honesty of the critic, and because these casual accusations of dishonesty that he directs at Italian critics in general and *Cinema Nuovo* in particular are quite undeserved.

Letter to a Marxist Critic

Federico Fellini

Dear Massimo [Massimo Puccini, Italian writer and critic], I read your letter with the greatest interest, just as I have read the articles by some left-wing critics with whom you agree, and I hope you will accept my frankness if I tell you that your criticisms, or rather your researches, whose good faith I don't doubt, don't seem to me very persuasive. Of course I'm not disputing the value of these criticisms, that's not my job; I'm simply saying they haven't persuaded me. And I think there must be something underneath all this. I think we must be starting from different principles and different premises which make it impossible, not for me to speak to you, because I simply put my film on the screen, but for you to listen and to respond. Perhaps it is the very principles you agree with that makes me doubt the rightness and coherence of your point of view; that is, your point of view as Marxists which, I must admit, makes your criticisms lose some of their value if I compare them with what is being said at present in Paris by Marxists who have seen my film. You will reply that the French communists can think what they like, that it is none of your business, but you must admit that, quite apart from having a particular value of its own, their opinion shows that your wish to offer advice and directives from your own point of view is seriously contested, and may be proved entirely wrong by anyone who starts from the same viewpoint as yourselves. You must admit that it is neither trifling nor irrelevant that a poet (and communist) like Aragon has said that he considers *The Gold Rush, Battleship Potemkin,* and *La Strada* the best films he has ever seen. And Jacques Doniol-Valcroze, who, as you know, is an exponent of the most orthodox left-wing culture, says, in his article about other forms of cinema, that "*La Strada* sends a great breath of pure healthy air through the cinema of 1955. This is the real avant-garde." In *Les Lettres Françaises,* Sadoul says of my film: "Goodness, love of men, faith and hope in the truth dominate all Fellini's work. How can we believe the biased lies of those who try to deny the profound significance of this film?" This is how he ends his article: "Time will pass over *La Strada.* We shall see the film again. And we shall see what success (or lack of

From *Fellini on Fellini,* trans. Isabel Quigly (London: Eyre Methuen, 1976), pp. 59–63.

success) it has. In any case we shall see it again. And I shall be very surprised if this film—at first sight so unexpected or so irritating—does not impress itself upon our memory and does not become a milestone in the history of the cinema. In any case I am certain that Fellini is a great creator, one of the greatest revelations the cinema has produced since the beginning of this half century."

Of course I should not have been so immodest as to quote these judgments if you had not quoted others which have appeared in Italy, and if you had not wanted to set up, not so much a dialogue, as a friendly discussion. Seeing you have quoted what someone else has written on the literary artifice which corrupts *La Strada,* allow me to reply with quotations which at least contradict it. Here, for instance, is what Jean de Baroncelli writes in *Le Monde:* "Fellini's art is essentially very far removed from any literary falseness and wrong sort of pathos. His poetry is natural, his mystery has no artifice about it. If he owes much to Chaplin, it can be said that the pupil is worthy of his master. To repeat what Cayatte said in Venice: *La Strada,* from this moment, is already a classic."

And here is what Charensol writes in *Les Nouvelles Littéraires:* "We are definitely in the presence of a poet who is like no-one else and in whom we should have total confidence."

Dear Massimo, I could go on for quite some time putting the criticisms you make of me into some sort of proper perspective, as well as those you quote and sum up in your letter. But you are well aware of the relative value of the quotations you cited, just as you are aware, I am sure, of the insufficient seriousness of your interpretation of my film's popular success. I should now like to add something more personal about what you say on the human and moral problem that is the basis of this film, and which is not, I believe, what you seem to think it is.

According to me, *La Strada* seeks to realize the experience which a philosopher, Emmanuel Mounier, has rightly said is the most important and the most basic in seeking to open up any social prospect: the joint experience between man and man. I mean that in order to learn the richness and the possibilities inherent in social life, today, when so much is said about socialism, what is more important than anything is for a man to learn to be, quite simply, with another. I think this is what every society must learn, and that if we do not solve this humble but necessary problem we may tomorrow find ourselves facing a society externally well organized, outwardly perfect and faultless, but in which private relationships, relationships between man and man, are empty, indifferent, isolated, impenetrable.

Our trouble, as modern men, is loneliness, and this begins in the very depths of our being. No public celebration or political symphony can hope to be rid of it. Only between man and man, I think, can this solitude be broken, only through individual people can a kind of message be passed, making them understand— almost *discover*—the profound link between one person and the next.

La Strada expresses something like this with the means available to the cinema. Because it tries to show the supernatural and personal communication between a man and a woman—Zampanò and Gelsomina, who would seem by nature to be the least likely people to understand each other—it has, I believe, been attacked by those who believe only in natural and political communication.

But the film also aspires to show things that are quite simply human and affective. It asks what function a woman may have in a relationship between individual people and how important feminine affectiveness (or, let us say, the poetry of woman) is in calling others to spirituality and love. The film shows a human example among the many possible examples, possibly the most unpromising case of human living together it would be possible to find, and tries to see how the greyness of this relationship slowly breaks out and flowers into an elementary, supernatural society. My ambition (perhaps my illusion) is that everyone can find similar cases to deal with in himself and around him, and that this film shows him how to do so, and above all gives him the wish to do so. If I am right, then our efforts will not have been in vain. If, in seeking to show how the essence of social will and the possibilities of social advance are born from a relationship, I used a situation that seemed so unsuitable and so abstract, so immediate, so drearily everyday, it is because I believe that if one is showing the transition from individualism to true socialism today, then, in order to be persuasive, this must be seen and analyzed as a need of the heart, as the impulse of a moment, as a line of action in the humblest part of our lives. 'Society' must be born as a profound need of existence; it is here that it must mature, and from here that it must be launched. You will not be surprised (or perhaps you will be) if I quote two passages from Engels to you: "The brutal indifference, the harsh isolation of each individual in his own private interests, appears all the more disgusting when these individuals are living close to one another in a small space"; "The dissolution of humanity into monads, each one of which has a principle of life of its own and a particular object: the world of atoms is here carried to extremes."

I think that this 'monadism,' this loneliness deliberately provoked, permeates the very essence of our life today, and that we should throw some light upon it and the forces that work against it. When a film shows suffering in a concentrated and what I should call a microscopic image (the dimensions of history do not, after all, matter in art) and, as far as it can, expresses the contrast between monologue and dialogue which is central to our life today and the source of so many of our troubles, it is dealing with a contemporary need, and examining it in depth; in other words, it is using realism in the way which seems to me most suited to the realist movement. I feel that the historical process which art must discover, support, and illumine, can be seen in far less limited, and, particularly, far less technical and political terms than those in which you see it. Sometimes a film, while avoiding any precise representation of historical or political reality, can incarnate in mythic figures, speaking in a quite elementary language, the opposition between contemporary feelings, and can become very much more realistic than another film in which social and political matters are referred to much more precisely. This is why I do not believe in 'objectivity," at least in the way you people believe in it, and cannot accept your ideas of neo-realism which I feel do not fully capture, or even really impinge upon, the essence of the movement to which I have had the honor, since *Open City,* to belong.

I should like to end with words from Pavese's diary (though I know Pavese is not in favor with you people nowadays): "You would think that nothing existed now except ideas of violent revolution. But everything in history is revolution; even a renewal, a slow, peaceful discovery. Away, then, with the preconceived idea of moral renewal which needs (on the part of the other people, the activists) violent action. Away with this childish need for company and noise."

The Road Beyond
Neo-Realism

Federico Fellini

Bachmann: I do not want to talk to you about one or another specific film, but rather more generally—about your attitudes toward filmmaking, your reasons for making certain films, and your philosophical and sociological approach to what you use as film material. For example, many critics have said that there is a deep symbolism in your work, that there are recurring motifs in all your films. Like the image of the piazza at night with a fountain, of the seashore, and others. Is there a conscious intention on your part in repeating these images?

Fellini: It is not intentional. In choosing a location, I do not choose it for its symbolic content. Things happen. If they happen well, they convey my meaning. Concerning the specific examples you mention, I'd like to say that all my films to date are concerned with people looking for themselves. Night and the loneliness of empty streets, as shown in the shots of piazzas you mention, is perhaps the best atmosphere in which I see these people. Also, it is quite possible that the associations which make me choose these locations are based on autobiographical experiences, for I cannot remove myself from the content of my films. Possibly what is in my mind when I shoot these scenes is the memory of my first impression of Rome—when I had left my hometown of Rimini and was in Rome alone. I was sixteen; I had no job, no idea of what I wanted to do. Often I was out of work, often I didn't have the money to stay in a hotel or eat properly. Or I would work at night. In any case, it is quite possible that the image of the town at night, empty and lonely, has remained in my soul from those days.

Bachmann: Did you intend to go into films when you first came to Rome?

Fellini: No, I didn't really know what I wanted to do. Still, my coming to Rome did have something to do with films: I had seen so many American films in which newspapermen were glamorous figures—I don't remember the titles, that was twenty-five years ago—but I was so impressed with the lives of newspapermen, that I decided to become one too. I liked the coats they wore and the way they wore

SOURCE: Gideon Bachmann, "Federico Fellini: An Interview," in *Film: Book 1,* ed. Robert Hughes (New York: Grove Press, 1959), pp. 97–105. A transcript of a radio program. Copyright © by Gideon Bachmann.

their hats on the back of their heads. Unfortunately, the job I found was very different from my dream—I became a cub reporter who was sent by the editor to hospitals and to the police to get the obvious news. Later I began to write for the radio—sketches, mostly. After that I was tempted by the stage; and I toured Italy with a small traveling musical show. That period was one of the richest in my life, and I still draw on many of my experiences from those days.

Bachmann: Certainly touring musical shows are one of the recurring motifs in your films. By the way, how did you finally begin working in films?

Fellini: First, I was a rewrite man—I used to add gags to the scripts of dull comedies. My first original screenplay was called *Avanti c'è posto,* and it was the story of a bus conductor. Freely translated the title would be "Please Move to the Rear." It was directed by Bonnard, who had taken to directing pictures when his fame as a matinee idol had faded. That was 1940. After that, I wrote many scripts. Too many. All were produced. They were comedies, mostly, in a pathetic vein. After the war, I met Rossellini, and for him I worked on *Open City* and *Paisan.* That's when I began to understand—or at least to suspect—that one could express deep things too in films. So I continued for two or three years writing scripts for the postwar Italian directors. After that, though, I became . . . I don't want to say disappointed, but when one really loves films, one cannot stop at the written page. I decided to direct. My first film was called *Luci del varietà* (*Variety Lights*).

Bachmann: You directed this yourself?

Fellini: Yes, I wrote and directed it. It was the story of the small troupe with whom I had spent a year on the road.

Bachmann: When did you write and appear in *The Miracle?*

Fellini: When I worked for Rossellini. Before I began to direct.

Bachmann: Your serious film career, then, began during the period of the flowering of Italian neo-realism. The relation between your films and "classical" neo-realism has been much debated by the critics. Do you feel that your work in any way derives from, or was influenced by the neo-realist directors with whom you have worked, like De Sica, Rossellini, Lattuada, etc.?

Fellini: Well, I was one of the first to write scripts for neo-realist films. I think all my work is definitely in the neo-realist style, even if in Italy today some people don't think so. But this is a long story. For me, neo-realism is a way of seeing reality without prejudice, without the interference of conventions—just parking yourself in front of reality without any preconceived ideas.

Bachmann: You don't mean simply to put the camera in front of "life" and photograph what's there?

Fellini: No, it's a question of having the feeling for reality. Naturally, there is always the need for an interpretation. What has happened in Italy is that after the war everything for us was completely new. Italy was in ruins; you could say everything you felt by just looking around. Later, the leftist press capitalized on this inadvertent one-sidedness by saying that the only valid thing to do in films is to show what happens around you. But this has no value from an artistic point of view, because always the important thing is to know *who* sees the reality. Then it becomes a question of the power to condense, to show the essence of things. After all, why are the films we make so much better than newsreels?

Bachmann: Though, of course, even newsreels are already one step removed from reality, through the selectivity of the cameraman who took them.

Fellini: Right. . . . But why should people go to the movies, if films show reality only through a very cold, objective eye? It would be much better just to walk around in the street. For me, neo-realism means looking at reality with an honest eye—but any kind of reality: not just social reality, but also spiritual reality, metaphysical reality, anything man has inside him.

Bachmann: You mean anything that has reality for the director?

Fellini: Yes.

Bachmann: Then the completed film is really *two* steps removed from nature: first the personal *view* of it by the director, and then his *interpretation* of that personal view.

Fellini: Yes, yes. For me, neo-realism is not a question of *what* you show—its real spirit is in *how* you show it. It's just a way of looking around, without convention or prejudice. Certain people still think neo-realism is fit to show only certain kinds of reality; and they insist that this is social reality. But in this way, it becomes mere propaganda. It is a program; to show only certain aspects of life. People have written that I am a traitor to the cause of neo-realism, that I am too much of an individualist, too much of an individual. My own personal conviction, however, is that the films I have done so far are in the same style as the first neo-realist films, simply telling the story of people. And always, in telling the story of some people, I try to show some truth.

Bachmann: Is there any underlying philosophy in your films? I mean besides the depiction of what is truth for you.

Fellini: Well, I could tell you what for me is one of the most pressing problems, one which provides part of the theme for all my films. It's the terrible difficulty people have in talking to each other; the old problem of communication, the desperate anguish to be *with,* the desire to have a real, authentic relationship with another person. You'll find this in *I Vitelloni,* in *La Strada,* in *Il Bidone,* and also in *Nights of Cabiria*. It may be that I'll change, but for now I'm completely absorbed in this problem—maybe because I have not yet solved it in my private life.

Bachmann: Do you feel that the reason for this difficulty in interpersonal communication is that we have created a kind of society which makes it hard for people to have true relationships?

Fellini: It is the fault of society only because society is made up of men. I believe that everyone has to find truth by himself. It is completely useless to prepare a statement for a crowd, or make a film with a message for everyone. I don't believe in talking to a crowd. Because what is a crowd? It is a collection of many individuals, each with his own reality. That is also the reason why my pictures never end. They never have a simple solution. I think it is immoral (in the true sense of the word) to tell a story that has a conclusion. Because you cut out your audience the moment you present a solution on the screen. Because there are no "solutions" in their lives. I think it is more moral—and more important—to show, let's say, the story of one man. Then everyone, with his own sensibility and on the basis of his own inner development, can try to find his own solution.

Bachmann: You mean to say that by "ending" a problem, the film-maker takes away from the audience the feeling that what they are seeing is the truth?

Fellini: Yes, or even worse. For when you show a true problem and then resolve it, the spectator is beguiled into feeling that the problems in his own life, too, will solve themselves, and he can stop working on them for himself. By giving happy endings to films, you goad your audience into going on living in a trite, bland manner, because they are now sure that sometime, somewhere, something happy is going to happen to them, too, and without their having to do anything about it. Conversely, by not serving them the happy ending on a platter, you can make them think; you can remove some of that smug security. Then they'll *have* to find their own answers.

Bachmann: This would seem to indicate that you're not just making pictures to make pictures, but because there are certain things you want to say.

Fellini: Well, I don't start that way. What usually starts me on a film idea is that something happens to me which I think has some bearing on other people's experiences. And the feeling is usually the same: to try, first of all, to tell something about myself; and in doing so, to try to find a salvation, to try to find a road toward some meaning, some truth, something that will be important to others, too. And when, as often happens, people who have seen my films come to visit me—not to discuss my films, but to talk to me about their personal problems— I feel I have achieved something. It is always a great satisfaction for me. Of course, I can't help them clarify their problems, but it means the picture has done some good.

Bachmann: When you say you don't start that way, do you mean to say that the real "message" of your films develops out of the material?

Fellini: Well, a picture is a mixture of things. It changes. That is one of the reasons why making films is such a wonderful thing.

Bachmann: Could you tell me about the process in your film work? A kind of step-by-step description of your work on any given film?

Fellini: First, I have to be moved by a feeling. I have to be interested in one character or one problem. Once I have that, I don't really need a very well-written story or a very detailed script. I need to begin without knowing that everything is in perfect order; otherwise I lose all the fun of it. If I knew everything from the start, I would no longer be interested in doing it. So that when I begin a picture, I am not yet sure of the location or the actors. Because for me, to make a picture is like leaving for a trip. And the most interesting part of a trip is what you discover on the way. I am very open to suggestions when I start a film. I am not rigid about what I do. I like the people with me on the film to share this new adventure. Certainly, I do remember that I am shooting, sometimes.

When the picture is finished, I would, if possible, like not to see it. I often say to my producer, joking: "Let's not cut this one; let's make a new one instead." But I cut all my own films. Cutting is one of the most emotional aspects of film-making. It is the most exciting thing to see the picture begin to breathe; it is like seeing your child grow up. The rhythm is not yet well identified, the sequence not established. But I never reshoot. I believe that a good picture has to have defects. It has to have mistakes in it, like life, like people. I don't believe that beauty, in the sense of perfection, exists—except maybe for the angels. A beautiful woman is attractive only if she is not perfect. The most important thing is to see to it that the picture is alive. This is the most rewarding moment in making films: when the picture begins to live. And I never go back to look at what I have already done—I edit the whole film right through. When it's finished, and I go into the projection room to see it for the first time, I like to be alone. I can express exactly what happens. I look at the picture; the picture looks at me. A lot of things happen. Some ideas are born; some die. Later I begin to "clean" the picture. In Italy we do not use the sound we shoot on location, but redo the whole track in the studio. But the first answer print still has the location sound on it. Once that is removed, something happens again. The answer print still has a flavor of the adventure of making the film—a train that passed, a baby that cried, a window that opened. I remember the people who were with me on location. I remember the trip. I would like to retain these memories. Once they put the clean, new track on it, it's like a father seeing his little girl wear lipstick for the first time. You have to get to know this new creature that is emerging; you have to try to like it. Then when you add the music, again something is added and something is lost. Every time you see it again, there is some new feeling. When it is completely finished, you have lost the objective point of view. Then, when others see it, I react personally—I feel they have no right to say anything about *my* picture. But I listen carefully, nevertheless—I am trying to find out whether for them the picture is alive.

Bachmann: Do you feel that in all the films you have made you have always remained faithful to what you were trying to say when you started the picture?

Fellini: Yes, I do.

Bachmann: Do you feel there is a relation between your work and that of the current crop of Italian writers, like, for example, Carlo Levi and Ennio Flaiano?

Fellini: Yes, I think this core of neo-realism in films has influenced all the arts.

Bachmann: Have you, yourself, done any writing except scripts?

Fellini: No. Just some short stories when I worked for newspapers. But not since I've worked in films. It's a different medium. A writer can do everything by himself—but he needs discipline. He has to get up at seven in the morning, and be alone in a room with a white sheet of paper. I am too much of a *vitellone* to do that. I think I have chosen the best medium of expression for myself. I love the very precious combination of work and of living-together that film-making offers. I approach film-making in a very personal way. That's why I consider myself a neo-realist. Any research that a man does about himself, about his relationships with others and with the mystery of life, is a spiritual and—in the true sense—religious search. I suppose that is the extent of my formal philosophy. I make movies in the same way that I talk to people—whether it's a friend, a girl, a priest, or anyone: to seek some clarification. That is what neo-realism means to me, in the original, pure sense. A search into oneself, and into others. In any direction, any direction where there is life. All the formal philosophy you could possibly apply to my work is that there is no formal philosophy. In film-making, as in living, you must take the experiences that life presents, those which apply to yourself and to others. Except that in film-making only the absolute truth will work. In life I may be a swindler or a crook, but that wouldn't work in a film. A man's film is like a naked man—nothing can be hidden. I must be truthful in my films.

Reviews and Commentaries

Reviews

When *La Strada* was first presented at the Venice Film Festival in 1954, it was in competition with a number of major works: Akira Kurosawa's *The Seven Samurai;* Kenji Mizoguchi's *Sansho the Bailiff;* Alfred Hitchcock's *Rear Window;* Elia Kazan's *On the Waterfront;* Luchino Visconti's *Senso;* and Renato Castellani's *Romeo and Juliet.* Quite without Fellini's approval or backing (given his distaste for his Catholic upbringing), Fellini's film was championed by a number of right-wing Catholic or anti-Marxist critics. As a result, the leftist or Marxist critics who were supporting Visconti's film felt obliged to attack Fellini.

The final awards managed to offend everyone. In an obvious attempt to avoid controversy, Castellani received the coveted Golden Lion. Four Silver Lions were awarded (two to the Japanese entries, one to Kazan, and one to Fellini); Visconti was completely ignored. When Fellini went to the podium to receive his award, the supporters of Visconti and Fellini began to shout and blow whistles at each other. Feelings were running so high that Moraldo Rossi, Fellini's assistant director, fell upon Franco Zeffirelli, Visconti's assistant director, and snatched his whistle away from him. The polemical debates that erupted at the Venice Festival spilled out into the film journals and newspapers of Europe and America for the next several years. If much of what was written can today safely be ignored, this quarrel nevertheless produced a number of the most important essays or interviews ever written on *La Strada* (essays by Bazin and Aristarco, for example, or several statements by Fellini himself, all reprinted in this volume in the section entitled "The Crisis of Neo-realism").

For many years during and immediately after this "crisis of neo-realism," critical attention to Fellini in Italy and France was far more acute and interesting than in Great Britain or America. The report from Venice by Francis Koval, however, manages to capture some of the flavor of the heated debate. British reviews of Fellini were, for the most part, superficial and often entirely beside the point. Good examples of such critical reactions may be found in a review by Gavin Lambert, who declares that Fellini strives to be a poet when he is not, or another anonymous review that accuses the director of sparing his audience "nothing in the way of bestiality and degradation." While an anonymous reviewer in *Newsweek* and John McCarten in *The New Yorker* seem to agree with their unsympathetic British counterparts, doubting that Fellini has much to offer the spectator, American audiences were fortunate to have a number of first-rate critical appraisals of Fellini and *La Strada*. Arthur Knight's review and Vernon Young's longer review essay (here much abridged) can still be read with profit today for their sensitive appreciation of Fellini's originality, as can the shorter but no less intelligent piece in *Harper's Magazine* by "Mr. Harper."

Films in Review

Francis Koval

The eagerly awaited Italian film *La Strada,* with Anthony Quinn and Richard Basehart (both dubbed, of course), was well received tonight by the public. This may have been partly due to the high quality of the acting by the three leads (the third: Giulietta Masina, the wife of the film's director, Federico Fellini). With great sensitivity she portrayed a poor, slightly dim-witted girl "sold" by her mother to a traveling showman (Anthony Quinn) who was much too primitive to appreciate her devotion— until it is too late. After witnessing a fight in which her master kills another circus artist (Richard Basehart), the girl loses her senses, is abandoned by the roadside, and later dies miserably. While many of my colleagues found all this to be significant Italian neo-realism, I felt somewhat afflicted and sorry that Fellini, having impeccably developed his idea in the first part of the story, quickly slipped into the quagmire of cheap melodrama. . . .

Although public opinion seemed evenly divided between *Romeo and Juliet* and *On the Waterfront,* the award of the Golden Lion of San Marco to the Anglo-Italian picture met with such enthusiastic applause that Castellani could hardly master his emotion when he came to the stage. As the four silver Lions were awarded to *On the Waterfront, The Seven Samurai, Sansho the Bailiff* and *La Strada,* the applause weakened progressively in that order and in the case of *La Strada* a few whistles of disapproval were heard, chiefly from Visconti-ites.

From "Venice 1954," *Films in Review* 5, no. 8 (1954):396–97 (abridged).

Sight and Sound

Gavin Lambert

Among new directors, the Italian Film Week showed us only Federico Fellini. . . . Fellini has of course been well known for some time as a scriptwriter, working with Rossellini (on *Open City, Paisà, S. Francesco, Europa '51*), writing the original story of *Il miracolo;* with Lattuada (*Delitto di Giovanni Episcopo, Senza pietà,* and co-directing *Luci del varietà*); and with Pietro Germi (*Cammino della speranza*). His two films, *I Vitelloni* and *La Strada,* show the eclecticism that such a career might suggest. Both are original in intention and both fail to make a really personal impact. . . . More than anything else, *La Strada* suggests a director striving to be a poet when he is not; the insistence on bare and desolate landscapes, the Chaplinesque mime of the waif, the constant intervention of "picturesque" episodes—a village festival on the edge of the marshes, a strange hooded little boy ill in bed in a great deserted room, a religious procession, a traditional Fool from a traveling circus who "understands" the waif—all these reflect Fellini's desire to load his story with atmosphere and symbols of profound meaning. But the "meaning" isn't there. To begin with, the crux of the idea is unconvincing: why should Zampanò, the moronic strong man, have his incoherent revelation that man is more than brute years after, when he learns Gelsomina has died? Unmoved by her tragicomic sufferings, abandoning her when she is ill, he has continued his old life with no sign of interest or involvement in her ultimate fate; and he has, besides, at another time shown complete indifference to death. This apart, the presentation of Gelsomina strikes a consistently false note; as played by Giulietta Masina, undoubtedly a gifted mime but a mature woman, the result is only a sophisticated grotesque of innocence, a clever little goblin masquerading as a waif. Unless one can believe in Gelsomina's innocence and youth, the character is merely pathological. Perhaps this incongruous sophistication is typical of

From "The Signs of Predicament," *Sight and Sound* 24, no. 3 (1955):150–151 (abridged).

Fellini. Inventive and versatile, he has an eye for the momentarily expressive image and a gift for atmospherics; but both *I Vitelloni* and *La Strada,* in their different ways, show the limitations of shallowness.

The Times (London)

La Strada was one of the films given at the Italian Film Festival in October last year, a festival which showed Italian films as deserting the formula of neo-realism which gained such glory for them in the immediate postwar years. . . . *La Strada,* which goes to the Curzon Cinema today, is indeed far from being a pretty film; it melodramatically stresses the ugly facts and facets of life, whereas the classic Italian films were content imaginatively to present them. Its theme is grim to a degree. Zampanò, an animal of a man (Mr. Anthony Quinn) who travels the country giving a one-man show breaking chains with his chest, buys a half-witted girl (Giulietta Masina) as his assistant. They fall in with a circus and Zampanò kills an acrobat (Mr. Richard Basehart) in a fight. The girl pines away with ill-treatment and unhappiness and eventually dies—off-screen, as it were. Zampanò gets drunk and "alone on the seashore," as the synopsis puts it, "trembles and weeps before his unknown destiny."

In directing this piece of vagabondage, Federico Fellini spares the audience nothing in the way of bestiality and degradation; this is realism crowing on a dung-hill. The film is impressive in a displeasing sort of way, and is given distinction by Giulietta Masina's performance as the girl. There is a look of Stan Laurel about her. She has the face of a lost and tragic clown, and she manages to make the girl's response to a word of kindness infinitely moving. Altogether, however, the film can hardly be called a successful example of American-Italian cooperation.

From "A Grim Italian Film," *The Times* (London), 25 November 1955, p. 3.

Newsweek

A film which has been having a great success in Europe for more than two years reached the U.S. this week. *La Strada,* Italian-made, won a second-place award at the Venice film festival in 1954, ran for seven months at London's fashionable Curzon Street Theater, and is now going into its second year in Paris. That it will have a comparable success in this country is doubtful. . . .

Anthony Quinn as the strong man and Richard Basehart as a derisive rival are excellent. As the girl, Giulietta Masina is extraordinarily touching and gives a performance hard to forget, though one does discover as time goes on that one can tire of something touching. It is an unusual movie. But Americans are very apt to get the feeling, again and again, that now THE END is at hand, only to find themselves wrong.

SUMMING UP: Novel and arguable.

From "The Strong Grow Weak," *Newsweek,* 16 July 1956, p. 84 (abridged).

Saturday Review

Arthur Knight

It has often seemed during the past few years that the Italian film-makers have reached both an artistic *impasse* and a philosophical dead end. *Umberto D.*, which Vittorio De Sica made in 1952, appeared to be the last stop on the neo-realist line. From the breadth of vision, the lifelike mingling of tragedy and humor, the urge to put on the screen an uncompromising image of "the way things are" (to use the neo-realists' favorite phrase) the Italian film had degenerated into a sleazy succession of exploitation pictures featuring well-endowed damsels in situations that permitted them to display as much of their endowment as the producers thought they could get away with. There was still lip-service to realism, if realism can be defined simply in terms of natural backgrounds and the seamiest side of life—drugs, perversion, adultery, and prostitution. But the high ideals of the neo-realist movement, using the film to create a greater understanding among people in the building of a better world—these had all but disappeared.

La Strada (Trans-Lux) is the first film in a long time to suggest that they have not disappeared completely. This moving and compassionate work, written and directed by Federico Fellini, is neo-realism on a new plane. Where Rossellini and De Sica recalled the documentary film in creating a precise and unadorned picture of society Fellini's approach is an intriguing mixture of realism and poetry. . . . From start to finish *La Strada* has been shaped with a sure feeling for overtone, for symbol, for a sensory rather than a literal form of perception. And what makes it completely extraordinary is the way its poetry, its symbols, its modest philosophy all flow from incidents so commonplace that only in their juxtapositions do they begin to acquire significance. It is like a modern morality play, set along the fringes of our urban society.

In any formal sense *La Strada* has no story. Its structure, like its title, suggests the straight line of the highway, beginning at the seaside by day, ending at the seaside by night. A brutal, bestial, itinerant strongman buys

From "Italian Realism Refreshed," *Saturday Review*, 30 June 1956, pp. 23–24 (abridged).

a simple-minded girl from her impoverished mother to serve as an assistant in his act, his slavey and concubine. He teaches her a few simple tricks, much as he would train a dog, then takes to the road, doing his pitiful chain-breaking routine in the village squares and fairs of northern Italy. For a time they join a small circus on the outskirts of Rome, but a clown persists in goading the strongman to a fury. When Zampanò pursues the clown with a knife the police step in and the circus moves on without him. Gelsomina, the girl, has been invited to accompany the troupe but, suddenly serious, the clown gives her a reason to wait for Zampanò. Perhaps he needs her. "All in this world serves some purpose," he tells her. Perhaps her whole purpose in life is to serve Zampanò. And Gelsomina awaits her master with a new sense of dedication. Later, on the road, they meet the clown by accident—and by accident Zampanò kills him. When the girl's whimpered reproaches become too much for him Zampanò abandons her by the roadside. At the end, alone and suddenly filled with the terror of his solitude, the strongman sobs out his agony before the infinity of sea and night sky—"like a dog," the clown had said earlier, "a dog that wants to talk to you and only barks."

Somber as this may seem, it is not handled either as a tragedy or even heavy drama. The central character, Gelsomina, is like the foolish, warm-hearted innocent that Harry Langdon used to play—and, like Langdon, Giulietta Masina fills the role with droll yet touching humor and bits of pantomime that are pure enchantment. Richard Basehart is the clown—gay, buoyant, tender, but possessed of a devil that drives him relentlessly to his own destruction. Even Zampanò, superbly acted by Anthony Quinn, has his own rough humor and, it develops, a trace of humanity. The constantly shifting backgrounds of circuses and small towns add a purely visual fascination; while Nino Rota's affecting score creates an emotional continuity filled with sweetness and sudden moments of wild joy.

What Fellini is saying through his parablelike yet human people is the echo of John Donne's "No man is an island." But Fellini says it in the poetry of film—images created with the haunting clarity of a Cartier-Bresson photograph come to life, emotions pantomimed through a scarcely perceptible widening of the eye or stretch of the hand, scenes imagined with such intensity that their physical details are simply the clues to their fullest significance in the contour of the film. . . . With *La Strada* Fellini takes his place as the true successor to Rossellini and De Sica.

The New Yorker

John McCarten

The Italian film called *La Strada* (The Road) takes us on a long, strange journey, and if our interest flags a bit before we've reached the end of it, there is still the satisfaction of having travelled some unusual cinematic byways. Directed by Federico Fellini, who can set a scene with the best of them, the picture roams all over the Italian countryside as it seeks to examine a couple of truths about life that are often overlooked. What Fellini would have us remember is that everyone and everything on earth has a particular purpose, and that loneliness is one of the greatest tragedies of all. These ideas, of course, are fairly elementary, but to establish them he has employed odd characters and odd situations. . . .

In following his performers about, Fellini happens upon all manner of interesting sights, from lovely landscapes to dramatic carnival uproars in small Italian towns. But there is, alas, a good deal of monotony about his characters. The strongman, played by Anthony Quinn, never, until the long-delayed end, displays anything in the way of human emotion, and the unfortunate girl, played by Giulietta Masina, who has been done up to resemble Harry Langdon, has a limited range of expression, registering joy and sorrow but nothing in between. As the clown, however, Richard Basehart is a mercurial type, and he helps out considerably when everybody else becomes too leaden for comfort.

From "Protracted Parable," *The New Yorker,* 28 July 1956, pp. 48–49 (abridged).

Harper's Magazine

"Mr. Harper"

With the art of film in the state of general desuetude into which it has currently fallen, I am ashamed to have to report that the best film I've seen in several seasons is Italian. Time was when "Italian"—or, before that, "French"—was a synonym for excellence. Time passed, and they turned into synonyms for sentimentality. The Unhappy Ending became not only a stereotype but a standard of judgment, and European movies seemed to devote themselves to elaborating the theme of "We never had it so bad." Meanwhile Hollywood was apparently rescuing realism from its friends, and burying in B-pictures the stuff of genius. Or so I happily thought. This has not invariably been, may I now candidly confess, the case.

The motion picture which forces me to this reluctant admission is called *La Strada*. It concerns, to oversimplify, the picaresque experiences of a rather fey girl who becomes the companion, on "the road" in Italy, of a brutal carnival strongman. Superficially, it bears full resemblance to the hard-luck tales that set the style—

Bicycle Thief was both good and bad enough to represent the type. *La Strada*, like the rest, is low-life in context, somber in tone, and without hope in message. For once, the difference is almost purely one of art. To the extent that *La Strada* is *not* a work of morbid pseudo-realism, it reveals the difference between true cinematic feeling and the many kinds of plausible movie-making ability that try to take its place. This is a lyrical expression of self-confidence, in which the limits of technique are stretched beyond the ordinary by technicians who know precisely what they are doing. They are even able, in *La Strada*, to build an entire picture around the sort of equivocal ambiguity that film conveys as no other medium can.

La Strada often borders on the sentimental—as it borders on fantasy and facile symbolism—but every time you think it is going over the edge it fools you. No character is quite what you have been led to assume; no incident has quite the obvious moral that you expected. The way *La Strada* moves within a consistent reality of its own creating, without fumbling

From "Movie Milestone," *Harper's Magazine* 213 (August 1956):81–82.

or straining for effects, gives a suddenly new impression of what movie-making competence might be like. It does strain, and sometimes fumbles, but always for achievements of a fineness and complexity far beyond those that have hitherto been highly praised. It makes other movies seem self-satisfied, and for that alone should restore the lost laurels to the country that produced it.

Hudson Review

Vernon Young

Fellini is the new princely name in films—Federico Fellini: seven syllables, like Vittorio De Sica, to be pronounced lyrically or fatefully. Associated in the immediate postwar years with the more widely known Roberto Rosselini and Alberto Lattuada, he has lately won recognition as a creatively important writer-director, yet the recognition is secure, and subject to revision even so, among Italian and French critics only. *Lo sceicco bianco* (*The White Sheik*), his first independent directorial achievement and the most artful Italian comedy short of *Miracle in Milan* with which I am familiar, was hooted down by political factions at the Venice Film Festival, 1952. It fared little better in New York City this April where, despite generally cordial notices, it was dismissed with arrant condescension by Mr. Crosley Bother, who keeps moviegoing safe for the film-page readers of the New York *Times*. A widespread assumption among entrepreneurs and exhibitors attributes to Mr. Bother the power of making or breaking a foreign film (exceptions acknowledged) in Manhattan, which determines its subsequent distribution in the country as a whole: not that he speaks with any authority demonstrable by reference to a film's visual or intellectual content, but that his unmistakable sincerity is so essentially middle-class as to be accepted without question by the multitude in search of its own image. *I Vitelloni* (1953) was equally a slow starter in Italy, which obliged Fellini to sell the film outright, whereupon it unforeseeably became a national success, though it did not escape vilification in all quarters. *La Strada,* a Venice prizewinner, 1954, has proved either baffling or irritating to every British reviewer I've come across, while *Il Bidone* (1955), excoriated in Venice, was exalted to the rank of "masterpiece" by certain Parisian critics. For the United States, the latter film, retitled *Con Men,* will be the victim of voice-dubbing, that process clearly derived from the principle—Nothing alien is human to me. . . . All of

From *"La Strada:* Cinematic Intersections," *Hudson Review* 9 (1956–57): 437–444 (abridged).

which suggests that Fellini is a dangerous man, and makes one wonder if he mightn't be a great one. . . .

From the actuality of the Italian middle-class family's tyrannical cohesion and bankrupt aims, Fellini derived the social substance of his unspectacular milieu. But he is a film poet, which is to say one whose images mean more than meets the eye. To a poet the social situation is never a closed system, the phenomenal opens to vistas, terrible or inceptive. *I Vitelloni*, circumscribed by its modest subject of incomplete illumination, none the less flashes with light from sources beyond the circle. Fellini's direction of this film was supple and alert, as if he were restraining impulses more intensely lyrical and searching for conveyances more stark.

La Strada is the consequent testimony of such a deduction: the most uncompromising fable yet evoked from the material of Italian naturalism, a mordant reproval of the deaf who have missed the deeper resonance in its voice. Not *cinematically* remarkable, for it is directed and photographed with a conventional technique, the film is metaphysically astounding; longitudes of implication extend as awesomely as the ocean, on the strand of which it begins and ends. As a crystalline conception it belongs with much of the pure literary art of

our time—with *Death in Venice,* for instance, or *The Man Who Died,* with a lyric by Jeffers or Yeats. Like any deeply felt and realized symbol, *La Strada* is at once nuclear and radiating; within its deceptively simple span, an eternal pattern and a prophecy are established.

From the one foot of water into which they have plunged, the performing seals of Social Outlook (who bark and clap flippers only when promised a literal fish) have retrieved the discovery that *La Strada,* like *Umberto D,* has something to do with "problems of communication." Indeed it has. Very likely it would yield a wealth of analyzable (or unanalyzable) problems for classification by the tools of Motivational Research. . . . Beyond the reach of death, McCann Erickson and David Riesman, to say little of the English, *La Strada* is nothing less than a rite of passage, a vision of perennially failing pig-man.

Zampanò is *here,* at the center of a debased culture once again: a spiritually abandoned savage who, trudging in a circle, makes a show of breaking voluntarily assumed chains—his destiny to burrow at last in shifting sand with the tide coming in and the sky bereft of illusion, having rejected the Clown and destroyed the Fool in himself.

Commentaries

Peter Harcourt's general introduction to Fellini's poetic world of images and metaphors focuses upon *La Strada*'s central place in the director's entire production. Written some twenty years ago, it remains one of the most compelling interpretations of Fellini that has appeared to date. Frank Burke's more recent essay is entirely devoted to a consideration of how *La Strada* presents the character of Gelsomina. It also reflects the contemporary move away from a strictly Catholic interpretation of the film to a discussion of problems of a philosophical or psychological nature. Critical commentary on *La Strada* since its appearance has, in general, fallen short of providing rigorous or convincing analyses of the film, in spite of its perennial popularity.

The Secret Life of Federico Fellini

Peter Harcourt

. . . as far as my personal feelings are
concerned, the film I'm fondest of is
La strada.[1]

. . . I believe in prayers and
miracles.[2]

T here is a sequence in *La strada* that is crucial for our understanding of the films of Federico Fellini. It begins with a wedding celebration taking place in the open air. To one side of a long banquet table, really quite unnoticed by the wedding party, Zampanò and Gelsomina are performing one of their tatty numbers, a kind of raggle-taggle conga. Zampanò is seated and is playing the drum, his huge form made awkward by the crumpled position necessary for him to hold the drum between his knees, while Gelsomina is performing her stiff little dance. Bowler hat on her head and clown's makeup on her face, she hops about in time to the music, thrusting her arms forward on every fourth beat. All about them both is the litter that is always associated with any festivity in Fellini; and although she is ignored by the wedding party, scarcely noticed by the adult world, while Gelsomina dances, a number of children in the background dance in unison with her. They respond in sympathy to what she is doing and imitate her movements. One of the guests offers Gelsomina some wine which, after a hurried sip, she passes on to Zampanò. Then the lady of the house calls them to come and eat, and the sad little performance ends. On her way to the house,

From *Film Quarterly* 19, no. 3 (1966):4–13, 19. © 1966 by The Regents of the University of California. Reprinted by permission of The Regents and Peter Harcourt. Another version of this article appears as a chapter in Peter Harcourt's *Six European Directors* (Harmondsworth: Penguin Books, 1974).
1. Gilbert Salachas, *Federico Fellini* (Paris: Éditions Seghers, 1963), p. 103. Translations from the French have been done with the help of Sue Bennett.
2. Delouche Dominique, "Journal d'un Bidoniste," in *Les chemins de Fellini*, by Geneviève Agel (Paris: Éditions du Cerf, 1956), p. 129.

however, Gelsomina is led away by the children who have been so attentive to her dancing. There is apparently something that they want her to see.

She is led up a narrow flight of stairs by the side of the house and along a network of corridors where she almost loses her way. At one moment we see a little boy dressed in a black cloak gliding along. We've never seen him before in this film and we'll never see him again; but the magical fascination of his sudden appearance holds us for that moment and gives us the sense of something festive about to take place as well as perhaps of something that we can't quite understand. Who is this boy? What is he doing here? What is going on?

Gelsomina is then led into a large dark room, all the windows shuttered to keep out the sun, at the end of which crouches Osvaldo, a little boy in a big bed. There are two small mobiles suspended above him, little universes that rotate before his eyes. Indeed, his eyes stare out of his misshaped head, for he is apparently some kind of spastic, in the film regarded as a little idiot boy. The children ask Gelsomina to try and make him laugh, but her imitative bird flutterings only strike more terror into the boy's already terrified eyes. Finally, in a moment impossible to describe without limiting its implications, she draws close to him—he staring in confused terror at her, her own eyes opening wide to receive the full impact of this stare. Then, abruptly, she and all the children are chased out of the room by a nun.

What is the meaning of this moment in *La strada*? What is it that she receives from those wild staring eyes? Is it that in this misformed child she recognizes some affinity with her own gentle strangeness? *Un po' strana,* as her mother described her at the beginning of the film. Or is it that she senses in this blank unmovable face something beyond the powers of her simple goodness to affect in any way? And is it, then, a feeling of real terror that communicates itself to her, the result of a sudden recognition that at the end of long corridors hidden away in some sunless room there might lurk something terrible, something beyond our understanding, something deeply buried away and kept from conscious sight, but something terrifyingly real nevertheless?[3] In the film, it is a moment of great power as Fellini creates it for us; and like the tatty party and the fleeting appearance of the bright-faced little boy, it is a moment that can remind us of similar moments in other films by Fellini. Yet it is essentially dumb. It defies confident interpretation. Just as the idiot boy's eyes do not fully give up their meaning to the

---

3. Geneviève Agel (*Les chemins,* pp. 5ff.), in the course of an immensely sensitive but predominantly Christian interpretation of Fellini's work, sees Osvaldo as marking one of the four stages in Gelsomina's development.

inquisitive Gelsomina, so the scene holds back its full significance from us. It is a moment where something deep and irrational passes between these two people; and if we are temperamentally attuned to Fellini's particular universe sufficiently to receive it, then something equally deep and irrational passes through to us.

But the sequence continues. We cut to the kitchen where Zampanò and the woman are stuffing themselves with food and talking about marriage. She is explaining how her first husband had been as big as he is and that no one subsequently has had any use for his clothes. Gelsomina appears and tries to tell Zampanò about the sick boy she has seen; but she fails to communicate anything to him and is left alone with her meal and with the gradual realization of what is going on as Zampanò and the woman go upstairs together, to see about those clothes.

Then a fade onto a typical Fellini post-festivity scene. The light of day has almost totally disappeared, making the foreground dark while the sky is still luminous beyond. Rags of streamers are hanging down from the house and posts nearby, and a single tree is isolated in midframe as one remaining couple carry on dancing to the sound of a lonely accordion player. Suddenly we notice a light-bulb dangling in the upper righthand corner of the frame, appearing comically out of place and apparently without function. But as we draw back a bit, we see that Gelsomina is in fact contemplating this scene from a barn widow and the light-bulb begins to make a little more sense.

Zampanò is trying on his new clothes, absurdly self-involved in his new-found pinstriped elegance. Meanwhile, Gelsomina begins to hum her little tune and relates how she had first heard it one day in the rain while standing by an open window. She wonders what it is called and asks Zampanò if he will teach her to play it on the trumpet. But as he continues to ignore her, she gets angry with him and stomps about the barn, finally falling down a hole where she decides to spend the night.

A cock crows as we dissolve into morning. Gelsomina is determined to take her stand. She is going to leave Zampanò and return home, not because she doesn't like the work but because she requires some human recognition. *Io me ne vado,* she keeps screaming to an unresponsive Zampanò and later to the stillness of the morning; but then, after changing back into the togs she wore originally, taking care to return all of Zampanò's property, she sets out on her way, waving in spite of herself at whomever she sees in a field nearby. There is no real sense of where she is going, simply the desire to get away.

After a bit (another dissolve), she sits down by the roadside, apparently in gloom. Then she notices a lady-bug or some such small creature and cannot help but become fascinated by it. She places it on her finger and blows it away. And immediately, without preparation, without a hint of plausibility in any social or psychological terms,[4] a characteristic Fellini miracle occurs. Her sense of wonder is renewed. The impulse to live again surges up inside of her as does her determination to continue her lonely journey in life. A little circus band of three musicians appears in the middle of a field, walking along by the side of the road, and in her turnabout way, she dances after them into town. Once in town she will come across another procession—a religious celebration—and, also in the rain as when she first heard her little tune, she will encounter Il Matto—the Fool—wearing an angel's wings and balancing precariously in the sky. Throughout the rest of the film, we will be aware of a strange affinity between Il Matto and Gelsomina, the stripes on his tights matching the stripes on her jersey as he also shares with her her little tune which he plays on a tiny violin.

> There are more Zampanòs in the world than bicycle thieves, and the story of a man who discovers his neighbor is just as important as the story of a strike.[5]

> I believe that everyone has to find truth by himself. . . . That is . . . the reason why my pictures never end. They never have a simple solution. I think it is immoral (in the true sense of the word) to tell a story that has a conclusion. Because you cut out the audience the moment you present a solution on the screen. Because there are no "solutions" in their lives. I think it is more moral—and more important—to show, let's say, the story of one man. Then everyone, with his own sensibility and on the basis of his own inner development, can try to find his own solution.[6]

In essence, the whole of Fellini can be found in this sequence from *La strada*. His thematic center is here. To begin with, reinforced by the title itself, there is the sense of life as a journey, as a constant tearing away from things known and a plunging into the unfamiliar. Unlike Bergman, however, whose allegoric wanderings are generally from place to place—in *Wild Strawberries,* the journey from Stockholm to Lund parallelling old Borg's journey along the path of increased self-knowledge—in Fellini, there is seldom any sense of direction or eventual goal. The form of his films tends to be circular, the characters usually ending where they began.

---

4. Although recently Fellini has related how just such a little band did one day improbably appear.
5. Dominique, "Journal d'un Bidoniste," p. 129.
6. From an interview with Gideon Bachmann in *Film: Book 1,* ed. Robert Hughes (New York: Grove Press, 1959), p. 101.

This restlessness of movement can work in different ways. Occasionally, as with the nuns in *La strada,* there is the feeling that we must give up things dear to us before we get too fond of them; but more frequently there is the feeling that only by moving on, by probing and searching, can we ever come to know the purpose of life. Fellini's fondness for processions is obviously related to this. Indeed, it sometimes seems as if the celebration of movement such as we witness in processions may by itself *provide* the purpose, as if in terrestial terms there may be, in fact, no goal.

Of course, Fellini would reject such intellectual speculations. For Fellini is an intuitive in his response to life, a great muddle-headed irrationalist with very strong feelings and no clear thought. He lives life from the senses, yet his intelligence has informed him that the senses can deceive. Hence, the intellectual indecisions, the apparently inexhaustible interviews with all their self-contradictions. Yet, hence too all the passionate affirmations of his films. It is as if Fellini recognizes that "truth" must lie somewhere, though locked up in subjectivity, but he is unable to seize it with the merely rational surface of his mind. Hence all the turbulence, all the restless energy, the endless traveling along streets and long corridors. Whether it is the Vitelloni wandering about the beach or the town at night or Moraldo setting off at the end on his own for we don't know where; whether it is the peasant families at the end of *Il bidone* (the little children with ricks on their backs recalling the first shot of Gelsomina) that walk by beyond the reach of the dying Augusto; or whether it is the complete Fellini-Anselmi entourage descending that vast structure at the close of *8½* and dancing round and round the circus ring together in an infinity of perfect movement—whatever the context and whatever the film, this perpetual movement is central to Fellini. And it is also central to his irrational view of life that the movement should be without origin or goal.

But in this sequence from *La strada,* there are also some examples of the twin experiences that this directionless journey through life must entail—experiences of the freshness and unexpectedness of innocence which are immediately followed by the experience of something dreadful that in a world freed from the devil is now without a name. On the one hand, we have the presence of Gelsomina herself and of the somewhat querulous Il Matto who appears from on high; but more characteristically we have the fleeting image of that little boy in the cloak passing along the corridor that charms us so gratuitously. For it is also a part of Fellini's irrationality that especially childhood innocence should so often play such a formally gratuitous role in his films, that children should simply appear and then disappear—providing us with a momentary pleasure and perhaps renewing our faith in the wonder of life but remaining essentially apart from the troubled business of life in Fellini's adult world. This goes a long way in *La dolce vita* towards explaining the floating presence of Paola, the little Umbrian angel, who has so universally been disapproved of as a facile resolution to that troubling, too-long film.[7] Initially, Paola simply passes into a short bridging sequence and passes out again, like the boy in the cloak. We see her setting the table at a seaside restaurant, misunderstanding Marcello's difficulties yet attracted by some quality in him, while deriving simple enjoyment from the loud assertions of "Patricia" playing on the juke-box, a simplicity that is emphasized by the later degradation which we experience toward the end of the film when Nadia strips to the same tune. But Paola has been placed here so that when she appears in the epilogue to the film as a kind of *diva ex machina,* she may suggest a quality in life that has been ignored in the compulsive distractions we have been witnessing. Dramatically in any conventional way, she may leave much to be desired; but she is perfect for suggesting Fellini's sense of youthful trust that, although beautiful, is presented as ineffectual and so exists somewhat apart. And we may remember in *I vitelloni* Moraldo's child companion of the railways, with whom he discoursed about life and the stars, who is left to return to the hopelessness of the town, balancing precariously along the rails. Or we might remember the children toward the end of *La strada* who (as if in gentle rehearsal for the end of *8½*) are dancing in a ring round a young tree while their mother (we assume) is hanging out her washing and singing Gelsomina's tune. And of course, there are the young people who appear out of the woods at the end of *Le notti di Cabiria*: "We have lost our way," one of them says as they begin to circle round her while another barks at her in a way that might remind us of the wild compère in the nightclub toward the beginning of the film. In spite of the hopelessness of her present position, the lack of "solution" to any of her problems, she cannot help but return their smiles and their "*Buona sera.*" And of course in *8½*, when the lights dim and the ring of dancers vanish and even the circus performers disappear from the scene, it is the young Guido Anselmi-cum-young-Federico Fellini who is left alone in the spotlight and who moves with it to the side of the ring, leaving the screen in darkness. Although there's never a solution to any of the problems, there's always the sense of something young and fresh left to carry on.

Yet, if on the one hand there are children, representing the possibility of new forms of life, on the other there is the recurring presence of this dreadful nameless thing, the presence of some form of evil, of some kind of threat.

7. See, for example, Eric Rhode in *Sight & Sound* 29 (Winter 1960/61):34.

In all of Fellini's films, there are these disturbing images, moments of disillusion that serve to challenge simple faith. There is the sinister homosexual who so disappoints Leopoldo in *I vitelloni,* as there had been the more-than-disappointing flesh-and-blood reality of the White Sheik before. But in *I vitelloni* more powerfully and more like Osvaldo is the woman in the cinema who so easily tempts Fausto and who is again encountered one day on the beach. Within the subterranean depths of Fellini's imagination, she serves as a link between Osvaldo and La Saraghina and simply appears at odd moments as a threat to the flesh. Also in *I vitelloni* there is the married man in the dark glasses who tempts Olga away. He too is first encountered on the beach; but most ominous of all is the shot of his dark car just before they drive away: it is almost hidden by the early morning shadows in the street while the light glares out above it threateningly, like a scar. And if in *Cabiria* there is of course the deceitful Oscar, more in keeping with the irrationality of these images of threat is the devil-dressed magician who through hypnosis turns innocence toward evil ends.

Excluding for the moment La Saraghina, who is a more complex incarnation of this kind of nameless threat, simultaneously described as "evil" yet *felt* to be beautiful, in *La dolce vita* we have a summary of this sort of effect in that strange blob of a fish that pollutes the stretch of beach at the end of the film and forms the imaginative counterpole to the young Paola waving to Marcello across the protective inlet of the sea. It is as if something deep in Fellini recognizes that in childhood and childlike responses to existence, there is beauty and affirmation of a frequently troubling kind, troubling because unconscious of the terrible threats and temptations that can lurk in the unknowable depths of adult life; and in the way that so frequently these polar elements seem more an accompaniment of the main theme than a formally intrinsic part of his films, it is as if at this stage of his development, Fellini cannot consciously work out the exact relationship between these two extremes or even to find a settled place for them within the narrative structure of his films. Constantly he creates situations for which he can find no earthly solution and his characters encounter difficulties beyond their means to control. So for the end of *La dolce vita,* it is as if the gods themselves must be evoked to bring about the closing affirmation. Failing to communicate anything helpful to Marcello, the little Umbrian angel looks straight at the camera, and at us. What do we make of it all? What do we feel about innocence by the end?

> I make movies in the same way that I talk to people—whether it's a friend, a girl, a priest, or anyone: to seek some clarification. That is what neo-realism means to me, in the original, pure sense. A search into oneself, and

into others. In any direction, any direction where there is life. All the formal philosophy you could possibly apply to my work is that there is no formal philosophy. . . . A man's film is like a naked man—nothing can be hidden. I must be truthful in my films.[8]

Among many film enthusiasts, especially in Great Britain, Fellini has been undervalued and, I think, misunderstood. Before the appearance of *8½, I vitelloni* had often been regarded as his most successful film. And so it is—on the social realist level. Along with *Il bidone* in its somewhat grimmer way, *I vitelloni* is the only Fellini film that truly works on the level of social observation. It is balanced in its narrative, minutely observant, beautifully paced, and very funny. Yet from a slightly deeper level, it can also make a more personal appeal. When looked at sympathetically, it is not *essentially* that different from Fellini's other films. Beneath its realist exterior, it too can make its more subliminal appeal.

One of the difficulties that Fellini's films pose for more rational minds—indeed, we could even say, one of the limitations of Fellini's particular kind of cinematic art—is that he has too often been too careless about the surface credibility of his films, confusing and alienating all but the most sympathetic of his viewers as the conventions of his films have seemed so strange. Yet at their best—excluding the colorful excesses of *Boccaccio '70* and *Giulietta degli spiriti*—they are strange only to the expectations of literary narrative and of psychological realism. Fellini's conventions are not at all strange to the language of painting which, beneath the narrative surface of his films, is the language that he most frequently employs.

For there is in all real films—in all films that have the lasting interest that characterizes a work of art—what I find it convenient to call a subliminal level, a level largely of images plus the complex associations of scarcely perceived sounds. Although we are often not really conscious of these vital ingredients, especially on a first viewing, we can nevertheless be immensely moved by their power to affect us. Indeed, it is generally these elements that give a film its atmosphere or mood.

If there are in Fellini certain constantly recurring themes or motifs, there are also certain constantly recurring images and effects that, when responded to, can make an extraordinary impression upon us and which are then cumulative in their power. For these images to be discussed at all, criticism has to lean away from the comfortably confident tone of literary-cum-film analysis and draw upon the tentativeness of art appreciation. For the central fact about art criticism is the

8. Interview with Bachmann, *Film: Book 1*, p. 105.

elusiveness of the total power of the image when talked about in words and of the apparently greater subjectivity of the way paintings speak to us, moving toward music which is the most subjectively elusive of all. Images and sounds cannot be argued with. They either affect us or they don't. When talking about a painting, there is always so much that we cannot *know.* The discursive element in painting is automatically much less than it can be in literature and the speculative element in interpretation correspondingly that much more. Once again, we might think of that moment between Osvaldo and Gelsomina, the inscrutability of which I've taken some pains to describe; but in Fellini's films, there are images of greater tentativeness than this.

If we look at a painting by Jean Carzou, for example, *The Bay of Dreams,* there are many things that we might want to say about it, about the gentle flowing lines of the figure in the foreground moving through a variety of shapes and objects in extended perspective to the sharply jagged quality of the mountains in the rear. But one of the most striking formal elements in the picture and part of what is for me the forlornness of its mood is the lateral shadow that cuts across its middle, intensifying its sense of space and further distancing these two contrasting worlds. If we next look at an image from *I vitelloni,* just after the departure of Moraldo's pregnant sister on her shotgun honeymoon, if we are responding to the impact of the images in the film and not just waiting for the next point of characterization or development of plot to emerge, we might be affected in much the same way. Similarly, if we contemplate the effect of the foreground shadow in Giorgio de Chirico's *The Rose Tower*[9] and remember that the entire proposal scene between Oscar and Cabiria is similarly played in shadow with the landscape and buildings luminous behind, we might feel that by the very light itself, both de Chirico and Fellini, working independently in their quite different ways, have employed these foreground shadows to lend a worried aspect to the scene and yet to suggest that there is something worthwhile in the distance, something worth achieving beyond.

In fact, de Chirico, perhaps because as an Italian he, too, has been particularly sensitive to Italian space and Italian light, can be used again and again to illuminate by analogy the images in Fellini. Along with images of the sea and of isolated trees,[10] the Italian town square with its fountain in the middle is a recur-

9. For a better understanding of the painting of de Chirico, I am indebted to Peter Greenaway, painter, film-maker, and himself a perceptive student of Fellini.
10. For a more detailed account of Fellini's recurrent imagery, see Agel, *Les chemins* or, following that, the excellent chapter on Fellini in John Russell Taylor's *Cinema Eye, Cinema Ear* (London: Methuen, 1964).

rent image in Fellini. It is generally seen at night or in the early morning, generally presented as a place of reckoning and is divorced from its more sociable associations of being a place where people meet. In Fellini, the town square is never felt to be the social center of a community. De Chirico, too, seemed to be sensitive to the empty feeling of such places at unused times of day—indeed, to the very irrelevance of such vast structures to the little intimacies of human life. And so in de Chirico, we find a number of such paintings that depict huge buildings and exaggerated shadows, where the tiny figures serve both to emphasize the hugeness of the structures (as do the miniature trains that we frequently see puffing away on the horizon) and to give a feeling that the little human things don't really belong in such a space. Sometimes this feeling is further emphasized by the presence of some stray object in the foreground, some object made bizarre by being torn from the context of its function—like that light-bulb in *La strada* or the railway carriage that we see in *Anguish of Departure* in the middle of the square.

So with Fellini, in the much-admired beach sequence in *I vitelloni* (admired for its sensitive observation of these five men imprisoned in their own apathy and defeated by the feeling that there is nothing they can do), Fellini emphasizes their own feeling of irrelevance and functionlessness by the many apparently useless structures that we see sticking up out of the sand. Skeletons of summer changing-huts and odd inexplicable bits of wire frequently dominate the scene and create the feeling of something strange with an almost surrealist intensity. Everywhere throughout the film, as throughout every Fellini film, there is the recurring presence of the bizarre.

In fact, this recognition of the bizarre is at the center of Fellini's world, the physical parallel of his response to the irrational, the source both of his humor and of his sense of dread. For if humor is uppermost in most films by Fellini, beneath the comic observation of the discrepancies of human life there is always this feeling of something beyond our control, something not fully known to our rational selves—like that grotesque fish at the end of *La dolce vita* or like Osvaldo in that guarded-over room.

The first image we see in the first film directed by Fellini himself is an image of a structure sticking up out of the sand with a piece of cloth blowing in the wind. In front of this structure with his robes also blowing sits the White Sheik on his horse in all his phony splendor—an opening image of immense absurdity as indeed are so many of the images in this extraordinarily funny film. But it is really in *Cabiria* that this purely visual absurdity acquires its most consistently surrealist force. Constantly surrounding Cabiria's boxlike house is a litter of people and objects apparently devoid of function and deprived of any context of psychological plausibility. At one moment as we track along we see a post with a for-sale sign on top and a bicycle leaning against it, a baby in a stroller a little beyond, and a woman squatting in the field further beyond that. At another moment as we see Cabiria stomping back from her unfortunate dunking in the river, wearing her characteristic vertical stripes, we see the bulbous Wanda in the background, beside her some washing, a stray horse, and behind her quite inexplicably a little black creature with an umbrella in the field, and behind all that, above yet another box of a house, there is a kite sailing aimlessly in the sky. But most absurd of all and most characteristically Fellinian is the strangely functionless structure that exists outside Cabiria's house. How did it come to be there and what purpose does it serve? Questions like that can have no answer on any rational plane, but the presence of this structure dominates a number of scenes in the film; and of course it is related both to the beach structures that we've seen more naturalistically in *The White Sheik* and *I vitelloni* and that structure to end all structures that looms over *8½*. And as in *8½* where throngs of people are always walking up and down this unnecessary construction, so in *Cabiria* little boys are constantly clambering about these poles that exist outside her home. Like the circus itself so important in Fellini, like the apparently gratuitous accomplishments of the clown or aerialist, it is as if this kind of purposeless activity that nevertheless can give pleasure and even a kind of physical meaning to the absurdity of life should exist as an emblem of Fellini's view of the world— movement without direction, life essentially without a goal.

> Visually, I've often made use of the theme of circus life which is a mixture of spectacle, risk, and reality. My characters are often a bit bizarre. I'm always talking to people in the street who seem rather unusual or out of place or who have some physical or mental affliction. Also, there is naturally the theme of beaches that recurs in all my films, but that has been talked about so much that I don't want to go into it! Since all these elements form a part of me, I don't see why I shouldn't introduce them into my films.[11]

So far in this account of Fellini, I have been concerned only with the thematic consistency of his work and with the peculiar force of his imagery. Taken all together, Fellini's films create a world that is uniquely and personally his own.

---

11. From another interview with Gideon Bachmann in *Cinéma 65*, no. 99.

They manage to enact his vision of the universe. But all this, although true, tends to ignore the great differences between Fellini's individual films, differences of surface characteristics but also finally of quality as well. For much as I respond with enormous pleasure to nearly everything that he has produced—even to much of *Giulietta degli spiriti*—I recognize that if Fellini is a man of immense inventiveness, he is also a director of uncertain control over the many elements that his mind, with apparently so little effort, can with such energy invent. Also, if Fellini is a man who has created for us an immensely personal view of life on the screen, I recognize that it is just that—an *immensely personal view of life* which is frequently egotistic, self-indulgent, sentimental, and above all willfully irrational, courting mystery at every corner and asking from us as much compassion for all these difficulties as he has bestowed upon them himself.[12]

So the critics who have preferred *I vitelloni* to anything that Fellini has subsequently done—at least until *8½*—have probably done so because of all his films, *I vitelloni* least imprisons us in Fellini's private world. There is in the film such a wealth of surface detail that we can get a good deal from it without being too closely attuned to its more subjective elements. Whereas *La strada* presents Fellini's private world with a minimum of props.

In *La strada,* unless we are sensitive to the subliminal level on which the film is really operating and are sympathetic to Fellini's concern through his images to unite Gelsomina with Il Matto and the two of them with the sea while at the same time he is enmeshing Zampanò in his own chains of earth and fire and brute insensitivity, unless we are sensitive to the suggestive power of the imagery, the film will either make very little sense to us or it will seem terribly naive. If by way of "meaning" we carry away from *La strada* only Il Matto's disquisition on the usefulness of pebbles, then we will come away with what we could rightly call a sentimental experience. But if we have been moved by the little children dancing round that tree and are aware that it is Gelsomina's beloved sea—both her natural home and her constant friend—that is washing up on the beach during that final image where Zampanò lies crushed by a kind of dumb and brutal grief, then the intellectually self-indulgent and sentimental elements will be buoyed up by some sort of aesthetic charge as well, by the sense of some depth of feeling and perception being communicated to us beyond what our merely rational selves can readily receive.

For if it is true that there is nothing in Fellini's films that we can properly call

12. Again, see John Russell Taylor's account in *Cinema Eye, Cinema Ear* for the "womblike" quality of Fellini's affection.

thought, there is nevertheless evidence of an intelligence of a totally different kind. Everywhere in his films there is the presence of a mind that responds to life itself on a subliminal level, that is acutely conscious of the natural metaphors to be found in the trappings of day-to-day life and which struggles to find a structure both flexible and persuasive enough to contain them within his films. Even in a film as distended and episodic as *La dolce vita,* there is an intricate interweaving of sounds and images that help to bind together this elongated experience. When the lifeless statue of Christ is being flown to St. Peter's at the opening of the film, only a handful of *ragazzi* follow its shadow through the streets of Rome; while at the injunction of the pneumatic Sylvia to "Follow me everybody," this laughing, living goddess, this beatific creature who is more at home with little kittens than with the temptations of the flesh, gains an active and excited response as people follow her dance about the nightclub floor. I've already mentioned the ironic repetition of the "Patricia" tune which should help to give a slightly more settled place to the presence of Paola—if we're fully attentive to the soundtrack of the film, we should be remembering Paola while we're watching Nadia strip—but also at Steiner's party certain things occur that acquire a formal relevance by the end.

In fact, the portrait of Steiner offers a convenient example of how Fellini's compressed characterization works in this sprawling fresco of his own uneasy mind.[13] As his German name might suggest (and he is played by a French actor!), Steiner is the modern *déraciné* eclectic, a man with only intellectual allegiances. For him, all experience is filtered through the mind. He is a *dilettante,* as he himself says, "too serious to be an amateur and not serious enough to be a professional." He remains outside experience, unattached, and strives to bring to life the order and clarity of a work of art. In his self-created isolation, he draws what sustenance he can from the culture of all nations and epochs. When we first see him, he is carrying a Sanskrit grammar in a modern church and, after a few tentative chords of jazz, we hear him playing a Bach toccata on the organ.

For Steiner, life has meaning only if he can contemplate it as he can a work of art. Even natural sounds, the roar of the wind and the sea, are recorded on tape and listened to like music; and his delight in his daughter is largely the delight he takes in her fondness for words, in her own instinctive gifts as a poet. For Steiner, real life is apparently too much and he tries, through art, to find an escape. Of course, he fails; and through his failure Fellini would seem to be, too schematically, insisting that there can be no path into the future through intellectual

13. This description of Steiner is adapted from an account of *La dolce vita* I wrote for *Twentieth Century,* Jan. 1961, pp. 81ff.

activity or through art. Yet, by the end of the film when we're confronted with the final beach scene and by our necessary Paola,[14] we should recognize that those very same sounds of the wind and the sea that Steiner had listened to as music are part of the disturbance that, along with the intrusive inlet of the sea, keeps Paola from communicating with Marcello. They are part of her "natural" protection from his jaded world. And although I shouldn't want to make great claims for the power of such effects to hold together this too insistent film, nevertheless they do reveal the presence of an artistic intelligence of a rare intuitive kind.

> I don't like the idea of "understanding" a film. I don't believe that rational understanding is an essential element in the reception of any work of art. Either a film has something to say to you or it hasn't. If you are moved by it, you don't need to have it explained to you. If not, no explanation can make you moved by it. That's why I don't think my films are misunderstood when they are accepted for different reasons. Every person has his own fund of experiences and emotions which he brings to bear on every new experience—whether it is to his view of a film or to a love affair; and it is simply the combination of the film with the reality already existing in each person which creates the final impression of unity. As I was saying, this is the way the spectator participates in the process of creation. This diversity of reaction doesn't mean that the objective reality of the film has been misunderstood. Anyway, there is no objective reality in my films, any more than there is in life.[15]

14. Gilbert Salachas, with nice perception, sees Paola as the guest of honor—"*l'hôtesse d'honneur*"—in *La dolce vita. Federico Fellini*, p. 2.
15. Interview with Bachmann, *Cinéma 65*, p. 85.

La Strada

Frank Burke

With *La Strada* (1954) we come to a landmark both in Fellini's career and in European film of the past thirty years. Though the film created controversy among Italian Marxists, who deplored its poetic (i.e., nonneorealist) style, it was enormously successful, enjoying a three-year run in New York City, receiving more than fifty international awards, and bringing Fellini his first Oscar. The film's historical importance seems equaled by its importance to Fellini himself. He has said: "*La Strada* will remain the crucial point in my life." [1] And, even twelve years after completing the film, he remarked: "*La Strada* is really the complete catalogue of my entire mythical world. . . ." [2]

Fellini's continued concern with conformity, mediation, and estrangement is reflected in the way the film's title relates to the story. A road is something already laid out—a civilized "convention"—which encourages everyone to travel the same restrictive route. (The railroad has similar significance in some of Fellini's preceding films.) The road is also a purely physical form of relatedness which comes, in *La Strada,* to be the only way people can connect in a world without love. Its capacity to separate eventually exceeds its ability to unite, and in failing to lead people to fulfillment, the road becomes an avenue to violence, death, abandonment, and alienation. . . .

One of the principal concerns in *La Strada* is the loss of potential, the elimination of creative possibility. A sense of loss is established right from the beginning with the reported death of Rosa—Gelsomina's sister whom Zampanò is seeking to replace. Though Rosa remains undefined, "unrealized" in the film, her name links her with a mandalic symbol of wholeness. . . .

A sense of loss is present not only through Rosa but through the diminishment of all three of the film's major figures—Gelsomina, Il Matto, and Zampanò— who are the most advanced characters to this point in Fellini's career. Gelsomina

From Frank Burke, *Federico Fellini: "Variety Lights" to "La Dolce Vita"* (Boston: Twayne, 1984), pp. 37–53 (abridged).

1. Quoted in Angelo Solmi, *Fellini* (London: Merlin, 1967), p. 116.
2. "The Long Interview: Tullio Kezich and Federico Fellini," in *Federico Fellini's Juliet of the Spirits,* ed. Tullio Kezich, trans. Howard Greenfield (New York: Orion Press, 1965), p. 30.

is the first Fellini figure capable of real growth. Her active intelligence and her ability to respond creatively to experience set her apart from the Checcos, Wandas, Moraldos, Sandras, and Rosannas that preceded her. Il Matto is a superb *artiste* (violinist, high-wire performer, clown) who uses his artfulness with great ingenuity to mask his loneliness and vulnerability. Zampanò, though he might seem terribly limited, is associated with a full range of positive human values: love (his relation with Rosa, his need for Gelsomina), creation and communication (his life as an artist), the "marriage" of home and profession (his van), as well as an active life on the road. Moreover, he surrounds himself with evocative symbols—an owl, snake, mermaid, and crossed swords—that bespeak an imagination struggling to express itself. Even his strong-man routine, the breaking of a chain with his pectoral muscles or "heart," is a metaphoric representation of his urge to free himself through love. It is the failure of Gelsomina, Il Matto, and Zampanò to act out their positive impulses that makes *La Strada* such an intensely tragic film.

The narrative process of *La Strada* is (like that of "A Matrimonial Agency") one of "*adult*-eration." Gelsomina, the childlife naif, is brought by Zampanò into an adult environment of work, money, discipline, convention, and linear thought, and she is destroyed. Her life quickly becomes fragmented, polarized; she is forced to sacrifice her identity; and her intelligence is compromised to the point of madness.

In the opening sequence, Gelsomina is an image of childhood promise, and a figure wholly in tune with her natural surroundings. . . . Once she is summoned to her mother and to Zampanò, this marvelously natural creature enters the world of civilized structure, economic and social forms, control. . . . Money is introduced as we discover that Zampanò has in effect bought Gelsomina. . . . Social propriety is emphasized as the children are ordered to say "thank you." Subtly, but most significantly, discipline and domination manifest themselves as Zampanò equates the education he intends to give Gelsomina with the training of dogs.
   In effect, Zampanò represents the point at which nature and civilization meet. Moreover, as someone who will introduce Gelsomina to planned, rather than purely spontaneous, behavior (repetition, rehearsal, memorization, performance), he embodies a rudimentary form of civilized intelligence crucial to the awakening of Gelsomina's mind. . . . From the beginning, Gelsomina's life with Zampanò is compartmentalized and based on role. The nature-civilization division of the first sequence becomes a split between personal and professional aspects of existence. The presence of each is evident in Gelsomina's function as both a companion ("wife") and a theatrical assistant and in Zampanò's use of the van as both home and workplace. An alternation between roadside (personal) activity and public performance suggests a relative balance at first. However, the balance proves more apparent than real. The first, and most extensive, roadside scene is given almost entirely to theatrical training, and Zampanò only turns to more "intimate" matters (forcing Gelsomina to spend the night in the van) after she has succumbed to his brutal professional "education." Though Zampanò eventually seems to develop a sense of appreciation for Gelsomina, it is the result not of genuine personal interaction . . . but of their success (largely through Gelsomina's performance in the ["Lifle"] routine) as *artistes*. In fact, what he seems to value most about her—the fact that she is "amusing"—is the very thing that has helped make them professionally successful.
   As Zampanò refuses to deal with Gelsomina in a truly personal way, she is forced to rely on her professional identity for satisfaction. She experiences a series of contrasts between acceptance as an *artiste* and rejection as a person. . . .

The subordination of personal identity to artistic persona is particularly clear from the way in which Gelsomina's powers of awareness awaken. During the roadside training sequence, as Zampanò tries a variety of comedic hats on her, Gelsomina's face, eyes, and imagination come fully alive. She responds with her own little dance, only to be quashed by Zampanò and forced to repeat the phrase "Zampanò is here" while she mechanically beats a drum. The fact that Gelsomina is awakened only by costuming suggests her need—given the limitations of personal life—to escape into make-believe. The fact that her attempt to unite make-believe with her own natural expressiveness is thwarted by Zampanò suggests that when she *does* escape into "art" and persona, it will be at the cost of originality.

During the wedding sequence, Gelsomina's awakening consciousness is again linked to costuming and her life as an *artiste*. She has two vivid moments of awareness: her encounter with Osvaldo and her recognition that Zampanò is going off to have sex with Teresa. Yet, in each case the face that is illuminated by sudden understanding is that of a clown. For the first sustained period in the film, Gelsomina is dressed wholly as a performer and has abandoned her cape whose "wings" suggested her capacity for self-transcendence. She is now dressed in a long, masculine, military overcoat. Moreover, both moments of awareness occur in the very midst of playacting. She is in the process of entertaining Osvaldo when she has her epiphany of kinship and wonder, and she and Zampanò exchange highly theatrical winks of complicity (their moment of greatest—yet most artificial—rapport) just before Gelsomina realizes what is really going on.

Her experience with Osvaldo is particularly significant as an indication of what has happened by this point in the film. . . . Through Osvaldo, Gelsomina encounters the very things which are being muted—or preserved only on the level of "art" or spectacle—in herself. Seeing herself in him, she experiences (her own) uniqueness only as abnormalcy, leading to isolation and fear. Self-consciousness becomes consciousness only of alienation. As a result, she is further inclined to suppress her originality and to deny true awareness by finding less demoralizing substitutes.

The Osvaldo sequence also highlights an emerging split between head and spirit, body and matter. Osvaldo's name means "the power of godliness." Gelsomina must ascend a flight of stairs to reach him; he is guarded by a religious representative, and Gelsomina's encounter with him is profound, numinous, awe-inspiring. At the same time, Zampanò is on ground level, gulping down food, talking with the self-assertively physical Teresa, and about to descend into the cellar to have sex. As Gelsomina's intelligence develops and as Zampanò continues to repress his own, they begin to live their lives on separate levels. In this instance—and indicative of what will recur throughout the film—she ends up back down on his, defeated by his unfeeling behavior.

Finally, in serving as a mirror or "projection" through which Gelsomina encounters herself, Osvaldo suggests that Gelsomina is becoming increasingly externalized—that her loss of identity has reached the point where she is about to begin living only through others. (The notion of "God" is introduced at this point as an abstraction and convention on which people begin to rely once they have lost their own godliness or capacity for self-transformation.)

Gelsomina's next moment of awakening—following Zampanò's adventure with Teresa—makes clear that she is, indeed, beginning to live largely through externals. Angered and depressed by Zampanò's infidelity, she is suddenly revived by the memory of a song she heard on the radio, and she asks Zampanò to teach her the trumpet. Her brightening of mood seems largely inspired by the light bulb she has been standing next to. The song and the radio are also external and, even more than the light bulb, can be seen as forms of surrogate consciousness. (They are "voices" that invade and take over the mind.) The song is particularly significant, for it will later be associated with Il Matto, which clearly comes to function as Gelsomina's "borrowed" intelligence.

Gelsomina's sudden preoccupation with the song is a denial of her present situation. For the first time since she started communicating with Zampanò, she fails to confront him directly with her concerns about his behavior. Moreover, enlightenment, which was earlier equated with self-expression and creativity (her dance with the comedic hats), is now equated with escape.

This urge to escape, in turn, leads to a failed attempt to leave Zampanò— which is established largely in terms of the personal/professional division we discussed earlier. . . . Here she clearly sets things out in terms of alternatives: her work versus her personal relationship with Zampanò. Moreover, in stating a preference, she chooses her "career." This strongly suggests that her eventual return to him will offer no chance for a direct or personal relationship but will be based on Gelsomina's need for the life of an *artiste*.

By the time Gelsomina makes her temporary break with Zampanò, her identity and individuality have been eroded to the point that she has little initiative. As soon as she reaches a major thoroughfare, she runs out of energy and sits down by the side of the road. She must be fueled by the appearance of three musicians. . . . Once they appear, she is reduced to a follower. Moreover, she is led to a town filled with narrow streets and alleys (the "road" at its most restrictive), where a religious procession is in progress. Here she is pushed and pulled, directed and redirected, forced to go with the flow of the mob.

Throughout her journey, she is associated with images of crucifixion and martyrdom. And when she is confronted by the procession, Gelsomina does, in a sense, martyr herself—kneeling and adoring the images paraded in front of her.

Born out of this is Il Matto. A heavenly apparition on his high wire, he is a "god" to be "worshipped." Known only by a stage name, he is pure role. First seen as a shadow on the side of a building, he is a projection more than a person. Dressed as an angel (a religious and theatrical "cliché") and born out of the religious, institutional, life of the town, he is strongly associated with tradition and convention. Finally, "crucified" on the cross formed by his tightrope and balancing pole, he is another image of martyrdom. He personifies, in short, everything to which Gelsomina is falling prey.

He also introduces a new phase in the film's analysis of the civilizing process. Whereas Zampanò introduced civilization at the point where it met and dominated nature, Il Matto embodies it when nature and natural relatedness are replaced by illusion. Whereas Zampanò introduced rudimentary, practical intelligence, Il Matto will promote idealization, fantasy, higher but *false* consciousness (the only kind that can emerge in a society that has lost touch with reality). His false consciousness, in turn, will become a form of "madness" as the meaning of his name—"the mad one"—suggests. (He is called "The Fool" in subtitled and dubbed prints, a name that is also indicative of his function in the film.)

In effect—and though Gelsomina does not realize it—Il Matto's appearance provides a "solution" to her dilemma with Zampanò. She can compensate for living with him by projecting everything of value onto Il Matto. The fact that her identity is about to become caught up in his is suggested moments before she is tracked down by Zampanò, when she is called *matta* (the feminine of *matto*) by a *vitellone* in a town square. . . .

As Gelsomina projects herself onto Il Matto, selfhood disappears and is replaced by the mere illusion of identity and meaningful existence. The crucial moment in this process occurs when Zampanò is jailed and Il Matto is momentarily given free rein to fill Gelsomina's head with his philosophy or rationale for life: everything, even the smallest stone, has a purpose, but only God knows how or why. Both his thesis and Gelsomina's wholesale acceptance of it illuminate all the major problems that now exist within the film.

1. Characters have stopped thinking for themselves. . . .

At this point, another stage in *La Strada*'s analysis of the civilizing process begins. A world that has imposed artificial structure at the cost of natural connection and has substituted false consciousness for reality, reaches the dead end of consciousness. Intelligence starts to self-destruct, and regression toward a primitive, precivilized state begins. Here we recall a crucial statement by Fellini quoted in our introduction: "There is a vertical line in spirituality that goes from the beast to the angel, and on which we oscillate. Every day, every minute carries the danger of losing ground, of falling down again toward the beast." [3]

2. All possibility for unity *within* experience is gone. . . .

3. Life, purpose, and love are reduced to bleak instrumentalism—a natural outgrowth of the purchase of Gelsomina. . . .

4. The split between reality and illusion has become irremediable. . . .

The characters' forced abandonment of the circus following the fight between Zampanò and Il Matto is a seeming return to reality from a world of artifice. However, the roles and illusions acquired in the circus environment make it impossible for the characters to reintegrate with the real world. . . .

The denial of nature and reality is best exemplified by the convent sequence. Convent life is, in itself, a retreat from the world, and as an isolated, entirely female, community dedicated to "God," the convent in *La Strada* proves to be even one step beyond the circus as an artificial "family" committed to illusion. . . .

Gelsomina's willingness to embrace the institution of marriage is another sign that she, through Il Matto and the nun, has succumbed to tradition and convention. . . . More profoundly and tragically than ever in Fellini's work, marriage as an institution is seen as a substitute for meaningful union.

The withdrawal of Zampanò and Gelsomina into separate realms of criminality and pseudotheology is one of the many ways in which divisiveness continues to grow. A more obvious indication lies in the initial absence of Il Matto. The "Angel" and the "Beast" can no longer live in the same world. The moment they come together, one is destroyed.

In the absence of Il Matto, Gelsomina takes on the role of Angel. *She* begins to call Zampanò a beast and to imply sharp distinctions between mental activity and mere mindless, physical, existence: "You're a beast. You don't think." In so doing, she not only externalizes herself further (becoming *La matta,* as it were),

---

3. "The Game of Truth," in Gilbert Salachas, *Federico Fellini* (New York: Crown, 1969), p. 114.

she further erodes any chance for unification. Instead of trying to balance or alternate opposites through Il Matto and Zampanò, remaining open to both options, she now becomes one-half of the division herself. Consequently, despite her thoughts to the contrary, she is irrevocably alienated from Zampanò.

By now, the division between Angel and Beast, mind and body, has become an outright divorce between ineffectual consciousness and brute physical necessity. Having lost all touch with reality, consciousness or thought can no longer influence it and, concomitantly, reality is now unredeemed by spirit or imagination. . . .

The killing of Il Matto is the crucial event in the film's analysis of a false and self-destructive civilizing process. It marks the end of everything even remotely associated with higher consciousness. Not only is Il Matto gone, but Gelsomina reacts to his death by surrendering all intelligence and withdrawing into a state of shock. . . .

Gelsomina's madness reveals the extent to which she has sacrificed her identity. She has allowed Il Matto to function so completely as her surrogate consciousness that when he dies, so does her own mind. His death, in effect, becomes hers.

Though Zampanò, by the time of Il Matto's death, has been reduced almost entirely to brutish behavior, he has not sacrificed his humanity altogether. . . . He can still feel an extraordinary sense of need for Gelsomina, becoming uncharacteristically solicitous as she falls ill and can no longer assist him. Moreover, Gelsomina serves as his conscience: her condition repeatedly reminds him of Il Matto's death. Both his sense of need and his surrogate conscience link him, however tenuously, with a social universe. When he casts Gelsomina off, however, the links dissolve and there is nothing left to prevent Zampanò's final tragic deterioration.

His abandonment of Gelsomina marks a major event in the growing predominance of "absence" in the film. At the beginning, things such as consciousness, identity, and meaning were to a large extent present *within* Gelsomina and her world. However, through projection and abstraction, she became increasingly "absent" to herself—a process which culminated when she so thoroughly identified with the dead Il Matto. Moreover, meaning came to depend not on immediate experience but on the remembered words of people absent . . . and even more conclusively on a God who never manifests Himself. Finally, meaning itself disappeared with the death of Il Matto and of conscious intelligence. Now that Gelsomina has been cast off, virtually everything in the film will be articulated in terms of absence, loss.

In the film's final phase, years after he has abandoned Gelsomina, Zampanò hears a young woman humming the song Gelsomina had inherited from Il Matto. She is, for a moment, "reincarnated." However, the manner of her reincarnation only serves to emphasize that she is irrevocably gone. Moreover, she and everything she embodied are "dead on arrival" in the very act of reincarnation. (A poster advertising the American film *D.O.A.* is prominently displayed behind Zampanò as the woman recalls Gelsomina.) Not only do we discover that Gelsomina has died, but she has no identity in the present. She is referred to only as a "girl" by the woman—and is not referred to at all by Zampanò. (The latter is a subtle indication of how repressed Zampanò's humanity is by now.) . . . Even Gelsomina's consciousness is dead in the retelling. . . . Gelsomina has evaporated and been replaced by the young woman who, in hanging out laundry, is herself repeatedly disappearing behind sheets.

Like Gelsomina, Zampanò is largely dead on arrival. When we first see him, he is solitary, mechanical, and unfeeling as he rejects the company of a female performer and wolfs down most of an ice-cream cone in one bite. He has apparently cast off his van, the emblem of his independence and openness to experience. He has made no attempt to replace Gelsomina, as he once replaced Rosa, to fulfill an urge for relatedness and love on some level. With the absence of his mobile home and female companionship, he is now definable solely in terms of work. (Unlike the Giraffa circus, the one he is now with shows no evidence of family or community.)

The story of Gelsomina offers him one last opportunity to awaken. Unfortunately, as his failure even to refer to her suggests, he is not up to it. He remains mute at the end of the woman's story and does not act on her suggestion that he find out more from the mayor. The next time we see him, he is performing his chain act in a state of complete numbness. (He fails to break the chain before we dissolve to the next scene.) Then, he represses awareness by getting violently drunk.

At this point, the final stage of regression occurs. Zampanò abrogates all social bonds by getting in a fight, hitting the one person who has identified himself as his friend and, most important, shouting, "I don't need anyone. I just want to be alone." These final words make clear that Zampanò has jettisoned his one remaining tie to the human race: his sense of need.

He then stumbles in darkness and in a stupor beyond the town and circus, beyond all civilized structure, out to the sea. He returns not only to the origins of the film (without the crucial presence now of either Gelsomina or of light) but to the origins of evolution. He douses himself with water in a clumsy, drunken way that bespeaks the very impossibility of baptism or a sacramental relation to nature. He then stumbles back onto the shore and collapses to a sitting position. Looking tragically simian, he experiences one final burst of sentience as he looks to the heavens and confronts the outer image of his own vast emptiness. He can respond only with grunts of terror. Then he slumps forward, face down, turned away from the last bit of dim illumination offered by the night sky. He lies motionless, "dead" upon the beach. The fall back to the beast and beyond even that—to mere inanimate existence—is complete. Complete also is Fellini's apocalyptic vision of a fatally flawed civilizing process that bears the seeds of its own destruction and leads only to the ultimate denial of civilization and humanity.[4]

The importance of *La Strada* in Fellini's growth as an artist is, for the most part, self-evident. The film marks a major advance in complexity in terms of both characterization and narrative structure. The metaphoric richness, in turn, generates the "poetic" style for which the film was attacked by Marxists and praised by virtually everyone else. Without sacrificing the concreteness upon which aesthetic experience depends, Fellini abandons realism, verisimilitude, in order to articulate things more purely and directly in imaginative terms. Characters are not "people" first and embodiments of aesthetic significance second, nor are events "real" first and foremost. They are defined principally by what they embody on an imaginative level. They possess the concreteness of imaginative, spiritual experience rather than the concreteness of quotidian reality.

Because Fellini is able in *La Strada* to invest his characters with so much potential and complexity, he is able to create a world more fully human and—in its ultimate destruction—more fully tragic. The growing strength of his characters moves him yet closer to stories such as *The Nights of Cabiria* and *8½*, in which potential and worth are realized rather than sacrificed.

4. I recognize that my view of the final scene runs counter to the more common critical view that Zampanò is somehow awakened and redeemed at the end—a view which Fellini himself has tended to encourage by talking of the film in terms of enlightenment. All the evidence, it seems to me, is to the contrary. The film is, indeed, about an enlightenment (Gelsomina's), but about an enlightenment that is ultimately negated.

Filmography and Bibliography

Fellini Filmography, 1950–1985

1950 *Luci del varietà* (*Variety Lights*), directed with Alberto Lattuada
Screenplay by Fellini, Lattuada, Tullio Pinelli, Ennio Flaiano, based on a story by Fellini.

1952 *Lo sceicco bianco* (*The White Sheik*)
Screenplay by Fellini, Tullio Pinelli, Ennio Flaiano, based on a story by Michelangelo Antonioni, Fellini, and Pinelli.

1953 *I vitelloni* (*I Vitelloni, The Young and the Passionate*)
Screenplay by Fellini, Ennio Flaiano, Tullio Pinelli, based on a story by Fellini.

1953 "Un'agenzia matrimoniale" ("A Marriage Agency,"), an episode in *Amore in città* (*Love in the City*)

Screenplay by Fellini and Tullio Pinelli.

1954 *La strada* (*La Strada*)
Screenplay by Fellini, Tullio Pinelli, Ennio Flaiano, based on a story by Fellini.

1955 *Il bidone* (*Il Bidone, The Swindle*)
Screenplay by Fellini, Ennio Flaiano, Tullio Pinelli.

1957 *Le notti di Cabiria* (*Nights of Cabiria*)
Screenplay and story by Fellini, Ennio Flaiano, Tullio Pinelli, with additional dialogue by Pier Paolo Pasolini.

1959 *La dolce vita* (*La Dolce Vita*)
Screenplay by Fellini, Tullio Pinelli, Ennio Flaiano, Brunello Rondi, based on a story by Fellini, Pinelli, and Flaiano.

1962   "Le tentazioni del dottor Antonio" ("The Temptations of Doctor Antonio"), an episode in *Boccaccio '70*
Screenplay and story by Fellini, Ennio Flaiano, Tullio Pinelli, in collaboration with Brunello Rondi and Goffredo Parise.

1963   *Otto e mezzo (8½)*
Screenplay by Fellini, Ennio Flaiano, Tullio Pinelli, Brunello Rondi, based on a story by Fellini and Flaiano.

1965   *Giulietta degli spiriti (Juliet of the Spirits)*
Screenplay by Fellini, Tullio Pinelli, Ennio Flaiano, Brunello Rondi, based on a story by Fellini and Pinelli.

1968   "Toby Dammit," an episode in *Histoires extraordinaires* [France], *Tre passi nel delirio* [Italy], (*Spirits of the dead*).
Screenplay by Fellini and Bernardino Zapponi, based on a story by Edgar Allan Poe, "Never Bet the Devil Your Head."

1969   *Block-notes di un regista (Fellini: A Director's Notebook)*
Screenplay by Fellini and Bernardino Zapponi.

1969   *Fellini Satyricon (Fellini's Satyricon)*
Screenplay by Fellini and Bernardino Zapponi, freely adapted from Petronius Arbiter, *Satyricon*.

1970   *I clowns (The Clowns)*
Screenplay and story by Fellini and Bernardino Zapponi.

1972   *Roma (Fellini's Roma)*
Screenplay and story by Fellini and Bernardino Zapponi.

1973   *Amarcord (Amarcord)*
Screenplay and story by Fellini and Tonino Guerra.

1976   *Il Casanova (Fellini's Casanova)*
Screenplay by Fellini and Bernardino Zapponi, based on Giacomo Casanova, *Storie della mia vita (Story of My Life)*.

1979   *Prova d'orchestra (Orchestra Rehearsal)*
Screenplay by Fellini, in collaboration with Brunello Rondi, based on a story by Fellini.

1980   *Città delle donne (City of Women)*
Screenplay by Fellini and Bernardino Zapponi, in collaboration with Brunello Rondi, based on a story by Fellini and Zapponi.

1983.   *E la nave va (And the Ship Sails On)*
Screenplay and story by Fellini and Tonino Guerra.

1985   *Ginger e Fred (Ginger and Fred)*
Screenplay and story by Fellini, Tonino Guerra, and Tullio Pinelli.

Selected
Bibliography

Scripts and Screenplays

Casanova. Edited by Federico Fellini and Bernardino Zapponi. Turin: Einaudi, 1977.

I clowns. Edited by Renzo Renzi. Bologna: Cappelli, 1970.

La Dolce Vita. New York: Ballantine, 1961.

Early Screenplays. New York: Grossman, 1971.

8½. Edited by Charles Affron. New Brunswick, N.J.: Rutgers University Press, 1987.

E la nave va. Edited by Federico Fellini and Tonino Guerra. Milan: Longanesi, 1983.

Fellini Satyricon. Edited by Dario Zanelli. Bologna: Cappelli, 1969.

Fellini's Casanova. Edited by Bernardino Zapponi. New York: Dell, 1977.

Fellini TV: Blocknotes di un regista/I clowns. Edited by Renzo Renzi. Bologna: Cappelli, 1972.

Il film "Amarcord." Edited by Gianfranco Angelucci and Liliana Betti. Bologna: Cappelli, 1974.

Ginger e Fred. Edited by Mino Guerrini. Milan: Longanesi, 1986.

Juliet of the Spirits. Edited by Tullio Kezich. New York: Grossman, 1965.

Moraldo in the City and A Journey with Anita [unrealized projects]. Edited by John C. Stubbs. Urbana: University of Illinois Press, 1983.

Le notti di Cabiria di Federico Fellini. Edited by Lino del Fra. Bologna: Cappelli, 1965.

8½ di Federico Fellini. Edited by Camilla Cederna. Bologna: Cappelli, 1965.

Il primo Fellini: Lo sceicco bianco, I vitelloni, La strada, Il bidone.

Edited by Renzo Renzi. Bologna: Cappelli, 1969. *Quattro film*. Introduction by Italo Calvino. Turin: Einaudi, 1974.

Roma di Federico Fellini. Edited by Bernardino Zapponi. Bologna: Cappelli, 1972.

La Strada. Edited by François-Regis Bastide, Juliette Caputo, and Chris Marker. Paris: Éditions du Seuil, 1955.

La Strada. L'Avant-Scène du cinéma 102 (April 1970): 7–51.

La strada: Sceneggiatura originale di Federico Fellini e Tullio Pinelli. Rome: Edizioni Bianco e Nero, 1955.

Three Screenplays. New York: Grossman, 1970.

Drawings and Photographs

Betti, Liliana, ed. *Federico A.C.: Disegni per Il Satyricon di Federico Fellini*. Milan: Edizioni Libri, 1970.

————, and Del Buono, Oreste, eds. *Federcord: Disegni per Amarcord di Federico Fellini*. Milan: Edizioni Libri, 1974.

De Santi, Pier Marco. *I disegni di Fellini*. Rome: Laterza, 1982.

Monti, Raffaele, ed. *Bottega Fellini: "La città delle donne": Progetto, lavorazione, film*. Rome: De Luca, 1981.

Strich, Christian, ed. *Fellini's Faces*. New York: Holt, Rinehart & Winston, 1982.

————, ed. *Fellini's Films*. New York: Putnam's, 1977.

Criticism

Agel, Geneviève. *Les chemins de Fellini*. Paris: Éditions du Cerf, 1956.

Alpert, Hollis. *Fellini: A Life*. New York: Atheneum, 1986.

Angelini, Pietro. *Controfellini: Il fellinismo tra restaurazione e magia bianca*. Milan: Edizioni Ottaviano, 1974.

Bazin, André. *What Is Cinema?: Vol. II*. Berkeley and Los Angeles: University of California Press, 1971.

Betti, Liliana. *Fellini: An Intimate Portrait*. Boston: Little, Brown, 1979.

Bondanella, Peter, ed. *Federico Fellini: Essays in Criticism*. New York: Oxford University Press, 1978.

————. *Italian Cinema: From Neorealism to the Present*. New York: Frederick Ungar, 1983.

Burke, Frank. *Federico Fellini: "Variety Lights" to "La Dolce Vita."* Boston: Twayne, 1984.

Costello, Donald P. *Fellini's Road*. Notre Dame: University of Notre Dame Press, 1983.

de Miro, Ester, and Mario Guaraldi, eds. *Fellini della memoria*. Florence: La Casa Usher, 1983.

Fava, Claudio G., and Aldo Viganò. *I film di Federico Fellini*. Rome: Gremese Editore, 1981.

Fellini, Federico. *Fare un film*. Turin: Einaudi, 1980.

————. *Fellini on Fellini*. Translated by Isabel Quigly. London: Eyre Methuen, 1976.

————. *Intervista sul cinema*. Edited by Giovanni Grazzini. Rome: Laterza, 1983.

Ketcham, Charles B. *Federico Fellini: The Search for a New Mythology*. New York: Paulist Press, 1976.

Marcus, Millicent. *Italian Film in the Light of Neorealism*. Princeton: Princeton University Press, 1986.

Murray, Edward. *Fellini the Artist*. 2nd ed. New York: Frederick Ungar, 1985.

Pecori, Franco. *Fellini*. Florence: La Nuova Italia, 1974.

Perry, Ted. *Filmguide to 8½*. Bloomington: Indiana University Press, 1975.

Prats, A. J. *The Autonomous Image: Cinematic Narration and Humanism*. Lexington: The University Press of Kentucky, 1981.

Rondi, Brunello. *Il cinema di Fellini*. Rome: Edizioni Bianco e Nero, 1965.

Rosenthal, Stuart. *The Cinema of Federico Fellini*. New York: A. S. Barnes, 1978.

Solmi, Angelo. *Fellini*. London: Merlin Press, 1967.

Stubbs, John C., with Constance D. Markey and Marc Lenzini. *Federico Fellini: A Guide to References and Resources*. Boston: G. K. Hall, 1978.